"What would Paul say to contemporary Wes
and Keesmaat have written one of the most
rent interface of biblical, cultural and politic
of Colossians and the urgent questions of ou
wit and surprise as well as scholarship and i
under a global empire posed particular cha
compels us to engage with the equivalent qu

N. T. WRIGHT, *Bishop of Durham, a
Christian Origins and the Question of Go*

"Walsh and Keesmaat expertly bring the a
world of North America crashing together, a
of Scripture combine with penetrating, tren
sources (exegetes, philosophers, musicians)
culturally subversive ethic is persuasively pu
Not exactly a commentary, this book is muc
our times. Take up and read."

STEVEN BOUMA-PREDIGER, *Jacob*

"After they did all of their exegetical homew
sians touch our lives in the contemporary w
neither will the reader. Whereas Colossians
ment, this book shows how it becomes front
all of globalization. The book makes clear w
led imagination."

WALTER BRUEGGEMANN, *Emeritu
Columbia Theological Seminary*

"This book is a Molotov cocktail lobbed into the midst of contemporary biblical studies and the American empire. It is full of illuminating exegesis of Colossians, rooted in solid knowledge of the Old Testament background and the first-century Roman imperial context of the New Testament. Its most helpful—and controversial—feature is that it demonstrates how a faithful reading of Colossians addresses head-on our contemporary idolatry of consumerism and the postmodern suspicion of truth that characterizes our culture."

J. RICHARD MIDDLETON, *Associate Professor of Biblical Studies,
Roberts Wesleyan College, Rochester, New York*

"A gripping, powerful and penetrating interpretation of Colossians for the third millennium! Based on responsible scholarship, enlivened by a discerning imagination and fired by commitment to Paul's gospel, this reading of Colossians by Walsh and Keesmaat is an outstanding contribution to the church's task of conceiving Christ rather than global consumerism as sovereign in our world. At the same time, it is a provocative stimulus to the church's mission of living out that alternative sovereignty in a community of compassion resistant to the forces of coercion from within and without."

ANDREW T. LINCOLN, *Portland Professor of New Testament, University of Gloucestershire*

"In my nearly twenty-five years of book selling I have seen few books which can rival *Colossians Remixed* for its sheer Christian audacity, its deep desire to be faithful in reading the Word in light of the burning questions of our time. Readers will be sure to be stunned—pondering, reacting, struggling with this fresh take on Scripture, as they are led to good insights about how to live out a transforming discipleship. If this proposal is taken seriously, the Bible will be heard anew, lives will be changed, and God will be pleased."

BYRON K. BORGER, *Hearts & Minds Bookstore, Dallastown, Pennsylvania*

"This creative and intellectually stimulating understanding of Colossians offers both a fresh reading of the letter in its first-century setting and a provocative attempt to challenge the cultural elites of the twenty-first century with Colossians' worldview. Not all will agree with its hermeneutical approach or its political positions. Everyone, however, will benefit from thinking with the authors about the ways in which the church has become captive to the dominant culture and the ways in which the domininant culture has too quickly dismissed the church."

FRANK THIELMAN, *Presbyterian Professor of Divinity, Samford University*

"Brian and Sylvia are phenomenally wise, profoundly formed by their immersion in biblical language, astutely aware of the pains and anxieties of residents in postmodernity, and outstandingly alert to the dangers of enculturated Christianity. This is a brilliant book—using multimedia of imaginative stories, probing conversations, alternative reading. Their targums alone are more than worth the price of the book because they make the Bible come alive with its deepest referents to Israel, to the community at Colossae and to our world, caught as it is in the throes of the empire."

MARVA J. DAWN, *author of* Unfettered Hope: A Call to Faithful Living in an Affluent Society *and* Powers, Weakness, and the Tabernacling of God

"*Colossians Remixed* is a book I've been waiting for eagerly; it's a tasty sample of postmodern engagement with a biblical text. It will provide a fascinating and readable entry into Colossians— and deeper into the essential message of Jesus and Paul. And in the process, it will expose readers to evocative and challenging new ways of reading and interpreting both Scripture and our culture."

BRIAN D. MCLAREN, *pastor and author of* A New Kind of Christian: A Tale of Two Friends on a Spiritual Journey

BRIAN J. WALSH AND SYLVIA C. KEESMAAT

COLOSSIANS
R E M I X E D

SUBVERTING THE EMPIRE

InterVarsity Press
Downers Grove, Illinois

for Bud Osborn

prophet, poet, priest

InterVarsity Press
P.O. Box 1400, Downers Grove, IL 60515-1426
World Wide Web: www.ivpress.com
E-mail: mail@ivpress.com

InterVarsity Press® is the book-publishing division of InterVarsity Christian Fellowship/USA®, a student movement active on campus at hundreds of universities, colleges and schools of nursing in the United States of America, and a member movement of the International Fellowship of Evangelical Students. For information about local and regional activities, write Public Relations Dept., InterVarsity Christian Fellowship/USA, 6400 Schroeder Rd., P.O. Box 7895, Madison, WI 53707-7895, or visit the IVCF website at <www.intervarsity.org>.

Scripture quotations, unless otherwise noted, are from the New Revised Standard Version of the Bible, *copyright 1989 by the Division of Christian Education of the National Council of the Churches of Christ in the USA. Used by permission. All rights reserved.*

"The Mad Farmer, Flying the Flag of Rough Branch, Secedes from the Union" is taken from Wendell Berry, The Selected Poems of Wendell Berry *(Washington, D.C.: Counterpoint, 1998). Used with permission. "Manifesto: The Mad Farmer Liberation Front" is taken from Wendell Berry,* The Selected Poems of Wendell Berry *(Washington, D.C.: Counterpoint, 1998). Used with permission of Counterpoint and North Point Press, a division of Farrar, Straus and Giroux, LLC.*

"Amazingly Alive," "Down Here" and "The Truth of Community" are taken from Bud Osborn, Hundred Block Rock *(Vancouver, B.C.: Arsenal Pulp Press, 1999). Used with permission.*

Every effort has been made to trace and contact copyright holders for additional materials quoted in this book. The authors will be pleased to rectify any omissions in future editions if notified by copyright holders.

Design: Cindy Kiple
Images: SEF/Art Resource, NY

ISBN 0-8308-2738-2
Printed in the United States of America ∞

Library of Congress Cataloging-in-Publication Data

Walsh, Brian J., 1953-
  Colossians remixed: subverting the empire/by Brian J. Walsh and Sylvia C. Keesmaat.
    p. cm.
  Includes bibliographical references.
  ISBN 0-8308-2738-2 (pbk.: alk. paper)
  1. Bible. N.T. Colossians—Social scientific criticism. 2. Rome in the Bible. 3. Globalization—Religious aspects—Christianity. I. Keesmaat, Sylvia C. II. Title.
    BS2715.6.R65W35 2004
    227'.706—dc22

                                                              2004017265

| P | 21 | 20 | 19 | 18 | 17 | 16 | 15 | 14 | 13 | 12 | 11 | 10 | 9 | 8 | 7 | 6 | 5 | 4 |
| Y | 21 | 20 | 19 | 18 | 17 | 16 | 15 | 14 | 13 | 12 | 11 | 10 | 09 | 08 | 07 | 06 | 05 |

CONTENTS

PREFACE

The idea of "remixing" carries with it ambiguous overtones. At its worst, remixing is a way to give some new shelf life to a past musical recording in order to generate continued income for washed-out rock stars and their mercenary record companies. Or sometimes a piece of music is remixed into a new song in a way that rips off the original artist both aesthetically and financially. But at its best, remixing is a matter of giving an older artistic expression new currency. In this sense, remixing is a matter of "revoicing," allowing the original song to be sung again in a contemporary context that is culturally and aesthetically different. Such a remixing honors and respects the integrity and brilliance of the original piece while helping it to be heard anew in the ears and lives of people with different cultural sensibilities.

Whether *Colossians Remixed* is an attempt to rehear an ancient text that should simply be left in its antiquated past, or a rip-off of the original author, or a revoicing of this ancient Christian letter in a way that allows it to be heard in the twenty-first century with integrity, is something that the reader will have to decide. But we should at least be clear about our intention. The epistle to the Colossians, we are arguing, was an explosive and subversive tract in the context of the Roman empire, and it can and ought to function in an analogous way in the imperial realities of our time. This letter proclaimed an alternative vision of reality, animating a way of life that was subversive to the ethos of the Roman empire. We believe that Paul's letter to the Colossians will only be read with integrity in our time when the radical vision of Christian faith encountered in this text engenders a similarly alternative way of life in our midst.

There is a sense in which this book is an "anti-commentary." While cognizant of the critical literature that has been written on Colossians, and not wanting to be totally dismissive of the writing of commentaries, our project attempts to go beyond the genre of commentary writing in three ways. First, the technical apparatus of commentaries is largely absent from this book. We know the intricacies of the Greek text (or at least Sylvia does!), we understand the arguments for and against Pauline authorship, and we have followed the debate about the identity of the "Colossian philosophy"; we know that these are valid and important topics. But we aren't overly interested in these issues because they do not bear heavily upon the questions that we bring to this text. Most of the issues raised by the commentaries remain mired in the problems of modernity, but ours is a postmodern culture (and we will offer our own nuanced reading of *postmodernity*). Our questions, therefore, seek to hear Colossians anew in our cultural context.

Second, commentaries are written for professionally religious people like pastors and professors. Both of us are professors and Brian is also a pastor, so we aren't denigrating these fine professions. It's just that we aren't writing for pastors and scholars, though we do hope that our colleagues in these guilds will find what we have written to be helpful to them. Rather, our audience is people like William, whom you will meet in the first chapter—people who have a hard time hearing the Scriptures speak in a way that addresses them where they are. Ours is a cultural, political, social and ecological reading of this text because these are the kinds of questions that our friends and our students ask. They are the kinds of questions that we ask. And that leads to the third way in which this is an anti-commentary.

Not only is our audience different from traditional commentaries, so also is our question. To illustrate, we'll tell you how this book had its origins: curiously enough, in conversation with a commentary writer.

In 1982 Brian began his doctoral studies at McGill University in Montréal where he met a young biblical scholar named Tom Wright. Tom was working on his Tyndale commentary on Colossians and Philemon at the time, and he asked Brian if he would read the manuscript. This began both a conversation that went on for a number of months and an enduring friendship. Tom would give Brian manuscript text on Tuesday afternoon; Brian would go home and read it that evening, and then they would meet and talk about it for a couple of hours Wednesday morning. The overriding question that Brian raised in these conversations was, "So what?" Tom's exegetical work around the meaning of things like "thrones, dominions, authorities and powers" was suggestive of so much more than he was allowing himself to address in the commentary. Brian wanted him to name contemporary names. Might the Pentagon or IBM or the International Monetary Fund be contemporary parallels to the rulers and authorities that put Jesus on the cross? And if it is true that Christ is the Creator and Redeemer of "all things" as the Colossian poem so eloquently puts it, then what might be the implications of such a breathtakingly comprehensive worldview for our ecological, political and economic lives?

Tom was writing a commentary, however, and these kinds of questions went beyond anything that such a genre could bear. So this book was born over twenty years ago. Brian has continued to teach and reflect on Colossians in pretty much everything he has done since those Wednesday morning conversations with Tom. Sylvia picked up on similar themes when she studied with Tom at Oxford from 1989 to 1992. When we married in 1993 it became clear that together we would eventually write a book that would attempt to answer the questions Brian had raised so many years earlier. And it also became clear that our answer to the "so what" question addressed to this ancient text would have to be embodied in the life that we would lead together as a couple and a family. As a result we made a commitment to each other, and we make it to you our reader, that we would not propose a way of life that we ourselves were not living out.

St. Paul knows that the vision that he is talking about makes no sense if it doesn't shape the Christian household as an alternative to the dominant Roman model of household life. And so the testing ground for anything that we say in this book is first and foremost our family. Our three children, Jubal, Madeleine and Lydia, did not have to "suffer through" the writing of this book. If they did then the book would in fact lack credibility. We did not "sacrifice" family life through long absences while researching and writing. So we offer the kids no apologies. Rather we thank them for grounding our lives in the important things like learning and housekeeping, playing and growing up, stories and nighttime prayers, tears and laughter.

Colossians is a subversive tract for subversive living, and it insists that such an alternative imagination and alternative way of life is formed and sustained in the context of community. So while this book began in our community with each other and with our friend Tom Wright, it immediately encompasses a larger community.

Food and worship pretty much sum up the human condition, and two communities have significantly contributed to our lives in these areas. First, we have been sustained with bread and wine, prayers and fellowship, baptisms and funerals, joy and sorrow, through our worship at the Church of the Redeemer in Toronto. This wonderful parish has been a place for us to serve as teachers and preachers, in ministry to the homeless and in pastoral care for the hurting and dying. And it has been a nourishing community that has sustained and encouraged our growth in Christian discipleship.

Second, the food side of the equation, is our involvement in a community called Karma Co-op. As one might tell from its name, Karma is a richly diverse multifaith community that runs a food cooperative, and it is as part of this that we buy our food. When we talk about the meaning of Paul's community ethic in chapter ten of this book and address it to how and what we eat, our debt to our friends at Karma will be clear.

Another important community is our students. The book begins with a student named William, and it is fair to say that the whole book has been written in conversation with our students. We have shared material from the book with students throughout Canada, the United States, New Zealand, Australia and Britain and have been enriched deeply through these conversations. The most sustained dialogue, however, has been with our students at the Institute for Christian Studies in Toronto, the Graduate Christian Fellowship and Wycliffe College (both at the University of Toronto), and the Creation Care Studies Program in Belize and New Zealand. We are indebted to many students who read all or large sections of this manuscript while it was in process and offered helpful challenges and corrections, probing questions and deep encouragement along the way.

Many others have also helped in the writing of this book. Tom Wright, Andrew Lincoln and Walter Brueggemann read sections of the book and provided encouragement. Thank you. Three friends, however, read the whole manuscript and gave us invaluable assistance. Janet Somerville confessed to us that she is more invested in relationships than in books and so finds that she doesn't read as much as she would like to. But when we asked if she would like to take a look at what was then a much longer manuscript, Janet immediately said yes. Her comments came at a crucial time in the development of this book, and for that we are deeply thankful. Richard Middleton is no stranger to things written by Walsh and Keesmaat, since he has coauthored works with both of us in the past. His insightful comments have helped us immeasurably, and we can also thank Richard for the overall three-part structure of the book. Byron Borger runs the best Christian bookstore in the world in Dallastown, Pennsylvania, called "Hearts and Minds." He is also the most well-read Christian that we know. His comments and suggestions on the manuscript will save us from some, but not all, of the criticisms that he anticipated. Janet, Richard and Byron aren't just generous colleagues who took considerable time out of their busy schedules to read a very long manuscript; they are fellow sojourners on the way, following the same Lord. With them at our side we find it just a little easier to stay on the path.

There is a fourth person who read the whole manuscript, and not just once! Jason Postma was our student assistant from the Institute for Christian Studies, and he carefully developed the indices that appear at the end of this book. A good index is a valuable asset to any book, and the production of such an index requires a careful and close reading of the text. Jason's work demonstrates something that goes beyond careful and close reading. This text, this rehearing of Colossians, *matters* to Jason, and the work he put into preparing the indices wonderfully demonstrates his enthusiasm for the project.

Sylvia's professional context while writing this book was the Institute for Christian Studies. She thanks her colleagues for their support and the Institute for sabbatical leaves to work on this book. Brian serves as a Christian Reformed campus minister to the University of Toronto and is grateful to the Christian Reformed Churches of Classis Toronto for their support and for a writing leave in 2004. A team of wonderful co-workers has always blessed Brian's ministry. Brian Lim, Charleen Jongejan, Alison Hari-Singh and Geoff Wichert have made ministry at the U of T both fruitful and fun. Their voices and lives can be heard throughout this book.

The Priscilla and Stanford Reid Trust provided the Christian Reformed Campus

Ministry (CRC) to the University of Toronto with two very generous grants in order to hire staff to assist Brian in his ministry and release him from some responsibilities in order to create time for the writing of this book. Professor Stanford Reid was a historian who insisted that his Christian faith was integral to his scholarship, and as such, he was a model of Christian scholarly discipleship to a generation of Canadian Christian academics. We are indebted to his ministry and grateful to the Trust for their financial support. We hope that this book does justice to the memory and heritage of Dr. and Mrs. Reid.

Rodney Clapp encouraged us to write this book when he was editor for academic books at InterVarsity Press. A change of publishing houses doesn't change friendships, and we continue to find great joy in our friendship with Rodney. Gary Deddo graciously took this orphaned contract and saw it through to completion with patience and grace. The copyediting of Ruth Goring has helped us achieve greater clarity and economy in our writing. Thank you.

Finally, this book is dedicated to our friend Bud Osborn—poet, prophet and priest. A priest because he mediates the pain of the most vulnerable, bringing it before the throne of God; a prophet because he proclaims to the powerful the cries of the suffering and demands justice; and a poet because it is through his poetry that he exercises his prophetic and priestly offices. Bud Osborn gives us courage to persist and to insist on life in the face of death, compassion in the face of cruelty and justice in the face of oppression. We dedicate this book to Bud because there is a profound kinship between the subversive poetry of Bud Osborn and the subversive vision of life we find in Paul's letter to the Colossians. Both root their subversion in following Jesus and in living for the kingdom that liberates rather than the empire that enslaves. At the end of his poem, "Down Here," Bud writes:

> let my words
> sing a prayer
> not a curse
> to the tragic
> & sacred mystery
>
> of our beautiful
> suffering
> eternal worth

If our words can echo the words of Bud Osborn, then we would be deeply grateful. This book, and these words, are dedicated to him.

Pentecost 2004

PART ONE

CONTEXT REMIXED

COLOSSIANS AND EMPIRE

— 1 —

PLACING OURSELVES

Globalization and Postmodernity

By some reckonings, the twentieth century had already ended in some parts of the world as we sat in a pub with William on December 31, 1999. It was good to see him for the first time in quite a while. He was now in law school, having recently returned from a stint working in international finance in London. That experience had led William to the conclusion that money is boring and that people who get excited about money are even more boring than the money itself. While we were wondering whether law school might lead him to simply intensify this already insightful conclusion, the conversation took a different turn.

"I've decided that I am a theist," he announced.

"Oh?" we asked. "And what does that mean?"

"Well, I guess that I've concluded that autonomy isn't all it's cracked up to be. I no longer believe that I am totally in control of my life. There is a higher power—God—with whom I must be in relation."

This confession had a familiar ring to it. Didn't the Gen X author Douglas Coupland offer a similar confession near the end of his book *Life After God*? "My secret is that I need God—that I am sick and can no longer make it alone. I need God to help me give, because I no longer seem to be capable of giving; to help me be kind, as I no longer seem capable of kindness; to help me love, as I seem beyond being able to love."[1] Of course, William didn't quite say all of that, but the sentiment was similar. And we knew William well enough to know that his abandonment of autonomy was his way of appropriating certain important features of postmodern culture and thought.

Autonomy was the clarion call of modernity, with its image of a self-made, self-centered ego. William had played with such a self-image and found it resulted in

---

[1]Douglas Coupland, *Life After God* (New York: Pocket, 1994), p. 359.

loneliness and confusion. Moreover, William's international finance experience, in which people made their fortunes and moved massive amounts of capital around the world every day, had been less than exciting and definitely not fulfilling. So William abandoned international finance and in the process abandoned autonomy and embraced theism.

This was quite a step for William. Raised in a Christian home that was deeply reflective and intellectually stimulating, with parents who had academic and pastoral ministries, William had become deeply alienated from Christian faith during his university studies. It was in that context that we'd first met. And now, a number of years later, William gave us a state-of-his-soul report by telling us of his embrace of theism. Needless to say, the news was received warmly both at home by his parents and in the pub that December afternoon.

But before we could pursue the issues further, William made an important clarification.

"This doesn't mean that I'm reading the Bible on any regular basis, though."

"And why is that?" we asked.

"My problem with the Bible is that as soon as I open it I bump up against the absolute. Actually, it is more that the absolute punches me in the face whenever I read this book."

As we inquired further to learn exactly what William was struggling with, certain themes began to emerge. For William there is an incredible tension between his lived experience and what he meets in the biblical text. In his lived experience everything is malleable, porous and changeable. He does not live in a world of unchanging, hard-and-fast absolutes. For William life is fundamentally a matter of interdependent relationships. And relationships are, by definition, dynamic, changeable and in process. So how does he read a text that seems to be set in stone, that seems to be full of absolutes? For William, such a text is not simply alien, it is offensive. This text proclaims a Truth (with a capital *T*), speaking with an absolute authority that is unrelated to William's lived experience. Actually, for William it is worse than that. This absolute is not only unrelated to his experience but also seems to be experience-denying and profoundly disempowering.

How then does William respond to the biblical text? Usually by reading a couple of verses and then slamming the book shut. His immediate impulse is to resist this text, question it, attack it. William responds to biblical texts with a deeply set hermeneutic of suspicion. And he has good reason for his suspicion. This text has been used—in his experience and throughout much of Christian history—as a repressive book of absolutes that silenced all questioning. Indeed the Bible seems to be a text suffused with certainty. And if there is one thing that William and his generation are certain of, it is that there is no certainty. Certainty needs to be abandoned because it claims too much for any human perspective.

Again we come back to William's problem with absolutes in the midst of a world of dynamic relationships. To be in relation is to be relative. Allan Bloom's depiction of the average university student at the end of the twentieth century fits William well: "There is one thing a professor can be absolutely certain of: almost every student entering the university believes, or says he believes, that truth is relative."[2] Of course truth is relative, replies William. Just consider the alternative! The modernist pretense to have objectively grasped a total reality invariably results in a totalitarian social practice. Failing to recognize that human knowledge is always constructed in particular historical contexts, "total systems" are invariably achieved "only at the cost of violence, by repressing what doesn't fit and erasing the memory of those who have questioned it."[3] At least implicitly agreeing with Jean-François Lyotard that modernist totality thinking has given us "as much terror as we can take,"[4] William has renounced the quest for a total scheme of things because it is both unattainable and inherently violent. In this important respect William is postmodern.[5]

So, given this postmodern allergic reaction to absolutism and any and all large claims to have understood, grasped and become a spokesperson for the Truth, what happens when someone like William attempts to read a particular biblical text like Paul's letter to the Christian community in Colossae? Essentially the allergic reaction sets in.

When William opens up a text like Colossians, the first thing he is struck by—indeed the first absolute to hit him in the face—is the claim the author is making for himself.[6] "Paul, an apostle of Christ Jesus by the will of God" (1:1). Given that introduction, is this a text that is likely to invite dialogue? Is this a text that might give the reader enough room to beg to differ on any subject that it addresses? Not likely. The author identifies himself in such a way that not only does he have divine authority but so also does the text that he writes.

Things only get worse as the salutation continues: "To the saints and faithful brothers and sisters in Christ" (1:2). After asking whether the sisters were really mentioned in the original (they were not; this is a contemporary inclusive translation), William is concerned that there is here a fundamental exclusionary dichotomy. If some folks are saints and faithful, then others must be sinners and faithless, and William is wor-

---

[2]Allan Bloom, *The Closing of the American Mind* (New York: Simon & Schuster, 1987), p. 25.

[3]John D. Caputo, "A Cold and Comfortless Hermeneutic or a Warm and Trembling Hermeneutic: A Conversation with John D. Caputo," interview by James H. Olthuis, *Christian Scholar's Review* 19, no. 4 (1990): 351.

[4]Jean-François Lyotard, *The Postmodern Condition: A Report on Knowledge, Theory and History of Literature*, trans. Geoff Bennington and Brian Massumi (Minneapolis: University of Minnesota Press, 1984), p. 81.

[5]See J. Richard Middleton and Brian J. Walsh, *Truth Is Stranger Than It Used to Be: Biblical Faith in a Postmodern Age* (Downers Grove, Ill.: InterVarsity Press, 1995), chap. 2.

[6]While our story about William so far has been reporting a real conversation, the account that follows is a loose fictionalization based on e-mail correspondence.

ried that he and his friends are in the second camp. So the text has, at least in his reading, already excluded him. Why would he continue to read?

But continue he does. Admittedly it is only a cursory read, but he notices that in the first twenty verses of this letter the author uses words like *all, everything* and *whole* something like twelve times. This author is certainly not afraid of making large claims! Given his religious perspective and divinely appointed authority, the author presumes to talk about how *all* of creation hangs together (1:17) and even to intimate that the point of his letter to these folks in Colossae is that they would come to *all* "wisdom and understanding" (1:9). But then if you presume to know how the whole world hangs together, it isn't such a big step to say that somehow you can impart that wisdom to anyone who will submit to your authority.

For William, things simply go from bad to worse in this text. While a lot of the imagery of the letter simply makes no connection whatsoever for him, William finds that much of the epistle seems to be little more than an attack on the corporeal self. Why such a preoccupation with sex and the flesh in chapter 3? With this attack on the body there also comes the repressive foolishness of Paul's admonitions to wives, children and slaves to obey their husbands, fathers and masters.

There, William insists, is where this whole letter was going from the beginning. "You posit a divine authority that structures and orders the world in a certain way, attribute that authority to yourself as author of the letter, wipe out any opposition that suggests things might be looked at differently, put clear restrictions on personal and communal life, and then top it all off with a divine sanction for patriarchy and slavery. And you want a postmodern person at the beginning of the twenty-first century to read this text, learn from it and maybe even receive it as divinely inspired Scripture? I don't think so!"

Discerning Our Context

Reading is always contextual. How one reads, interprets and responds to a text is influenced and formed by the context within which one does the reading. Latin American peasants, upper-middle-class North Americans and African villagers engage this text differently.[7] And so does someone like William. For William, the Bible is an alien and oppressive text of absolutes. How did William ever come to such a conclusion? It wasn't too difficult. You see, this is the Bible William met in Sunday school and while listening to countless sermons as a young person reared within a particular kind of Christian community. Within that Christian tradition the Bible is received as an authoritative text of absolute Truth. But we have seen that this is not the only context in which William lives his life. He is also a member of what has been dubbed

---

[7]See Fernando F. Segovia and Mary Ann Tolbert, eds., *Reading from This Place,* vol. 1, *Social Location and Biblical Interpretation in the United States,* and vol. 2, *Social Location and Biblical Interpretation in Global Perspective* (Minneapolis: Fortress, 1995).

Generation X and is comfortable describing himself as "postmodern." Interestingly, however, this Gen X postmodern has also dabbled in international finance and law school. All of this forms the context in which William reads and evaluates an ancient biblical text.

Reading is always *from* somewhere. We always read from a particular historical, cultural and geographical place. The question that we must ask is, how do we discern our particular place at the beginning of the twenty-first century? How do we "place" ourselves, how do we discern the times and spirits that invariably influence our reading of a text like Colossians? What are the questions, crises and opportunities that we necessarily (and legitimately) bring to this text? If we are not clear about these issues the biblical text will remain silent, unable to address (and confront!) us where we live.

Such discernment, however, is no easy thing. Indeed, cultural discernment in service of opening up the biblical text must be deeply rooted in that very text. Discernment of the spirits of our time must be directed by the Spirit who, we confess, has inspired this text. Another way to say this is that any worldview analysis of our cultural context that will serve the reading of the biblical text in that context must drink deeply from the wells of a biblical worldview.[8]

But cultural discernment is always a risky business. How do we discern between competing cultural visions, seemingly conflicting cultural trends and interpretations of our time that are in stark contradiction to each other? Consider two visions that would appear to be diametrically opposed.

Peter McLaren opens his hard-hitting critique of contemporary culture with these words:

> I will not mince my words. We live at a precarious moment in history. Relations of subjection, suffering, dispossession and contempt for human dignity and the sanctity of life are at the center of social existence. Emotional dislocation, moral sickness and individual helplessness remain ubiquitous features of our time.[9]

This emotional dislocation and sense of helplessness are the result, he says, of late modernity's "dehydrated imagination that has lost its capacity to dream otherwise."[10] And with this loss of imaginative creativity a "funky nihilism has set in; an aroma of cultural disquiet."[11]

Precariousness, helplessness, dislocation, dispossession, nihilism and cultural disquiet—that is one way to read the times. Consider another. In 1998 *Wired* maga-

---

[8]Brian J. Walsh and J. Richard Middleton, *The Transforming Vision: Shaping a Christian Worldview* (Downers Grove, Ill.: InterVarsity Press, 1984), pt. 2.
[9]Peter McLaren, *Critical Pedagogy and Predatory Culture: Oppositional Politics in a Postmodern Age* (New York: Routledge, 1995), p. 1.
[10]Ibid., p. 2.
[11]Ibid., p. 4.

zine delivered its "State of the Planet" statement in the form of an evocative photoessay.[12] In the opening of the essay we see contrasting images on two pages. On the left there are two photographs: the chest of a black man with the word *Terror* crudely (and cruelly) burned into his skin, and a densely smog-covered cityscape. The caption over these images looks something like this:

YESTERDAY
We lived in the shadow of nuclear
and environmental apocalypse.

On the facing page, however, we see a beautiful garden scene, lush in spring bloom with a tranquil, flowing stream. The caption strikes the contrast with the previous message:

We stand on the verge of an era
of peace, freedom,
prosperity, and
environmental
harmony.
TODAY
Not that we don't
have problems—
we do.

But we also
have real reasons
to be optimistic
about the future

because
things
are getting
better.

Funky nihilism or optimism? Precariousness or things are getting better? Contempt for the sanctity of life or environmental harmony? Suffering or peace? Emotional dislocation, individual helplessness and moral sickness, or peace, freedom and prosperity? Two visions, both powerfully alive in our culture. How do we discern between them?

We will investigate these two visions under the broad rubric of postmodern disquiet and cybernetic global optimism. After discussing each cultural dynamic, we will ask how they might be related.

---

[12]"Change Is Good," *Wired* 6.01, special fifth-anniversary issue (January 1998): 163-207.

Postmodern Disquiet

The performer has returned to the stage for an encore.[13] A solitary woman sits down at a grand piano, while the crowd shouts out the names of songs she has not yet performed in the concert. She quietly begins to play and then leans towards the microphone and sings, "Somewhere, over the rainbow . . ."

The crowd goes wild. Someone shouts out, "Toto!" But as she continues to sing, a hush, a deeply respectful silence, falls over the crowd. You see, if you aren't quiet you won't be able to hear this remarkable performance. The artist is Tori Amos, famous for her pathos-filled, post-Christian and postmodern songs of pain and loss.[14] And she sings this song of longing for home, this cultural icon from *The Wizard of Oz,* with an intensity and a pathos that are immediately arresting. When she gets to lines like "And dreams that you dared to dream really do come true," her voice trails off, and that last word of the phrase—*true*—is barely whispered.

It is clear that this is a song sung from the perspective of a terribly broken heart. In this performance there is no confidence that dreams can come true, that there might even be such a thing as truth, that the plot tensions of our lives might ever be resolved and we might finally be able to go back home. For Amos, and for many of her generation, there is no going home. She sings the song as if she is out of breath because she is all cried out. Her performance is a testimony to the ending of dreams and a profound loss of confidence in the hopes of a modernist culture. At heart, this performance questions not just whether the story of homecoming in *The Wizard of Oz* is still believable but whether the whole narrative of modern culture might have exhausted itself.

Amos embodies in her music precisely the kind of cultural disquiet that McLaren refers to. Her inability to return home mirrors the emotional dislocation of our time. And that sense of cultural disquiet, we suggest, is all-pervasive. We can feel it in our bones when we walk through a mall or turn on the television. Something is different "out there" and maybe even deep within ourselves. There is indeed a sense of cultural disquiet. We have a sinking feeling that we don't really understand what is going on, but we know that the changes taking place around us affect both what we believe and the way we believe it.

The term *postmodern* keeps being tossed about as a possible explanation for our present confusion and malaise. But what does it mean? The attempt to find an answer to this ques-

---

[13]Portions of this section have been previously published in three articles by Brian Walsh. "The Church in a Postmodern Age: Ten Things You Need to Know," *Good Idea! A Resource Sheet on Evangelism and Church Growth* 3, no. 4 (Winter 1996): 1-5; "Education in Precarious Times: Postmodernity and a Christian World View," in *The Crumbling Walls of Certainty: Towards a Christian Critique of Postmodernity and Education,* ed. Ian Lambert and Suzanne Mitchell (Sydney: Centre for the Study of Australian Christianity, 1997), pp. 8-24; and "Where Is Society Going? Education, Tall Tales and the End of an Era," *Christian Teachers Journal* 8, no. 2 (May 2000): 4-9.

[14]Tori Amos, "Somewhere over the Rainbow—Live," from the CD *Hey Juniper,* Atlantic Recording, 1996.

tion can be frustrating. Since the postmodern outlook is characteristically suspicious of definitions, what follows is necessarily more descriptive than an attempt at definition.[15]

The first thing that we need to say about postmodern culture is that it is a culture of betrayal. This is at the heart of our cultural crisis and is the emotional source for a widespread hermeneutic of suspicion—not just of ancient authoritative texts but of any systems or institutions of authority. Long before we begin trying to listen to what postmodern thinkers might be saying, we need to note that the experience on the street, and especially the experience of young people, is suffused with a sense of betrayal. In the song "bullet with butterfly wings" on the album *Mellon Collie and the Infinite Sadness,* the Smashing Pumpkins sing,

> the world is a vampire, sent to drain
> secret destroyers, hold you up to the flames
> and what do i get, for my pain
> betrayed desires, and a piece of the game.[16]

This quintessentially Generation X lament is permeated by a deep sense of betrayal. Someone has told them a story, spun them a line, about the good life, and it has proved to be a lie. When the lie runs as deep as this, it is not surprising that they experience the world not as a place of safety and opportunity but as a "vampire" that sucks the very lifeblood out of them. The world is decidedly malignant and dangerous. The best that one can expect in this world of betrayal is to simply get a piece of the game; but even this cannot be guaranteed.

Betrayal can breed either rage or numbness. While we meet rage at antiglobalization protests, the more prevalent postmodern emotional response is numbness and boredom.[17] For example, in the teen film *Pump Up the Volume* the young protagonist says, "There's nothing left to do anymore. Everything decent's been done; all the great themes have been used up and turned into theme parks." And the Smashing Pumpkins echo this sentiment when they sing,

> there's nothing left to do
> there's nothing left to feel.[18]

---

[15]Robin Usher and Richard Edwards note that the term *postmodern* is not a fixed description but a "loose umbrella term under whose broad cover can be encompassed at one and the same time a condition, a set of practices, a cultural discourse and a mode of analysis" (*Postmodernism and Education: Different Voices, Different Worlds* [New York: Routledge, 1994], p. 7).

[16]Smashing Pumpkins, "bullet with butterfly wings," from the album *Mellon Collie and the Infinite Sadness,* ©Virgin Records America, 1995. Lyrics by Billy Corgan.

[17]In the early 1990s Albert Borgmann described the mood of America as a passive sullenness evidenced by "the incapacity to be pained by things undone and challenges unmet" (*Crossing the Postmodern Divide* [Chicago: University of Chicago Press, 1992], pp. 6-7).

[18]Smashing Pumpkins, "jelly belly," on *Mellon Collie and the Infinite Sadness,* ©Virgin Records America, 1995. Lyrics by Billy Corgan. This song also includes the words "living makes me sick / so sick i wish i'd die / down in the belly of the beast."

We feel most passionately when we have a sense of newness to our life, projects to complete, dreams to fulfill. If there is nothing left to do, then there is nothing left to feel either. And if the guiding narrative of our culture breeds suspicion, not confidence, then history-forming action is paralyzed.

It is not surprising, therefore, that Lyotard's summary of postmodernity is the one most often cited: "Simplifying in the extreme, I define postmodernity as incredulity toward all metanarratives."[19] Again, the Smashing Pumpkins prove to be insightful. In their infinitely sad song "tales of a scorched earth," they sing, "and we're all dead yeah we're all dead / inside the future of a shattered past."[20] We live inside the future of a shattered past because that past told grand stories that have proved to be destructive lies. The grand story of a Marxist utopia collapsed along with the Berlin Wall. The heroic tale of technological progress blew up with the Challenger explosion. The progress myth of democratic capitalism that promised economic prosperity and social harmony strains under the weight of economic contraction, ecological threat, and an ever-widening gap between the rich and the poor, both domestically and internationally. The postmodernist ethos insists that stories such as these—stories that have so shaped our lives—are not stories of emancipation and progress after all but stories of enslavement, oppression and violence. And on such a view, any story, any worldview, that makes grand claims about the real course and destiny of history—including the grand narrative of God's redemption of all of creation in Christ found in a text like Colossians—will make common cause with such violence and oppression.

Of course, all of this creates profound uncertainty for human history-forming praxis. Alisdair MacIntyre is right when he says, "I can only answer the question 'What am I to do?' if I can answer the prior question 'Of what story or stories do I find myself a part?'"[21] But if all narratives—especially overarching and civilization-directing metanarratives—are met with postmodern incredulity, then it is not surprising that postmodern culture appears to have no fixed ethical anchors and is characterized by profound moral instability.

In his apocalyptic song "The Future," Leonard Cohen sings,

Things are going to slide in all directions
Won't be nothing you can measure anymore.[22]

Robin Usher and Richard Edwards make the same point: "Postmodernity, then, describes a world where people have to make their way without fixed referents and

---

[19]Lyotard, *Postmodern Condition*, p. xxiv.

[20]Smashing Pumpkins, "tales of a scorched earth," on *Mellon Collie and the Infinite Sadness,* ©Virgin Records America, 1995. Lyrics by Billy Corgan.

[21]Alasdair MacIntyre, *After Virtue: A Study of Moral Theory,* 2nd ed. (Notre Dame, Ind.: University of Notre Dame Press, 1984), p. 216.

[22]Leonard Cohen, "The Future," from the album *The Future,* ©Sony Music Entertainment, 1992.

traditional anchoring points. It is a world of rapid change, of bewildering instability, where knowledge is constantly changing and meaning 'floats.'"[23]

Postmodernity insists that all moral codes, all normative frameworks, are particular inventions of people in history. This means that the old idea that there are moral absolutes to which we all have access and to which we all, in principle, are subject has evaporated in the heat of a postmodern culture. And since there are no universally recognizable measures for human life, it is not surprising that Cohen confesses that "When they said REPENT / I wonder what they meant."[24] One can only imagine what happens when a text that speaks of "forgiveness" (Col 1:14) and being "blameless and irreproachable" (1:22) is read in such a context.

Together with moral instability and incredulity toward all metanarratives and totality systems, postmodern culture is a *postrationalist* culture. Simply stated, while the modernist penchant for seeking rational justification for all beliefs and actions lives on in some segments of our culture, it is all but dead in the street and in the real lives of people as they make economic, political, cultural and religious choices. Notice that few products are touted on television these days on the basis of being "scientifically proven." That doesn't impress the postmodern consumer. On the contrary we are all too aware that science can prove whatever we want it to and rational argumentation can be used for all kinds of terrible causes. Rather than being concerned with rational justification, the quintessential epistemological stance of a postmodern culture is "Show me." What will this idea accomplish? What are the implications for my life and the life of our culture and planet if we accept this perspective as true?

While we will argue in this book that such an epistemological stance is in important respects both legitimate and thoroughly biblical, it needs to be acknowledged that there is a cultural downside to all of this. The relative homogeneity of a modernist culture is replaced by the carnivalesque culture of postmodernity. Lacking any unifying story, rational justifications and normative anchors, postmodern culture fills the boredom of our time with a carnival of worldview options and consumer-directed faiths. An all-encompassing plurality of beliefs and perspectives are available for our tasting and consumption. Or perhaps we could say that we live in a mall culture: the carnival has simply moved indoors. And just as we mix and match our wardrobe items and our culinary tastes at the mall, so also do we find it increasingly unproblematic to combine beliefs from various religious traditions into one faith. The imposition of one set of beliefs is seen to be a hegemonic move to close down other options. Postmodernity is all about keeping your options open and not closing down new experiences, perspectives, rituals and beliefs without trying them out. If life is a carnival, then why not taste every-

---

[23]Usher and Edwards, *Postmodernism and Education,* p. 10.
[24]Cohen, "Future."

thing that is on offer? Being "all over the map" would appear to be a postmodern virtue.

Consider the "anything goes" attitude described by Kenneth Gergen: "Under post-modern conditions, persons exist in a state of continuous construction and recon-struction; it is a world where anything goes that can be negotiated. Each reality gives way to reflexive questioning, irony, and ultimately the playful probing of yet another reality. The center fails to hold."[25] Why place so much emphasis on coherence in our moral or spiritual lives, especially if such coherence would mean no longer being open to all of the diverse spiritualities, worldviews and lifestyles that we have to choose from? Why close down choice? In place of the blandness of homogeneity, postmodernists raise a toast to heterogeneity, the celebration of difference.[26]

But if we are to celebrate heterogeneity, then what are we to make of a text like Colossians that seems to strenuously close down choice in its attack on any kind of syncretism?

Perhaps we need to begin by acknowledging that an abandonment of coherence has debilitating personal and cultural consequences. Modernist homogeneity is easily replaced by postmodern fragmentation. Tom Beaudoin puts it this way: "For Xers, both our *experience* and our *imagination* of our selves are characterized more by inco-herence than coherence, more by fragmentation than unity." He goes on to say, "We seem to have many centers, each of them shifting and unstable.[27]

When one is accustomed to toying with a multiplicity of perspectives, identi-ties and worldviews, it is not surprising that life starts to feel fragmented. And when "difference" is experienced not just "out there in the world" but deep within our personal life, a biblical text that offers a path to integral wholeness (see Col 1:28—2:3) could only be received as odd at best, or as offering unrealistic pipe dreams at worst.

Postmodernity, then, can be described as a period of cultural disquiet. In the face of the betrayals and failures of past overarching metanarratives, culturewide suspi-cion and incredulity takes hold. A single story, providing coherence to personal iden-tity, grounding for ethical action and passion for life in history, is displaced by a car-nivalesque existence of fragmentation, numbness and boredom. Final decisions based on rational analysis give way to the undecidability of keeping all options open and the spiritual promiscuity of pop religion.

Cohen captures our cultural mood well when he sings,

---

[25]Kenneth Gergen, *The Saturated Self: Dilemmas of Identity in Contemporary Life* (New York: BasicBooks, 1991), p. 7.

[26]Our thanks to David Lyon for this phrase. For helpful exposition of our cultural times, see his book *Post-modernity* (Minneapolis: University of Minnesota Press, 1994).

[27]Tom Beaudoin, *Virtual Faith: The Irreverent Spiritual Quest of Generation X* (San Francisco: Jossey-Bass, 1998), p. 137.

The blizzard of the world
has crossed the threshold
and it has overturned
the order of the soul.[28]

The cultural disquiet we are here describing is not a shift that is taking place only "around us"; it is happening "within us." The postmodern blizzard has crossed the threshold and entered our homes. This is quite literally the case every time we turn on the television or surf the Internet. Christians do not live in a self-enclosed, hermetically sealed world. They breathe the same air as everyone else, and postmodernity is in the air.

So how do we read Scripture, specifically the letter to the Colossians, in such a context? Can Scripture continue to speak a fresh word, a radical word that has "voice and force in changed circumstances"?[29]

But things are more complicated than we have thus far suggested. Recall that postmodern disquiet is only one voice we need to hear as we discern our cultural context. There is another loud, persistent and powerful voice.

Cybernetic Global Optimism

Here's the problem. The same young adults who listen appreciatively to artists like the Smashing Pumpkins (and Tori Amos, Nine Inch Nails, Rage Against the Machine, Marilyn Manson, etc.) are often at the forefront of the cybernetic revolution with all of its super-hyped hope of a new era of economic growth along the information highway. Somehow, crushing despair and even nihilism capture the imagination of a generation that at the same time is buoyantly optimistic about the future. What we see here is both a sense of the emptiness, betrayal and ending of a particular cultural mythology and—at the same time and often in the same people!—a retrenchment, intensification and rebirth of that very same worldview or cultural myth.

While an artist like Leonard Cohen can apocalyptically intone that the story of modernity is "over, it ain't going any further" precisely because the poet has "seen the future baby, it is murder,"[30] that's not the way things look from the perspective of the cybernetic revolution. Indeed, IBM ran a three-paneled advertisement recently that confidently proclaimed in the middle panel, "We have seen the future. And it actually held still for a couple of photographs." Those photographs are on the other two panels, and they are, predictably enough, of IBM's most recent technology.

Wired magazine's photoessay "Change Is Good" illustrates well this transformation of apocalyptic anxiety and nihilism into the buoyant humanistic optimism of the cyber-

---

[28]Cohen, "Future."
[29]Calvin G. Seerveld, "Footprints in the Snow," *Philosophia Reformata* 56 (1991): 30.
[30]Again, Cohen, "Future."

netic revolution.[31] In this essay the past is presented as a time of terror, ignorance, hierarchical control and stifling pollution, while the future is depicted as a time of peace, Internet access to information, egalitarianism and natural harmony. We are confidently told that "for the first time in a long time, PROSPERITY in the world is expanding faster than the population" because we have entered "the Long Boom" with "the arrival of personal computers, open markets and globalization in the early 1980's."

It doesn't take too much imagination or suspicion to discern that all of this buoyant optimism is little more than a new, improved version of the very same modernity that Tori Amos and the Smashing Pumpkins feel has betrayed them. When a photo of a replica of Rodin's *The Thinker* sculpture being lowered into place by a crane bears the caption "In this economy, our ability to create wealth is not bound by physical limits, but by our ability to come up with NEW IDEAS—in other words, it's unlimited," it becomes clear that this is the same old modernity all over again. But this isn't just a retrenched modernity, it is modernity with an arrogant vengeance. It is almost as if postmodernity has managed to kick one or two modernist demons out the front door, only to allow seven more virulent demons in the back.

If the problem in late modernity was that it seemed as if it could not deliver on its socioeconomic and cultural promises, then the new and improved modernity is confident that information technology will be able to deliver on our deepest dreams and realize our most precious values. The *Wired* photoessay accompanies a picture of the Berlin Wall crumbling with the words "Networks are inherently decentralizing and anti-hierarchical"—as if the World Wide Web brought down the wall!

That this is warmed-over humanism is demonstrated in an advertisement from AT&T which shows us a group of people, all of whom have a globe in their hands— or on a laptop! The ad copy reads,

> Your world without limits. It's not about phones. Or faxes. Or the World Wide Web. They are just the tools for you to do what you want, be what you want, get what you want from life. Life? You get out of it what you put into it. Introducing AT&T Canada True Choice . . . A world of communication tools for the only world that matters. Yours.

With this technology, we are told, autonomous human beings once again have history under control, once again can determine for themselves what life is all about. There may well be a plurality of worlds, but they are all in our hands—*if* we have the right technology!

Contrary to the postmodern disquiet identified above, this optimism is fueled and propelled by the cybernetic revolution in communications technology and rooted in a metanarrative.[32] An extended citation from another article published in *Wired* magazine illustrates the point:

---

[31]"Change Is Good."

[32]Portions of the following analysis have previously been published in an article by Brian Walsh, "Will You Have Fries with That Faith?" *The Varsity* 120, no. 41 (March 7, 2000): 10.

We are watching the beginnings of a global economic boom on a scale never experienced before. We have entered a period of sustained growth that could eventually double the world's economy every twelve years and bring prosperity for—quite literally—billions of people on the planet. We are riding the early waves of a 25-year run of a greatly expanding economy that will do much to solve seemingly intractable problems like poverty and to ease tensions throughout the world. And we will do it without blowing the lid off the environment. . . . These two metatrends—fundamental technological change and a new ethos of openness—will transform our world into the beginnings of a global civilization . . . that will blossom through the coming century.[33]

This is pretty inspirational stuff! And *inspiration* is the right word! Think about it for a minute. Where else do we meet language about solving problems that have previously been intractable, radical new beginnings, transforming the world, an ethos of openness, and the blossoming of life? Doesn't all of this sound just a tad religious? In fact, we could find strikingly similar language in the epistle to the Colossians.

Of course, it could be asked how something so clearly materialistic as the shift to a centralized global economy could ever be confused with a religion. What could possibly be religious about a borderless economic order ruled by transnational corporations moving capital around in cyberspace and exploiting public resources for private economic gain? What could be religious about a free market of unrestrained competition in which we can all fish in each other's ponds without worrying about outmoded notions of national sovereignty or local control of resources? And how could the hope of a rising economic tide that will "lift all boats" ever be construed as a religious hope? Never mind the problem that only people with the capital resources to own fishing gear get to fish in other folk's ponds—and that if you don't actually own a boat then a rising tide is more like a Mozambiquan flood than a symbol of hope. Those are just glitches in the system. And while they may suggest at least some degree of blind faith is at work here, surely globalization isn't a religious vision, is it? We think it is.

This cultural force promises nothing less than the blossoming of a new civilization that will eventually bring an end to international conflict, resolve hitherto intractable problems like poverty and environmental degradation, and produce increased prosperity for all—even though all the current evidence seems to contradict these promises! We are dealing with something here that is bigger than free trade, the lifting of tariffs, money speculation and exploitation. We are facing the most powerful, fastest-growing and most successful religion in the history of the world. And what is fantastic about this religion is that it actually doesn't require any volitional choice of its converts.[34]

---

[33]Peter Schwartz and Peter Leyden, "The Long Boom," *Wired,* July 1997, p. 116.

[34]Harvey Cox puts it this way: "I am beginning to think that for all the religions of the world, however they may differ from one another, the religion of The Market has become the most formidable rival, the more so because it is rarely recognized as a religion" ("The Market as God: Living in the New Dispensation," *Atlantic Monthly* 283, no. 3 [March 1999], available online at <www.theatlantic.com/issues/99mar/marketgod.htm>).

In a famous essay, Benjamin Barber described the dynamics of globalization as the emerging "McWorld" culture. "McWorld is a product of popular culture driven by expansionist commerce. . . . It is about culture as commodity, apparel as ideology." In such a commodity culture, various products become "icons of a lifestyle," and shopping malls become "the new churches of a commercial civilization" in which everything is "constructed around image exports creating a common world taste around common logos, advertising, slogans, stars, songs . . . and trademarks."[35] Icons, churches, image, logos, songs. Do you see the pattern?

When a religion aggressively proselytizes and seeks to transform the world, its most important resource is its images. It is image that transforms the imagination, and it is imagination that engenders a lifestyle. And what globalization does better than anything else is transform the imagination. That is why the entertainment and advertising industries are the first wave of the emerging global consciousness.

In *Mustard Seed Versus McWorld,* futurist Tom Sine puts it this way: "Borders are melting and distance is dying as five billion of us now shop at the same macromall and stare transfixed at the same electronic images."[36] Those images, whether on a television set or a computer screen, are not simply about increasing free trade and free enterprise; rather, they "are working to redefine what is important and what is of value in people's lives all over the planet."[37] What is at stake in globalization is not only the production and consumption of products but, more important, the construction of a homogenized global consumerist consciousness. Globalism wants more than your pocketbook, it wants your soul.

"Wait a minute," someone is bound to say. "Capitalism is about capital, it's about money. Religion is about faith." Well, we're not so sure that capitalism isn't ultimately a matter of faith.[38] Faith is invariably rooted in overarching stories or metanarratives that give meaning and direction to life. (Precisely the kinds of stories that engender postmodern incredulity!) Such stories always entail certain foundational beliefs or assumptions. These assumptions and these kinds of stories are usually argued *from,* not argued *to.* They are the basis of any argument and are not, in the end, finally provable. That is, they require faith.

Given this little bit of phenomenology of faith, what might we say about globalization? To begin with, let's note that global capitalism is the most recent (and most virulent) chapter in a story that has its roots in the age of discovery, the industrial revo-

---

[35]Benjamin Barber, *Jihad vs. McWorld* (New York: Times, 1995), p. 17. This book is an expansion of the original article of the same title that appeared in *Atlantic* 269, no. 3 (March 1992): 53-63.

[36]Tom Sine, *Mustard Seed Versus McWorld: Reinventing Life and Faith for the Future* (Grand Rapids: Baker, 1999), p. 53.

[37]Ibid., p. 21.

[38]See Bob Goudzwaard, *Capitalism and Progress: A Diagnosis of Western Society,* trans. Josina Van Nuis Zylstra (Toronto: Wedge/Grand Rapids, Mich.: Eerdmans, 1979).

lution and the Enlightenment. This is *the story of progress,* which proclaims with all the certainty of faith that civilization will blossom, peace will reign, and we will enter into an age of prosperity if we allow human reason to freely investigate the world by means of the scientific method and transform that world through technological power. If we do these things, then we will realize our highest aspiration, economic growth. This belief in the ineluctable progress of autonomous humanity is the underlying faith or religion of Western culture.

Now this grand tale of progress is a myth that requires faith at the best of times, but especially when none of its promises have been realized. International tensions have increased over the last one hundred years, the environment continues to be raped, and the rise of prosperity for the wealthy has been accompanied by increased poverty, starvation, homelessness and misery for the majority of the world's population. There is something wrong with this story.

The story's foundational assumptions themselves require faith. For example, is it self-evidently true that a limited, finite world can sustain unlimited economic growth? Can we provide an empirical justification for the belief that economic prosperity for the controllers of capital will necessarily result in increased prosperity for all? Doesn't it require faith to believe that economic growth is the driving force of history? And on what basis, other than a perversely blind, self-interested faith, can we justify the assumption of global capitalism that it is permissible to ruin one place or culture for the sake of another?[39]

Globalization isn't just an aggressive stage in the history of capitalism. It is a religious movement of previously unheard-of proportions. Progress is its underlying myth, unlimited economic growth its foundational faith, the shopping mall (physical or online) its place of worship, consumerism its overriding image, "I'll have a Big Mac and fries" its ritual of initiation, and global domination its ultimate goal.

And now we come to a conundrum in our cultural analysis. Remember, we are trying to find a way to situate ourselves so that we are clear about the context from which we approach the biblical text and to which we want the biblical witness to speak. But we have met two seemingly irreconcilable perspectives on our cultural situation. Are we in a time of numbing cultural disquiet or riding the exciting wave of the cybernetic future? Are we really incredulous in the face of all metanarratives, or is the grand tale of global capitalism experiencing something of a revival? Do we really raise a toast to heterogeneity when our glasses are all full of the same beverages produced by the same international corporations and we are all wearing the same brand of blue jeans and using Microsoft technology to communicate with each other? Doesn't this look like homogeneity and sameness rather than heterogeneity and difference? Even if the

---

[39]See Wendell Berry's criticisms of capitalism in *Home Economics* (New York: North Point, 1987); *Sex, Economy, Freedom and Community* (New York: Pantheon, 1992); and *Another Turn of the Crank* (Washington, D.C.: Counterpoint, 1995).

world is a carnival, how significant is that if all the side shows are sponsored by the same international entertainment conglomerates? And what about moral flux? Are people in the global economy really having problems making life decisions, or are we mostly following the consumerist dictates of the market?

Ultimately, what all of this boils down to is the relationship between postmodernity and globalization. How are they related?

Postmodernity and Globalization

Empires are totalizing by definition. In the words of the psalmist, imperial "mouths lay claim to heaven, and their tongues take possession of the earth" (Ps 73:9 NIV). Empires are built on systemic centralizations of power and secured by structures of socioeconomic and military control. They are religiously legitimated by powerful myths that are rooted in foundational assumptions, and they are sustained by a proliferation of imperial images that captivate the imagination of the population.

What could possibly be further from the antitotalizing, antihomogenizing agenda of postmodern thought and culture? While postmodernity wants to celebrate diversity and otherness, empires are all about hegemony and sameness. So while it is clear enough that the ineluctable forces of globalization are indeed imperial in character, isn't postmodern disquiet something of a protest movement in the face of such globalization? Not necessarily.

Nicholas Boyle notes that the global market is nothing less than "the establishment of the one and only world-system there has ever been" precisely because it has no outsiders.[40] "Since 1945 a single overriding economic fact, the development of the global market, has determined not only the economic but the political and cultural life of the human world, and has been responsible for all the most striking changes those years have seen," including the rise of postmodernism as a cultural force.[41]

Walter Truett Anderson makes a similar point: "Globalism and a postmodern worldview come in the same package; we will not have one without the other."[42] The indissoluble link between them is precisely the "pluralism" that they both champion. As Boyle perceptively points out, "the belief that there is, not a single truth and a single world, but a multiplicity of mutually untranslatable perspectives, is strangely analogous to the belief that the market is a boundless medium within which perfect competition is possible between an infinite number of discrete commercial identities."[43] The postmodern multiplicity of perspectives is essentially the

---

[40]Nicholas Boyle, *Who Are We Now? Christian Humanism and the Global Market from Hegel to Heaney* (Edinburgh: T & T Clark, 1998), p. 74.

[41]Ibid., p. 75.

[42]Walter Truett Anderson, *Reality Isn't What It Used to Be* (San Francisco: Harper & Row, 1990), p. 25.

[43]Boyle, *Who Are We Now?* p. 152.

same as the multiplicity of products available on the global market. In such a pluralism, "the moral world, like the material world, is supremely represented as a shopping mall: it is now open to us to stroll between the shelves and pick out, or opt for . . . whatever takes our fancy."[44] In this discernment of our cultural context, postmodern emphases on choice, diversity, difference and otherness simply function as a smokescreen to cover the homogenizing forces of global capitalism.[45] Not only is postmodernity no real threat to the empire of consumerism, it also provides ideological comfort to that empire.

At heart, postmodernity and globalization share the same anthropology. For both, humans are understood primarily as units of consumption for whom choice is the defining characteristic. Again, Boyle is insightful:

> The market does not concern itself with whether my choice is rational, whether it is identical or consistent with choices I made yesterday or may make tomorrow, nor does it concern itself with any purposes I may have in making my choice or any consequences of my choice insofar as these do not themselves involve market decisions. Indeed, as far as the market is concerned, I exist only in the moment of making a single commercial choice.[46]

The fragmented self does not need to buy into any metanarrative of progress or make her choices according to any coherent or rational system of values. All she needs to do is make consumer choices. The Cartesian dictum "I think therefore I am" is replaced by "I consume therefore I am" (or "I shop till I drop").

The difference between modernity and postmodernity isn't all that great when looked at this way. The cult of the autonomous imperial ego, an "endlessly acquisitive conqueror and pioneer,"[47] devolves into a "commodious individualism" characterized by an "unencumbered enjoyment of consumption goods or commodities."[48] This ego may not be centered on a modernist self-image of conqueror or pioneer—indeed it may well have abandoned any notion of centeredness altogether. Nonetheless, it remains an endlessly acquisitive ego, consuming the products and, more important, the images that global capitalism serves up.

In late capitalism we see an almost total commodification of life. And once *everything* is commodified—including beliefs, worldviews and all cultural products—then

---

[44]Ibid., p. 80.
[45]Mark McClain Taylor, "Vodou Resistance/Vodou Hope: Forging a Postmodernism That Liberates," in *Liberation Theologies, Postmodernity and the Americas,* ed. David Batstone, Eduardo Medienta, Lois Ann Lorentzen and Dwight N. Hopkins (New York: Routledge, 1997), p. 169.
[46]Boyle, *Who Are We Now?* p. 153.   •
[47]Christopher Lasch, *The Minimal Self: Psychic Survival in Troubled Times* (New York: W. W. Norton, 1984), p. 137.
[48]Borgmann, *Crossing the Postmodern Divide,* p. 43.

the imperial hegemony of global capitalism has been established.[49]

Describing postmodern disquiet above, we noted that a postmodern culture appears to have no fixed ethical anchors and is characterized by profound moral instability. In the lives of many people that instability results in either a moral paralysis or an aimless wandering. But the economic globalism that we are here describing would seem to have a rather clear course through history, directed by the mandate to acquire and consume. The difference is that this is a course directed by no overarching ethical framework or guiding narrative. The young entrepreneur making a killing in e-commerce may be playing the same game as capitalists before him, but he does so without the benefit (or, it would appear, the need) of any grounding, legitimating or directing worldview or ideology beyond personal self-aggrandizement and security. Hence we see the ability to personally identify with the depressing nihilism of Gen X culture while at the same time being a full and energetic participant in global economics.

Stanley Hauerwas puts it this way: "Too often postmodernists turn out to be liberals in their ethics and politics who no longer believe in the conceits of liberalism but have nowhere else to go."[50] Economic globalization is late capitalism without the framework of a modernist ideology of progress to provide it a narrative foundation and ethical direction.

Returning to William

So now we return to William. By his own admission, he has played the game of economic power in a global economy and found it lacking. Moreover, the anthropology of the autonomous ego constructing itself in a world of endless possibility has proved untenable. So he acknowledges that he needs God. He needs a source, an origin, a meaning beyond himself to give direction and accountability to his life. Another way to look at this is to say that in a world of imperial control, in a world that is suffused with the rhetoric, symbolism and images of empire, we need to have appeal to a power, a sovereignty greater than the empire, if we are to have any hope. In William's struggle with his own Christian faith, he goes deep into the heart of the beast known as the empire—he plays at international finance—and comes out the

---

[49]Peter Berger anticipated the commodification of belief in a radically pluralist society in *The Sacred Canopy: Elements of a Sociological Theory of Religion* (New York: Doubleday, 1967). He argued that once culture recognizes the constructed character of reality, religious traditions can no longer be imposed (to say nothing of "assumed"); they must be marketed. Religion "must be 'sold' to a clientele that is no longer constrained to 'buy.' The pluralist situation is, above all, a *market situation*. In it, the religious institutions become marketing agencies and the religious traditions become consumer commodities" (p. 138). Anderson concurs: "Never before has any civilization openly made available to its populace such a smorgasbord of realities. . . . Never before has a society allowed its people to become consumers of belief, and allowed belief—all beliefs—to become merchandise" (*Reality Isn't What It Used to Be,* p. 188).

[50]Stanley Hauerwas, "The Christian Difference: Or, Surviving Postmodernism," in *Anabaptists and Postmodernity,* ed. Susan and Gerald Biesecker-Mast (Telford, Penn.: Pandora, 2000), p. 48.

other side with a longing for a God who might be able to disarm and demythologize this beast.

But that doesn't mean that he is reading Scripture. Why not? Because in the absolutism of the Bible and its authoritative interpreters he has met a force as disempowering and oppressive as he met in the empire of global consumerism. Why trade in one absolutism for another?

We wonder, however, whether for William—or at least for many people of William's generation—the aversion to absolutes might itself be paradoxically representative of the continued power of the empire over them. Think about it for a minute. If postmodern pluralism, with all of its rhetoric of "the other" and "difference," really is a smokescreen for the acquisitive, consumptive lifestyle of the empire of global capitalism, then might it not be that this aversion to absolutes is little more than a resistance to anything that might limit our consumer choice in the marketplace of ideas, beliefs and worldviews?

Don't get us wrong. We think that William has good reason to reject the absolutism of much conservative Christianity. In fact we will argue later in this book that the whole notion of "absolutes" is a bad idea that has been surreptitiously imposed on biblical faith. Nonetheless, perhaps a near-allergic reaction to a text that makes certain clear truth claims might be as indicative of a postmodern consumerist desire to "keep our options open" as it is representative of a healthy rejection of the oppressive strictures of a conservative religious worldview.

Let's put our cards on the table. William may want God, but the question is, which god does he want? And on whose terms will he accept this god? You see, the danger of wanting a god, without being willing to allow this god to speak in a voice that is radically *other* to our own voice, is that the god we end up with is like any other consumer product we take off the shelf. We would never be accountable before such a god, precisely because we never allow this god a voice that would actually call us to account. This consumer-friendly god, this god of postmodern construction, this generic off-the-shelf god would be no God at all. Rather, it would be an idol. And before idols like this the empire has nothing to fear, because ultimately such idols—such gods—are in the service of the empire.

There is, however, an important point we need to add here. We have already said that William has good reason to reject the Absolute Deity encoded in an Absolute Text of his past. He also has good reason, we suggest, to be wary of trading one absolutist system (of the empire) for another (of Christian faith). It will be incumbent on us in our engagement with Paul's ancient letter to the Colossians to demonstrate both how this letter is seriously misread if approached as an Absolute Text and how the kingdom this text proclaims is radically different from the violent absolutism of the empire. Before we proceed, however, we need to reflect for just a few more pages on that violent absolutism.

September 11, 2001, Postmodernity and Empire

No attempt at cultural discernment post-September 11, 2001, can fail to take into account the culture-shaping and history-shifting significance of the tragic events of that day and the response that these attacks evoked.[51] If we are at all correct in referring to the culture of global consumerism—a culture that has become essentially synonymous with America—as an empire, then the events of September 11 and its aftermath only served to confirm the analysis. Indeed, if we are attempting to engage in cultural discernment of the shape of the twenty-first century, then it could be said that the twenty-first century began not with William in the pub on December 31, 1999, but on September 11, 2001.

The tragic events of September 11 cannot be fully understood apart from the dynamics of empire. Remember that we said earlier that empires are built on systemic centralizations of power and secured by structures of socioeconomic and military control. Moreover, empires are religiously legitimated by powerful myths that are rooted in foundational assumptions, and they are sustained by a proliferation of imperial images that captivate the imagination of the population. So what happened on September 11? In a stroke of perverse, counterimperial genius, America was attacked at the site of its socioeconomic and military control. The World Trade Center and the Pentagon were, of course, the perfect targets. This attack went to the systemic center of American culture—its economic control and military power. But just as important, these were targets of profound symbolic significance. These institutions are at the heart of the powerful myth that legitimates the empire identified with America. As Benjamin Barber puts it, this was an "astonishing assault on the temple of free enterprise in New York City and the cathedral of American military might in Washington, D.C."[52]

Clearly American political leaders understood that the battle at hand was of mythical proportions. This is why the language of myth was sharply in focus during the president's brief address to the nation on the evening of September 11. The attack, he said, was an attack on "freedom" which was intended to inflict chaos on the nation, but he was here to tell us that America was still in control. The president was in the White House, government services would be reopened in the morning, and, most important, "America is open for business."

America is open for business? Wasn't that a rather callous and irrelevant comment under such circumstances? Not at all. You see, "America is open for business" means the forces of chaos will not triumph because the forces of salvation are stronger. And

---

[51]Much of this section is dependent on an article by Brian Walsh, "Lamenting the End of the Empire," *Church Times,* no. 7231 (September 21, 2001): 9. See also Andrew Goddard, "Something Still Stands," *Third Way* 24, no. 8 (November 2001): 13-17; and the provocative poem "September 11th, 2001," by Godfrey Rust in the same issue.

[52]Benjamin Barber, "2001 Introduction: Terrorism's Challenge to Democracy," in *Jihad vs. McWorld,* exp. ed. (New York: Ballantine, 2001), p. xi.

as we have seen, in this myth salvation is found in an ever-expanding global economy. If America is still "open for business," then freedom still reigns! It is not surprising, then, that the litany repeated throughout the months following these attacks was two-fold. Yes, America will root out the terrorists and destroy them, together with anyone else perceived to be a threat to American freedom. But in the meantime, the highest patriotic duty of the American population was to go out and consume. We must not let the terrorists have the sweet victory of destroying our economy, our very way of life. Spend your money, fly on airplanes and take the kids to Disneyland! This was the moral admonition of the empire.

However, the American imperial mythology of invincibility, rooted in its economic and military hegemony and historically proved with the collapse of communism, had been shaken. When the president said that you can shake the foundation of a building but not the foundation of a nation, you knew somehow that this was not true. The foundation of the nation had indeed been shaken. For the first time in its history, an enemy of the nation had brought the pain, violence and bloodshed of war not only to the American mainland but to the heart of the American system of economic and military power. And you think that the foundations of the nation aren't shaking?

No wonder people on the street said that it all seemed so unreal, so much like a movie, rather than reality. How could this be reality? The American mythology has no way of interpreting such an event. In terms of the myth, the attack simply could not have happened. How could a nation that is so clearly virtuous, so moral, such a leader in civilizational progress ever be hated by anyone so much? Did they hate us, David Letterman asked, "because they don't get cable?" Is that it? Is this a matter of civilizational jealousy? Is it a matter of our just having more stuff than they do? The feebleness of Letterman's humor mirrored the superficiality of the culture that he entertains. So captivated by the consumerist imagination of the empire, and so immersed in the empire's self-justifying mythology and rhetoric, we find ourselves unable to fathom the depths of the crisis in which we now live.

If the myth is in crisis, who better to provide answers to our doubts than the official mythmakers of the empire—the media? And what better entertainment product but *The West Wing* to be the avenue for such myth refinement? In a special episode that was aired in response to September 11, an event of international terrorism has hit the United States, and the White House is subject to a security shutdown. But a group of bright high school students is now locked into the White House, and all of the show's regular characters arrive to discuss the issues with the students. The heart of the show—its moment of mythological resolution—comes right at the end. The security situation is resolved, and the students are about to leave, when the presidential press secretary makes his final point. He tells the students that if they really want to get to the terrorists, if they want to get at them deep down where they really live, then "believe more than one thing. It drives them crazy."

Believe more than one thing. Embrace a plurality of belief. Keep your worldview options open. And these terrorists go crazy because they are capable of believing only one thing at a time.

Why do "they" hate us so much? Is it because of cable? Well, sort of. Perhaps they hate us because we are a cable culture of multiple channels mirroring a belief pluralism that just keeps too many options open. From the perspective of an Osama bin Laden, such pluralism represents not the maturity of an open society but the lack of moral courage and the conviction of a promiscuous society. Perhaps "they" hate us because we are the consummate consumers. Perhaps "they" find the consumption of belief so morally reprehensible that "they" are willing to risk everything in order to destroy such a civilization.

The culture we have just described is the global consumerist empire, with its postmodern multiplicity of perspectives. And now that empire is under attack. It is not only self-imploding under the sheer weight of its own consumer refuse but exploding under the attack of a counterimperial force.

And in such a context William wants to be a theist. But what will the God he now believes in have to say? And what might a text written by the apostle Paul in the context of the Roman empire possibly have to say to the twenty-first century—the third millennium—which began on September 11, 2001?

—2—

COLOSSIANS AND
DISQUIETED GLOBALIZATION

Ancient texts were not always ancient. That may seem to be rather obvious, but it is worth remembering. Paul's letter to the Christian community in Colossae was once a piece of contemporary correspondence to a particular community in a particular place and time. And like our time, theirs was a time of empire.

In the next chapter we will attempt to situate this letter more concretely in the context of the first century, and we will have occasion to return to the theme of empire at that time. But before we do that, let's stop and try an interpretive exercise. What would happen if a letter like this was written to us in a post-September 11 context of global disquiet, combined with the cyberoptimism of the so-called economic boom? What language would the author use if he listened to contemporary music, watched the World Trade Center towers collapse, and was culturally attuned to the challenges of being a Christian community in the twenty-first century? What would the letter to the Colossians look like if it was written not two thousand years ago but last week? And what would it say if its audience weren't the beleaguered Christian community in the town of Colossae in the Roman empire, but the Christian community trying to make sense out of being the body of Christ in the third millennium?

This isn't really such a novel way of approaching an ancient text. In fact, when rabbis read the Torah to the Jews of the Diaspora, they did precisely this kind of thing. Recognizing that their congregations did not understand Hebrew, the rabbis would have to translate the text as they read. And their translations were certainly not literal. Rather, they would update the text, apply it to the changing context and put it into contemporary idiom. The results of such interpretive exercises were called *targums*— extended paraphrases of the text. So before we dive into the world of the Roman empire, consider this targum on Colossians 1:1-14.

Colossians 1:1-14 Targum

Brian and Sylvia, disciples of Messiah Jesus by the grace of God, to the covenanted community of faithful brothers and sisters in Christ in the totally wired world of the new global economy.

At the dawn of a new millennium, and in the face of a world of terror, may you experience the all-encompassing shalom and wholeness that is received as a wonderful gift from God our Father.

We want you to know that thankfulness permeates our prayers for you. We continue to give thanks to God, the Father of our sovereign Messiah Jesus, as we hear the stories of struggling and daring discipleship that continues to characterize his followers. We have heard that your faith and trust in Jesus is proved true because it takes on the real flesh of love in your midst—a love that is manifest in your care for the poor, providing shelter to the homeless, food for the hungry and hospitality to the stranger. Such faith and love are inseparable: one cannot exist without the other. But neither is possible without hope. And here at the end of a century of such bloodshed, betrayal and broken promises, it is an amazing thing to be a community animated by hope. May that hope sustain you in a world addicted to violence.

But your hope is not the cheap buoyant optimism of global capitalism with its cybernetic computer gods and self-confident scientific discovery, all serving the predatory idolatry of economism. You know that these are gods with an insatiable desire for child sacrifice. That is why your hope is not the shallow optimism of the "Long Boom" of increased prosperity. Such optimism is but a cheap imitation of hope. Real hope—the kind of hope that gives you the audacity to resist the commodification of your lives and engenders the possibility of an alternative imagination—is no human achievement; it is a divine gift. This hope isn't extinguished by living in "the future of a shattered past," precisely because it is a hope rooted in a story of kept promises, even at the cost of death.

You didn't get this hope from cable television, and you didn't find it on the Net. This hope walked into your life, hollering itself hoarse out on the streets, in the classroom, down at the pub and in the public square, when you first heard the good news of whole life restoration in Christ. This gospel is the Word of truth—it is the life-giving, creation-calling, covenant-making, always faithful servant Word that takes flesh in Jesus, who is the truth. So it is not surprising that the Word of truth is no detached set of objective verities committed to memory and reproduced on the test. No, this Word of truth is active, bearing fruit throughout the cultural wilderness of this terribly scorched earth. From the beginning blessing, "Be fruitful and multiply," God has always intended that creation be a place of fruitfulness. Now the Word of truth is producing the fruit of a radical discipleship, demonstrated in passion for justice, evocative art and drama, restorative stewardship of our ecological home, education for faithful living, integral evangelism, and liturgy that shapes an imagination alternative to the empire's.

And when that kind of fruit is evident in your lives, you don't need to choke on the word *truth*—you don't need to whisper it through your tears. You see, once you have comprehended the grace of God in truth and your life bears witness to the power of this truth, then you can speak—indeed you can sing—of truth with integrity. You have learned all of this well from prophets and singers, teachers and preachers, artists and storytellers who have come before us, and again, they all testify to your love in the Spirit.

So ever since we have heard of your faith, love and hope, we have not ceased to pray for you. And our prayer is that in a world that has commodified knowledge, you will be saturated with the holistic, intimate knowledge of God's way with this world that he has created. May your lives be characterized not by the accumulation of disembodied, unconnected facts and information but by a playful, history-embracing, this-worldly, interconnected wisdom that traces the wise and loving way God engages this world in all of its rich diversity.

What we are praying for is that you will demonstrate a spiritual wisdom and understanding in all things, so that you can discern where the Spirit is leading the church in this new century. You see, such knowledge, wisdom and understanding are essential if you are to shape cultural life in a way that is worthy of the Lord. And don't miss the scope of what we are talking about here. What is at stake is nothing less than the pleasure of our Lord, a pleasure that he takes when every dimension of our lives bears the fruit of his kingdom.

But it is not simply a matter of growing in knowledge and then displaying the practical consequences or uses of that knowledge in our daily lives. No, that would be too much like the intellectualism that was the hallmark of modernity. The knowledge and cultural fruitfulness we are talking about feed off each other. Knowing the world in wisdom and discernment engenders a certain way of life that then leads to an increase in knowledge. Knowing grows in the doing.

But here's the rub. Everything in this monolithic culture of McWorld globalization is allied against you and will try to keep your imagination captive, stripping you of the courage to dream of alternative ways to live. When a culture is threatened, it becomes especially repressive of those who dare to live differently, subject to another vision of life, another Lord. So may you be strengthened with all strength and empowered with the weighty power of God in this disempowered culture of unbearable lightness. May your vision, your stubborn refusal to allow your imaginations to be taken captive, have the tenacity to hang in there for the long haul and a patience that doesn't need to aggressively realize the kingdom of God *now,* because your faith will work and wait for a miracle, for the coming of God's shalom to our terribly broken world.

You will have the resources of such patient endurance and be sustained for the long haul of radical obedience in the face of overwhelming odds if your life is embedded in gratitude. Joyful thanksgiving is deeply empowering.

And *what* we are thankful for provides us with a subversive imagination. While the cybernetic revolution will tell us that the world is in the hands of those with the most powerful computers and widest Net access, and while the forces of globalization arrogantly proclaim that those who control capital have a proprietary right to the resources of creation, we confess that this world is the inheritance of those who live in the light— not the dim light of the Enlightenment, nor the glittering lights of computer screens, televisions and gambling terminals, but the light that liberates us from darkness.

You see, friends, because we are not subservient to the empire but subjects of the kingdom of God's beloved Son, we have the audacity to say to the darkness, "We beg to differ!"[1] We will not be a pawn to the Prince of Darkness any longer, because we owe him no allegiance, and by God's grace, through our redemption and forgiveness, our imaginations have been set free.

What Was That?

Uh, excuse me, but your translation seemed to add an awful lot to the text.

Well, as we tried to explain, this isn't exactly a translation but rather something akin to the ancient rabbinic interpretive practice called *targum*.[2]

But you can't tell me that the ancient rabbis translated Scripture in ways that were so culturally explicit.

Of course they were culturally explicit—they could only write out of their own cultural context.

Yes, but this feels more like an imaginative construct that the two of you dreamed up. You've rewritten this text with such a strong message to a consumer global culture of anxiety and optimism that I wonder if you haven't changed it immeasurably. And while all your allusions to popular culture—like the Indigo Girls, Smashing Pumpkins and Tori Amos— make your targum exciting and relevant, I feel uneasy with it. I guess maybe the original text doesn't seem to have that exciting relevance, and I'm not sure it ever did.

I guess I'm just a little hung up on the liberties that you take with Scripture. It is all well and good to apply this biblical text to our very different cultural context, but is there any basis in the text itself for what you are doing? Don't get me wrong, I am no fundamentalist, but neither am I a postmodernist. I mean, you can't just do whatever you like with a text. So my question is: does this targum have any exegetical credibility?

Well, what are the parts of the targum that worry you?

Let's start at the beginning. How do you get from a simple and straightforward greeting from Paul, "Grace and peace to you from God our Father," to "May you experience the all-encompassing shalom and wholeness that is received as a wonderful gift from God our Father"? Not only is your version a lot longer, it seems to be saying more than would be present in a typical early Christian greeting. Why all the extra description?

That's a good question. "Grace and peace to you" is a greeting that is rich in meaning, if you can hear all of its overtones. And it seems to us that hearing overtones in

---

[1]Mary Jo Leddy, *Say to the Darkness, "We Beg to Differ"* (Toronto: Lester & Orpen Dennys, 1990).

[2]The noun *targum* is derived from the Hebrew verb *tirgem*, which carries the meanings both "to translate" and "to explain." It is important to note that a targumic translation of a Hebrew text was seldom literalistic. The rabbis invariably expanded on the text as they translated, and the collection of such translations is called the Targum. Philip S. Alexander explains the role of Targum as providing more than "a simple rendering of Scripture into everyday speech: it could be commentary as well as a translation, and impose a comprehensive interpretation on the original Hebrew." As such, targumim (the plural form) "achieve a degree of polyvancy in their readings of Scripture" ("Targum, Targumim," in *The Anchor Bible Dictionary*, ed. David Noel Freedman [New York: Doubleday, 1992], 6:329-30).

biblical literature is something that most of us are quite poor at. Let us suggest to you this fundamental hermeneutical principle: Always read the New Testament with Old Testament eyes—or to shift the metaphor, always hear the New Testament with Old Testament ears. Now this might just seem a little obvious to you, but take our word on it, it has been a contentious issue in the history of biblical scholarship for at least one hundred years.[3]

If a first-century Jew like Paul uses a word like *peace*—even if he is writing in Greek—then one cannot miss the overtones of the Hebrew notion of *shalom*. Here is a word that is overflowingly rich in meaning. On one level it refers to well-being: may things go well with you. But this is a well-being that encompasses all of life. Shalom has to do with blessing, richness, abundance and a far-reaching harmony that permeates and characterizes all of our relationships.

Since you are asking me to "hear with Old Testament ears," could you give an example of this from the Old Testament?

Sure—consider Ezekiel. On two occasions Ezekiel speaks of a "covenant of peace" that is characterized by a renewed fruitfulness in the land: there is no longer enmity between humans and wild creatures, drought gives way to showers of blessing, barren trees again can be harvested, the people of Israel experience political security because they are at peace with their neighbors, socioeconomic oppression is replaced by liberation, and the hungry are fed (Ezek 34:25-31). But such shalom, wholeness and well-being in all of our social, ecological, political, agricultural and economic relationships is rooted in a restored relationship with God. There can be a covenant of peace, says Ezekiel, only because God promises, "My dwelling shall be with them; and I will be their God, and they shall be my people" (37:27). We see then that for Ezekiel, peace is rooted in grace. There can be such wholeness, such creationwide shalom, only if God enters into our conflict-ridden, distorted, oppressive and broken reality with initiatives of grace.

And you were trying to convey that with "may you experience the all-encompassing shalom and wholeness that is received as a wonderful gift from God our Father"?

Well, yes, for those with ears to hear.

That's a pretty high expectation.

Why do you say that?

Because the ideas are so alien. This sense of shalom as well-being in all of our relationships is far removed from any notions of well-being that I meet in my life. I mean, not only is our culture preoccupied with individual well-being—"my" inner peace, "my" level of affluence and comfort—but there is no sense that such peace is rooted in grace.

Of course not. Grace, after all, is a fundamentally relational idea. We receive grace

---

[3]To get a thorough overview of this history, see Stephen C. Neill and N. T. Wright, *The Interpretation of the New Testament, 1861-1986*, 2nd ed. (Oxford: Oxford University Press, 1988).

as a gift from an other. But the idea of peace or well-being that you are describing is so individualistic that it could never depend upon an other. In fact, in the competition of the marketplace other people are usually an impediment to our success, rather than being the very foundation of shalom. But it goes even deeper than that. The problem isn't just individualism, it is the sense that well-being is an accomplishment, a product of our own ingenuity, skill and hard work. If this is true, then who needs grace?

The biblical understanding of grace—the whole matrix of understanding that lies behind Paul's use of the word—is predicated on the idea of a radical gift.

And our society knows nothing of gift, nothing of anything that is free, that cannot be commodified.

Precisely. So when Paul says something as seemingly unremarkable and innocent as "Grace to you and peace from God our Father," he is carrying a whole weight of meaning from the tradition of Israel, and saying something deeply subversive of a culture that views well-being in terms of the autonomous achievement of the solitary individual.

Why didn't you put all that stuff in the targum?

It would have got too long, and targum isn't the only genre we want to use in this book.

Can I ask one more question?

About the targum?

Yes.

Well, let's not talk the targum to death. There is an intentional evocative quality to this genre that perhaps gets lost if it is explained too much.

But the evocative nature of the targum is expressive of both your imaginative application of the text and serious exegesis. Right?

Yes.

Then let me ask one more exegetical question.

OK, shoot.

I want to hear more about your views of truth. You seemed to describe truth as personified. I think you said something about truth "hollering itself hoarse out on the streets." Are you suggesting that truth isn't so much something that we discover as it is something that discovers, or searches out, us? And if so, why?

Well, look at the text again. Paul describes the good news of Jesus as "the word of the truth . . . that has come to you" (Col 1:5-6). And then he goes on to say that this word of truth is active; indeed "just as it is bearing fruit and growing in the whole world, so it has been bearing fruit among yourselves" (1:6). Now try again to hear this text with Old Testament ears. Where have you ever met something like truth seeking folks out and having a dynamic effect in the lives of those who respond to its advances?

The only time in the Old Testament I can think of where truth seeks us rather than our seeking the truth would be in Proverbs, where we meet Wisdom calling and inviting people to follow her and not Dame Folly.[4]

There you have it. And where is she calling out?

In the streets, the public squares, at the busiest corners and at the entrance to the city gates.[5] All right, I see your point. But *where did you get that "hollering itself hoarse" line from?*

We borrowed it from a friend.[6]

So you are hearing in Paul's language of the word of truth "coming to you" a personification of truth similar to what we see happening with wisdom in Proverbs. But it seemed to me that you had more than that to say about truth. Didn't you relate truth to discipleship and to the practice of justice, art, stewardship, education and evangelism? How does truth relate to these things? And have you rejected the link between truth and verifiable knowledge, or truth and objective facts?

Let's start at the end of your question. First, remember that William's problem with the Bible is that every time he begins to read this ancient text he feels that he is getting "punched in the face with the absolute." We think the absolute he is meeting in the Bible is something that is alien to the text. What he is struggling with is a view of knowledge (or "epistemology") that aspires toward a sense of objective and absolute finality. And this, we contend, is an epistemology that is imposed on the text by those who have embraced Enlightenment definitions of truth. We want to encourage a reading of Scripture that unabashedly abandons such objectivism for a more holistic understanding of knowing.

Second, we acknowledge the force of the postmodern complaint that "all thought that pretends to discern truth is but an expression of the will-to-power—even domination—of those making the truth claims."[7] While the targum makes no explicit reference to the way postmodernity makes "truth" into a problem, these issues are in the background, and we will need to return to them later in this book.

But your questions about the targum have been exegetical. And this leads us to the third thing going on in the targum when we are expanding on the language of truth, knowledge, wisdom and understanding in the text. In stark contrast to an objectivist epistemology that esteems distance, detachment, universality and abstractness, we discern in the biblical literature an understanding of truth that affirms intimacy, con-

---

[4]Proverbs 1:9—9:18. Educational theorist Parker Palmer grasps this point beautifully when he writes, "I not only pursue truth but truth pursues me. I not only grasp truth but truth grasps me. I not only know truth but truth knows me. Ultimately, I do not master truth but truth masters me" (*To Know As We Are Known* [San Francisco: Harper & Row, 1983], p. 59).

[5]Proverbs 1:20-21.

[6]Calvin G. Seerveld, *For God's Sake, Run with Joy* (Toronto: Wedge, 1972), p. 33.

[7]J. R. Snyder, introduction to Gianni Vattimo, *The End of Modernity: Nihilism and Hermeneutics in Postmodern Culture* (Cambridge: Polity, 1988), p. xii.

nectedness, particularity and concreteness. At root, in the Hebrew Scriptures truth is a matter of fidelity. Indeed the Hebrew word *emeth* was translated in the King James Version as "truth" but is rendered "faithful" in almost all modern translations. To say that God is true therefore means "that he keeps truth or faith with his people and requires them to keep truth or faith with him."[8] Truth, then, is a decidedly personal, social and relational concept in the Scriptures. To know the truth, and to be known in the truth, is fundamentally a matter of covenantal faithfulness, manifest in the concreteness of daily life within a particular community at a particular time. No wonder the old English term for truth was *troth*. Parker Palmer puts it this way: "To know something or someone in truth is to enter troth with the known . . . to become betrothed, to engage the known with one's whole self, an engagement one enters with attentiveness, care, and good will."[9]

While this is striking all kinds of intuitive chords in me, I have trouble imagining what it would look like. Can you give me some Old Testament examples of this, as you did when we were talking about shalom?

Yes, in fact we can even connect this discussion about truth with shalom. Consider Psalm 85. This is a prayer that is concerned with the restoration of the land of Israel after the exile. Expectantly listening for "a word of shalom" from Yahweh (v. 8), the psalmist proclaims:

> Surely his salvation is at hand for those who fear him,
>   that his glory may dwell in our land. (v. 9)

And when that glory, that presence of the Holy One, takes up residence in the land again, then

> Steadfast love and truth will meet;
>   righteousness and shalom will kiss each other.
> Truth will spring up from the ground,
>   and righteousness will look down from the sky. (Ps 85:10-11, our translation)

Steadfast love, truth, righteousness and shalom are all inextricably related in a biblical worldview. And when God restores covenantal shalom to the land, then truth, or faithfulness, will permeate life so deeply and fully that it will seem as if truth springs up from the ground. To this understanding of truth as covenantal fidelity, notions of detached distance and abstract universality are decidedly alien.

Let me try to get at this a different way: in the modernist view of truth, when truth is absent the result is error. What happens if biblical truth is absent?

---

[8]Thomas Torrance, "One Aspect of the Biblical Conception of Faith," *Expository Times* 68, no. 4 (1957): 112; quoted by Miroslav Volf, *Exclusion and Embrace: A Theological Exploration of Identity, Otherness and Reconciliation* (Nashville: Abingdon, 1996), p. 259.
[9]Palmer, *To Know As We Are Known*, p. 31.

That is a great question. You can really know the truth, in this biblical sense, only when the truth is embodied or incarnated in the life of the community in the land. When truth "perishes" (as Jeremiah 7:28 puts it), then the sociocultural and ecological consequences are disastrous. Using the analogy of marriage, what happens if truth perishes in a marriage, if there is no more troth in the relationship and trust has been broken?

I guess that usually results in divorce.

That's right, and this is precisely the language we find in Hosea:

Hear the word of Yahweh, O people of Israel;
   for Yahweh has a divorce case against the inhabitants of the land.
There is no truth or steadfast love,
   and no knowledge of God in the land.
Swearing, lying, and murder,
   and stealing and adultery break out;
   bloodshed follows bloodshed.
Therefore the land mourns,
   and all who live in it languish;
together with the wild animals
   and the birds of the air,
   even the fish of the sea are perishing. (Hos 4:1-3, our translation)

Because truth is deeply relational, when there is no truth or intimate knowledge in the land, all human relationships are broken. Everything from our social and personal to our ecological relationships takes on the pall of death when there is no truth.

And "bloodshed follows bloodshed."

Yes, bloodshed follows bloodshed. There is something ironic about Hosea's comment when read in light of the postmodern suspicion that large-scale truth claims invariably serve to legitimate violence. In contrast, Hosea insists that it is the *absence of* truth that gives rise to ever-escalating bloodshed.

What about the way you interpret Paul's prayer that the Colossians be filled "with the knowledge of God's will in all spiritual wisdom and understanding" (1:9)? It seemed to me that you suggested a similarly relational and this-worldly approach to that language. Does this also have Old Testament roots?

Indeed it does. And here we meet a problem that doesn't come from postmodern suspicion about truth but, more tragically, from the church's own dualism.

What do you mean?

Well, whenever we meet language about "spiritual wisdom" and a knowledge that is related to God's will, we tend to think of some kind of otherworldly, spiritual realm that is related only tangentially to the here and now. But this is as bad a mistake as reading the language of truth through a modernist, objectivist lens.

Sort of like embracing Plato along with Kant.

Yes, that would be a good way to put it. Remember: hear the New Testament with Old Testament ears. Language of wisdom in the Hebrew Scriptures has nothing to do with otherworldly contemplation and everything to do with being attuned to the wise ways God engages creation. That is why the whole book of Proverbs is about wise life "in the land" (Prov 2:20-22), and Isaiah can illustrate what wisdom is by appealing to how a farmer knows when and where to plant crops and the proper way to harvest and process those crops (Is 28:23-29).

What is "spiritual" about that?

In biblical perspective, "spirit" has to do with the direction of one's life in creation. And just as truth must be enfleshed in sociocultural, political and ecological relations, so also is a spiritual wisdom and understanding a matter of knowing, or intimately discerning, the direction that God would have us go in our life at a given time.

Consider Isaiah's prophecy of the coming Messiah:

> The spirit of Yahweh shall rest on him,
>   the spirit of wisdom and understanding,
>   the spirit of counsel and might,
>   the spirit of knowledge and the fear of the LORD. (Is 11:2)

Here we have all the words that Paul employs in his prayer for the Colossians: *spirit, knowledge, wisdom* and *understanding*. And what will the Messiah do with this Spirit-endowed knowledge, wisdom and understanding?

> He shall not judge by what his eyes see,
>   or decide by what his ears hear;
> but with righteousness he shall judge the poor,
>   and decide with equity for the meek of the earth. . . .
> Righteousness shall be the belt around his waist,
>   and truthfulness the belt around his loins. (Is 11:3-5)

This wisdom and understanding, this knowledge that is received as a gift of the Spirit, is for justice. If the Messiah wears truthfulness (or faithfulness) as the belt around his waist and is filled with wisdom and understanding, then that knowledge will be evident in the way he redresses real, this-worldly socioeconomic injustice.

Then the text concludes with these words:

> They will not hurt or destroy
>   on all my holy mountain;
> for the earth will be full of knowledge of the LORD
>   as the waters cover the sea. (Is 11:9)

Isn't that amazing? Just as the psalmist talks about truth springing "up from the ground" (Ps 85:11), so does the prophet envision the whole earth as full of the knowledge of God.

If this is what Paul has in mind when he uses the language of knowledge, wisdom and understanding in his prayer, then we must read it as a prayer that the Colossian community will have a knowledge that will transform all of their communal life. Remember, Paul prays for this kind of knowledge to grow in the community "*so that* you may lead lives worthy of the Lord, fully pleasing to him, as you bear fruit in every good work and as you grow in the knowledge of God" (Col 1:10). Just as the word of truth is "bearing fruit . . . in the whole world," so also must the recipients of this truth, those who are filled with this knowledge, bear the historical, cultural fruit of the gospel in their lives. In our targum we attempt to envision what that might look like for us today.

So what you are saying is that Paul's language of truth, knowledge, wisdom and understanding in the first chapter of Colossians carries these kinds of Old Testament overtones, and that is why you employ Colossians against the modernist preoccupation with objectivity.

That's right.

Then I have two quick questions. First, are you relativists?

No, but that will have to wait for further discussion later in the book.

All right. Then second, would the first-century recipients of this letter have gotten the point? Would Gentile converts have heard these Jewish overtones in Paul's language? Or wouldn't they have been more likely to have heard this language of truth, knowledge, wisdom and understanding in terms of their own cultural context, which was influenced by Greek thought and Roman social and political structures?

This is another important question. But we need to spend some time in that first-century context before we can begin to answer it. So let us introduce you to Nympha.

—3—

PLACING COLOSSIANS

Discerning Empire

Nympha's Story

It began like every other day, with visits to my weavers and dyers in Colossae and inspection of their work.[1] After a few meetings with merchants to whom I was selling cloth, I enjoyed a leisurely visit with some friends, long unseen. Nothing out of the ordinary.

But then my day took a totally unexpected twist: a messenger arrived with news about a letter from Paul. That would have been exciting enough, but the letter was carried by *the* scandal of the house churches in Colossae: Onesimus, runaway slave. Can you imagine? Along with Tychicus, envoy of the apostle, Onesimus came as a bearer of a letter to the very community where his master, Philemon, was a prominent leader.

Even though I was only visiting Colossae (followers of Jesus meet in my house in Laodicea), I decided I had to be there for the reading of the letter. So I sent my tutor to cancel my evening appointment, and I hastened with some anticipation to the meeting where Paul's letter would be read.

But I can see that I have jumped in too quickly. Let me begin at the beginning, and maybe you will understand my excitement. My name is Nympha, and I am a textile manufacturer. My father was one of the most illustrious merchants and benefactors Laodicea has ever known. Over his lifetime he excelled in the careful craftsmanship that made his cloth and dyes sought after throughout the Lycus Valley and even beyond. As his reputation grew, so did his lands, with many farms around Laodicea,

---

[1]While the following narrative is fictional, we suggest that it is also historically plausible. See the reference to Nympha in Colossians 4:15.

Hierapolis and Colossae coming under his control. These farms are now the backbone of my wealth; on them I grow flax and wheat, olive groves and vineyards, and fertile pasture for my many oxen and sheep. The flax and sheep, of course, provide linen and wool for my business. As you may know, the dyers of Colossae and Hierapolis produce some of the most sought-after purple cloth in Asia Minor, and I am fortunate to have some of them in my employ.[2]

Of course, my farms do not only produce for my business. As is the custom here, I also for many years provided wheat and oil, wine and oxen for the imperial feast days and sacrifices in Laodicea. Indeed, until a year or so ago my business enabled me to be an important benefactor to my city, and my civic duties were considerable, as befits the daughter of a wealthy merchant. I have been high priestess of the emperor cult, priestess of Demeter, a priestess of the ancestral gods, one of the committee of ten responsible for public revenues and the collection of tax, a builder of the city gates and restorer of the gymnasium, and the provider of oil for the gymnasium during the imperial games.[3] And, of course, my dyers were privileged to be responsible for the provision of purple cloth to the provincial high priests of the imperial cult. I should perhaps mention that my husband is still one of the leading benefactors of our city.

As you can imagine, my business requires me to travel considerably within the Lycus Valley. It was during one of my visits to Colossae about a year ago that I met another textile merchant named Lydia, also a seller of purple cloth.[4] And she told me something that changed my world. She began by telling me the good news about Jesus, the anointed Messiah of the Jews and the savior not only of the Jews but of the whole earth! I questioned her closely and in some astonishment, for we all know that Caesar is the one worshiped as savior of the whole world, for he has brought peace and prosperity to the whole of his kingdom by the might of his arm and by the blessings of the gods on his rule.

My astonishment grew as Lydia responded to my concerns not with arguments but with a story, the story of the God of the Jews. Now, no doubt you are familiar with the stories about the origin of this Jewish people. I, at least, had heard how they had their

---

[2]"Colossae was famed for her wool, which was dyed purple/red. Its distinctive tint was known as *colossinus*" (Edwin Yamauchi, *The Archaeology of New Testament Cities in Western Asia Minor* [Grand Rapids, Mich.: Baker, 1980], p. 157).

[3]All of these positions were held by a wealthy woman, Menodora, daughter of Megacles from Sillyon in Pamphylia. See Riet van Bremen, "Women and Wealth," in *Images of Women in Antiquity*, ed. Averil Cameron and Amélie Kuhrt (New York: Routledge, 1993), pp. 223, 237n6; and Richard Gordon, "The Veil of Power," in *Paul and Empire: Religion and Power in Roman Imperial Society*, ed. Richard A. Horsley (Harrisburg, Penn.: Trinity Press International, 1997), pp. 135-36.

[4]According to Acts 16:14-15, Lydia came from Thyatira in Asia Minor. This gives us an interesting insight into how far a woman may have moved in her lifetime from her place of birth, since the impression one gets in Acts is that her household and her home are now in Philippi. On the importance for Thyatira for dyeing, see Yamauchi, *Archaeology of New Testament Cities*, p. 53, and references there. He also quotes a text in which Philippi honors a purple dyer named Antiochus, the son of Lykus, also a native of Thyatira.

origins in Egypt, from where they were expelled because the Egyptians feared conta-
gion from their skin disease, and how they wandered for seven days until they took
over Mount Sinai. Stopping there, they proclaimed the seventh day a sabbath for their
nation and took the precaution of not associating with foreigners because of their
condition. As I understood it, these were still their practices to this day.[5]

But this wasn't the story that Lydia told. Rather she began by talking about the
God who had made the whole world and everything in it. This God chose one man,
a wandering Aramean named Abraham, out of the nations of the earth, and promised that a great nation would come from him, a nation through which the whole
earth would be blessed. When this man's descendants were later made slaves by the
Egyptians, this God heard their cry and rescued them, drowning the Egyptian armies
in the sea. For forty years their God bore with them, nourishing them in the wilderness until they entered the land that was promised to them. This God gave the Israelites a king, David, and promised that one of his descendants would rule over all
other empires forever.

Well, this was certainly a different telling of the story from the way I had heard it!
But Lydia wasn't finished. She went on to say that God had kept his promise by sending a savior who was indeed a descendant of David: Jesus of Nazareth. This Jesus performed many signs and wonders, healing many who were sick and proclaiming the
coming of the kingdom of God. But the residents of Jerusalem and their leaders did
not understand that he was the one promised to them, and they handed him over to
the Roman governor, Pontius Pilate, to be crucified. His followers thought that was
the end. "Imagine their amazement," Lydia exclaimed, "when they discovered that
God had raised him from the dead! He now sits at the right hand of God, and those
who have his Spirit are able to do signs and wonders in his name, healing the sick
and casting out demons."

My head was spinning. But before I could interrupt, Lydia explained, "This is why
we proclaim him as Lord. Forgiveness of sins comes only through Jesus. Peace is
given only through Jesus. And he will come again, to establish his rule on earth in
righteousness." Her enthusiasm was both infectious and worrisome. And it seemed
to carry her on, as if she had to tell me the whole story right then and there.

Throughout the empire, Lydia told me, there are groups of people who worship
this Jesus as Lord and Savior. Some were God-fearers as she was, some have turned
from the worship of idols to this living Jesus, and some are Jews who have embraced
Jesus as the Messiah of their people.[6] Whoever they are, these people meet together

---

[5]This telling of the origins of the Jewish people is from Pompeius Trogus *Universal History* 36, found in
Justinus's *Epitome;* see Molly Whittaker, *Jews and Christians: Graeco-Roman Views* (Cambridge: Cambridge
University Press, 1984), p. 88.

[6]Gentiles who worshiped the God of Israel but had not undergone a complete conversion to Judaism (which
involved circumcision) were known as God-fearers. Acts 16:14 tells us that Lydia was a worshiper of God.

without distinction according to patron or client, slave or freeborn, Jew or Gentile, male or female. They share a feast that recalls the death and resurrection of Jesus, and they learn the story of the God of the Jews, whom Jesus proclaimed.

Well. What would you do if you heard such a story? It was the most bizarre thing I had ever heard—bizarre and downright dangerous. "Lydia," I said, "why on earth would you ever want to believe such a story? Why on earth would you ever want to worship such a king and lord? Look at you! You've got all that you need: money, prestige and social standing. You have contributed much to the glory of your city and the glory of the empire, and for that you have assurances of your own position and power. Why would you risk all that for the worship of this Jesus? Think of what could happen. Why, if someone unsympathetic heard you they might think you were suggesting that Caesar isn't our lord and savior. They might think you didn't appreciate the peace and prosperity that Rome has brought. Don't you see the kind of trouble you could get into with this way of thinking? Remember that although you are rich, you are still a woman. You could lose it all, just like that!"

"But that's the point," she said, "I *don't* believe that Caesar is our savior. I *don't* believe that he has brought peace and prosperity. And I *don't* worship him or any of the other gods, any more."

I must have had a stunned look on my face, because she continued more gently. "Look, Nympha," she said. "Look at the Roman peace. Yes, it is peaceful here, but at what price? Only if we promise subservience to the empire, only if we pay our taxes. And for those who don't? The land where this Jesus is from is Judea, and all the people of that land want is to live in peace and worship their own God, not Caesar. And has Caesar given them peace? No. Only death and destruction, demolishing their cities, enslaving the inhabitants, demanding taxes that drive the small landowners to slavery and revolt.[7]

"All over the empire we see the results of this 'peace': on the coins we are paid for our products, on the gates of our cities, in our temples, in the victory parades that accompany imperial worship. Our coins have Pax, the goddess of peace, on one side, and weapons on the other. Our gateways depict the emperor's victories over his enemies. This is peace by the blood of the sword.

"And yes, we benefit from this peace. You own many farms, Nympha, and you do so because of the taxes your tenants were unable to pay to Rome. Those taxes are supposed to ensure peace, but they also make it possible for the wealthy to buy peasant farms very cheaply and even take their owners into slavery. This peace is good for you. And it has been good for me, too. But it isn't good for everyone. This peace divides—it makes the peasants hopeless and the wealthy even wealthier.

"But the peace of Jesus is different. The peace of Jesus isn't imposed by violence.

---

[7]On imperial presence in Galilee and Judea see Richard A. Horsley, *Galilee: History, Politics, People* (Valley Forge, Penn.: Trinity Press International, 1995); and Warren Carter, *Matthew and Empire: Initial Explorations* (Valley Forge, Penn.: Trinity Press International, 2001), pp. 1-53.

Quite the opposite! You see, the reconciliation Jesus brings is accomplished through his own death on a cross, where he took evil upon himself until it had totally exhausted itself. This is a peace for the whole of the cosmos, for the whole of creation. This is a freedom for all people, slave and free, male and female, even the Scythian and barbarian. The peace of Jesus doesn't come just for those who have but for those who have nothing."

"But what does this have to do with the story of the Jews?" I asked. "How do the practices of this Jesus arise out of a religion which is about taking many holidays and despising foreigners?"[8]

Then she told me the story of Israel again, this time as the story of a God who came to free his people, who were enslaved under a foreign empire. According to Lydia, this God called Israel to establish a society of justice and righteousness, where the orphan and the widow were to be cared for and no one was to live in poverty. She told me how this God came in Jesus to save not only Israel but the whole world, not by arms and might but by his own blood, crucified on a Roman cross. Then she told me again that this Savior is the true Son of God, the One that God raised from the dead, and that he now sits as our true Lord at the right hand of God, our true Father.

I questioned her more closely about the followers of Jesus. Why would anyone want to risk worshiping this Jesus? Why believe that Jesus, not Caesar, brings peace? And what difference does this belief make in the way they live their lives?

Lydia continued to tell me about the communities that worship Jesus. She told me how they care for one another without regard for social status and how they challenge the economic system of the empire by sharing all that they have, so that none goes in need.[9] She told me stories of healings that have happened in some places. She told me how Jews and Gentiles are eating together at the same table, how women and men are proclaiming the gospel together, how slave and free are worshiping together as one. She told me how they practice forgiveness for all, reconciling their differences rather than fighting things out. She went on to explain how these communities are proclaiming a society counter to that of the empire by not accepting the social distinctions and divisions that we find everywhere we turn, by not accepting the way of vengeance. Rather, this community is proclaiming a gracious welcome and healing in Jesus that gives hope rather than despair. This is a community based on the kingdom of Jesus, she said, a fellowship grounded in love and forgiveness, rather than the hierarchical society of the empire based on status, wealth and race.

I don't need to tell you how upsetting this conversation was. In fact, it was deeply

---

[8]In the ancient world, the Jewish practice of keeping sabbath, together with the observance of food laws which inhibited social interaction with Gentiles, led to a reputation for sloth and despising strangers.

[9]On the early Christian community as an alternative economic community, see Anthony J. Riciutti, "The Economics of the Way: Jubilee Practice Among the Early Christians According to the Acts of the Apostles" (M.Phil.F thesis, Institute for Christian Studies, 2001).

disquieting. Proclaiming a lord other than Caesar could result in immediate impris-onment and a closer view of the imperial games than anyone would want—not as a spectator but as a participant on the losing side. I was glad that Lydia and I were speaking in the women's quarters of the house we were visiting. Although our tutors had accompanied us to oversee business transactions in town, they were not permit-ted into this wing of the house and were passing their time on the street outside. However, their presence nearby reminded us of our tenuous social standing.

You see, what Lydia was telling me was nothing less than treasonous, a threat to the empire. When, in a hushed tone, I told her so, she acknowledged that the follow-ers of Jesus were being persecuted, and the persecution came from both sides. While some claimed that they were blasphemers against the God of Israel, others insisted that they were a threat to the security of the empire. In fact, she was carrying messages from a follower of Jesus, Paul, who was in prison in Philippi and who had proclaimed the good news to her. He sent words of encouragement to the assemblies of believers in the regions of Lydia and Phrygia and throughout the empire.

We talked far into the night about this Jesus, and when we did retire, mine was a restless sleep. As we parted in the morning I remained unconvinced. Everything around me testified that Caesar was lord and that peace and prosperity had come through him. And such peace and prosperity testified to his status. Didn't Horace write, "Thine age, O Caesar, has brought back fertile crops to the fields"? And didn't Horace also say that the emperor "has wiped away our sins and revived the ancient virtues"?[10] Ever since I was a little girl during the glorious reign of Augustus, I had been taught that Caesar brought us forgiveness of our sins. After all, were not the gods blessing us in all that we did?

Throughout the next few weeks I gazed around as I went about my business. Ev-erywhere I turned there were images of Caesar. When I walked to the market, I saw his image in the square. I saw his image in the theater, in the gymnasium, in the tem-ples. And the coins with which I transacted my business all bore his likeness. Even my household was full of his image, from the idol of the emperor in the atrium to images on my jewelry and utensils and paintings on my walls.[11] I noticed that my clay lamps were decorated with symbols of Roman victory, and my father's seal ring, which I kept but no longer used, was decorated with a kneeling Parthian, a symbol of Rome's dominance over its enemies.[12]

---

[10]Horace *Odes* 4.15.

[11]Paul Zanker sums up the ubiquitous character of imperial images well: "Soon political symbolism could be seen on every imaginable object made for private use, indeed on virtually everything that could be decorated at all: jewelry and utensils, furniture, textiles, walls and stuccoed ceilings, door jambs, clay facings, roof tiles, and even on tomb monuments and marble ash urns" (*The Power of Images in the Age of Augustus* [Ann Arbor: University of Michigan Press, 1990], p. 266).

[12]Ibid., pp. 266-67.

But it wasn't just what I looked at. The whole rhythm of my life, especially in the city, was shaped by the empire. There were an astonishing number of feasts and festivals, all dedicated to the emperor and his reign.[13] Even the athletic games and the gladiatorial fights were all in honor of the emperor and the wonderful blessings he had bestowed on us. Such games and festivals were indeed for the upbuilding of the community: we were all, slave and free, rich and poor, united in thanksgiving to the emperor for all he had given us.

The more I looked, however, the more I noticed that nothing ever changed. For example, I had never before noticed, or perhaps I had never really cared to notice, that the very structure of the theater for the games was set up so that slave and free never needed to see each other. We were all worshiping the emperor, but we were doing so within the clearly prescribed roles that the empire had set for us. At the banquets, I ate the double portion due to a benefactor of the city, while the slave next door ate his much smaller and inferior portion, all in honor of the emperor.

I began to notice other things that Lydia had mentioned. I visited my farms near Laodicea, and for the first time I saw the despair in the eyes of those who were now slaves on the land they once owned. I saw that while peace had brought prosperity for me, it had also brought greater poverty to these proud farmers. Was Caesar indeed good news for these people?

I was disturbed. Lydia had offered a challenge to my faith in the empire. I knew that her story and mine couldn't both be true. Either Caesar had brought forgiveness of our sins, fruitfulness and peace through the great victories he had wrought, or Jesus had brought forgiveness of our sins, fruitfulness and peace through his paradoxical victory on a Roman cross. But this seemed impossible, unimaginable!

It was also clear that Lydia's story of Jesus could not be happily accommodated by the imperial regime. Devotion to Jesus was not like devotion to Isis or Apollo. These gods and their cults were no threat to the empire. Actually such private devotion, it was believed, made one a better citizen and enhanced one's public duty to the empire. Jesus, however, created a problem. His lordship clearly precluded Caesar's, and the guarded privacy of my conversation with Lydia notwithstanding, it was clear that following Jesus could not be a private matter but would have to be a public faith, transforming public life.

I decided that I needed to see what the society created by this Jesus would look like, but I was nervous about doing that at home in Laodicea. So the next time I was in Colossae, I sought out some followers of Jesus.

I was astounded by what I saw. It was pretty much as Lydia had said: men and

---

[13]According to Zanker, there were sixty-seven days of regularly scheduled games (ibid., p. 147). In addition, there were occasional festivals to celebrate the safety of the emperor and to extol his victories over enemies. See John K. Chow, "Patronage in Roman Corinth," in *Paul and Empire: Religion and Power in Roman Imperial Society,* ed. Richard A. Horsley (Harrisburg, Penn.: Trinity Press International, 1997), p. 107.

women, slaves and free, Jews, Scythians, barbarians and Romans all meeting together in peace to talk about this Jesus, pray to him, share a meal in remembrance
of him, and struggle with what following Jesus meant for their daily life in the empire. It was an unheard-of gathering of people in the Roman empire. This isn't to
say there weren't struggles. Social divisions and hierarchical relationships that have
been entrenched for ages and reinforced by the emperor do not change overnight.
But at least these people struggled! At least they had some vision and hope for a
better way to live together![14]

And that hope was rooted in the memory of Jesus—a memory they kept alive with
an astounding meal. At this meal none appeared to be superior to the other. All received equal portions of bread and wine, and none went without. I was amazed at the
love they had for one another and for this Jesus they worshiped.

What also astonished me was how they saw their actions as a prophetic witness
against the rule of Caesar. They knew that their actions, the way they embodied their
faith together in their community, challenged all that Roman society held dear. They
spoke of themselves as a new family, a new humanity, those who had left darkness for
light,[15] who were now bringing, through their small house meetings, nothing less
than reconciliation for the whole world.[16] They saw themselves as a living embodi-
ment of the forgiveness and healing Jesus had brought for the world.

I went away deeply disturbed and wrestling with what the worship of Jesus would
mean for my life. These Christians had such a comprehensive vision, but following
Jesus would come at a high cost for me. Living such a life would mean ceasing to be
a benefactor for the emperor cult, giving up my position as provider of wheat and
oxen for the imperial festivals, purging my house of all that bore the image of Caesar
and his victories. It would mean ceasing to participate in the imperial festivals and
games. It would mean refusing to participate in the give-and-take of benefactor and
client, bestowing monetary and social favors on those who sang my praises and
danced attendance on me. It would mean distancing myself from the communities
and societies that had given my life meaning.

I began to attend more regularly the meetings of those who follow Jesus. They wel-
comed me in, even though they knew that my position in the community could prove
a threat to their security. They were prepared to practice such a risky love, they explained, because their Lord embodied such love even to the point of death on a cross.
So I wanted to know more about this Jesus. The life of this assembly of Jesus followers
awakened in me an insatiable curiosity about Jesus and his story.

---

[14]The story of Acts records in a number of places such struggles in relation to economic sharing and the
inclusion of Gentiles. See Acts 5:1-11, 6:1-7 and chapter 15. See also 1 Corinthians 8 and 11:17-34, as
well as Galatians 2:1-14.
[15]See Colossians 1:13, Ephesians 5:8 and 1 Peter 2:9; and compare Romans 13:12.
[16]See 2 Corinthians 5:16-21 and Colossians 1:15-20.

I don't know how to explain it, but the more I met with this community and the more I learned about Jesus, the more I wanted to join them in following him. And the more I followed Jesus, the less enamored I became with Caesar.

One day in a conversation with these Christians I found I was using the word *we*. I had, almost without noticing it, thrown in my lot with Jesus and his followers. I had become a Christian. The Christian community in Laodicea now meets as an assembly in my house.

But it has not been easy. My husband wasn't at all impressed with my purging of the imperial imagery from our household, especially since some of our artworks had been commissioned in Rome and were quite expensive. And the question we have been struggling with as a community is this: how far do we need to go? What does it mean to be faithful to Jesus as Lord over all of our life?

We have begun to hear other stories of what following Jesus means: stories of slaves who are freed, stories of wealthy people who sold all that they had and gave it to the assembly. There are even stories of some who refuse to follow the empire's laws regarding compulsory marriage.[17]

In our communities here in Laodicea, Hierapolis and Colossae, tensions have been rising. We have tried to follow the lead of Judaism in resisting the emperor cult by observing alternative feasts and festivals, and by withdrawing as much as possible from the aspects of our culture which have been taken over by the empire. But the stories we hear have raised wider questions: Should we free our slaves? Should I indeed be selling my purple cloth to the imperial high priests? Should I give back the farms that became mine because peasant owners could not pay their debts? What does it mean to use my wealth for the pride of the city and the empire, now that I no longer honor the emperor? And underlying all of these is the question of the persecution that some in our communities faced already for our suspected resistance to Rome. Is this going to continue? How much are we expected to bear?

Now you can see why the news of a letter from the apostle Paul caused me to drop everything and rush off to the meeting. Surely Paul would have some wisdom for us on these issues. And if the runaway slave Onesimus accompanies this letter, then surely Paul will have something to say about the problem of slavery that has been vexing us. If Paul were here in person, our question would be clear. How ought we to be followers of Jesus at the heart of the empire? What does it mean to be Christians here in Colossae or Laodicea? Surely this letter would answer some of our concerns. I could hardly wait to hear it.

---

[17]On those who sold all and gave it to the assembly, see Acts 4:32-37. As part of his restoration of morality in the empire, Augustus passed legislation which contained "major penalties for those who remained unmarried . . . as well as rewards and privileges for parents of several children" (Zanker, *Power of Images,* p. 157). On refusing to follow imperial marital legislation, see 1 Corinthians 7.

The Colossian Context: Discerning Empire

Imagine that in the year 2200 a letter is discovered which had been written to a North American church in 2000. The discovery is incredibly exciting, because in 2050 the city in which the church was located was buried in an avalanche and almost no records remain to show what the city and the church were like. All our living witnesses to that city are gone. And now a letter suddenly comes to light. Would we be able to understand the letter? Would we be able to set the historical context of the church and the issues it might have been facing?

Even though little evidence might remain about the particular congregation to which the letter was written, there would be some important evidence to help us understand the letter. One would be the larger historical context. What were the issues facing the culture as a whole? What was the dominant worldview of the culture of which this city was a part? What were the nearby cities like? Does the letter seem to address any of the issues of this dominant culture? Does it refer to cultural events and symbols that were part of the larger culture? What can we infer from such references?

When reading the letter to the Colossians, we find ourselves in a similar situation. Colossae was destroyed by an earthquake somewhere around A.D. 60-64 and has never been excavated. We have much less knowledge of the context in Colossae then we do of other cities in the first century. But we do have some knowledge of the dominant worldview of Asia Minor in the first century. We know what some nearby cities were like (Laodicea, Hierapolis, Aphrodisias), and we know what some of the hot issues were for Christians throughout Asia Minor. *All* Christians at this time would have found themselves confronted with the worldview of empire.

To understand this letter, then, we need to understand something of the world in which Nympha lived and its parallels to our own world. To discern both the historical and the contemporary meaning of Colossians, we need to discern empire.

In chapter one we stated that empires are (1) built on systemic centralizations of power, (2) secured by structures of socioeconomic and military control, (3) religiously legitimated by powerful myths and (4) sustained by a proliferation of imperial images that captivate the imaginations of the population. This definition of empire will provide the contours for our discussion of Colossians in the context of both the Roman empire and our own imperial realities.

Systemic Centralizations of Power

Empires always guarantee the status quo of privilege and oppression through a centralization of power. In the Roman empire the *paterfamilias*—the patriarchal structure of marital, familial and economic relationships—was considered the empire's building block. In this "father-directed" hierarchy, power was centralized and the empire was socially encoded. The economic importance of women, children and slaves was carefully guarded in Roman law: the bulk of rulings regarding the guardianship of women and the various laws upholding the power fathers had over their sons was rooted in the practical necessity of safeguarding the family wealth.[18] Similarly, the legal code ensured that slaves, even if made free, continued to be legally under the power of their former masters.[19]

In fact, even freed slaves still fell under the strictures of the patron-client relationship which ensured the continuation of power amongst certain sectors of Roman society. The patron-client relationship, with its dynamic of the promise of benefit from the patron in exchange for the honor and praise of the clients, functioned as a powerful means of social cohesion and control. This same dynamic operated on the level of the society as a whole: the emperor was the ultimate patron, bestowing his benefits on those who lauded him.[20] Indeed, in the structure of the *paterfamilias* the emperor is the father supreme. The whole structure of society serves to secure his rule and authority.

It is astonishing how similar power relations in the context of global capitalism are to this first-century system. Andrew Wallace-Hadrill describes patronage in a way that demonstrates some striking parallels with contemporary economics. In the patronage system, withholding promised resources from the client served to strengthen social power in an effective manner because the patron's "power over a client derives not from generous and regular distribution, but from keeping him on tenterhooks with the prospect of access to resources which is in fact never fully granted."[21] Such a strategy, of course, is not alien to those of us familiar with the policies of the World Bank and the International Monetary Fund for keeping countries in the South dependent by means of structural adjustments and perpetual debt.[22]

Global economic structures reveal centralizations of power. Most major corporations use the equivalent of slave labor to produce clothing, toys, tools and some foods. Most of this labor is done by people in Asia, Latin America or Africa. While cash-crop farmers include both men and women, the majority of those who work in sweatshops, on coffee plantations and in the sex trade are women and children.[23] Al-

---

[18]On women see Bremen, "Women and Wealth," p. 234; Jane F. Gardner, *Women in Roman Law and Society* (London: Colin Helm, 1986), pp. 14-22. On the power of fathers over sons, see J. A. Crook, *Law and Life of Rome, 90 B.C.-A.D. 212* (Ithaca, N.Y.: Cornell University Press, 1967), pp. 107-11.

[19]See Chow, "Patronage in Roman Corinth," pp. 120-21. Whereas a patron-client relationship was usually of a voluntary nature, the relationship between a master and freed slave was governed by law. See Andrew Wallace-Hadrill, "Patronage in Roman Society," in *Patronage in Ancient Society,* ed. Andrew Wallace-Hadrill (New York: Routledge, 1989), p. 76; Crook, *Law and Life of Rome,* pp. 51-55.

[20]Wallace-Hadrill, "Patronage in Roman Society," p. 84.

[21]Ibid., pp. 72-73.

[22]Thus it is no surprise that for every dollar that is sent in foreign aid to Africa, four are returned in the form of debt servicing.

[23]See *New Internationalist* no. 347, *Inside Business: How Corporations Make the Rules* (July 2002); Naomi Klein, *No Logo: Taking Aim at the Brand Bullies* (Toronto: Vintage Canada, 2000), pp. 195-229. On the effects of globalization on women in Africa, see Omega Bula, "A Jubilee Call for African Women," in *Jubilee, Wealth and the Market* (Toronto: Canadian Ecumenical Jubilee Initiative, 1999), pp. 64-76.

though we live in a society that would deny it, such centralizations of power are still evident in the overwhelmingly white male face of corporate culture in North America and in the increasingly high levels of poverty and incarceration among aboriginal and black communities. Even in this brief sketch it is evident that although our culture does not openly subscribe to an ethos of patriarchy, racism and classism, the effects of the global economic market create the same kind of societal dynamic that was present in first-century Rome.

A question we will need to address when looking at Paul's advice to women, children and slaves in Colossians 3:18—4:1 will be whether Paul is reinforcing or undermining the *paterfamilias* of the empire in this passage. And how might his view of households inform our engagement of oppressive socioeconomic structures in our own time?

Socioeconomic and Military Control: An Economics of Oppression

Rome was renowned for its efficient military structure. Once a land had been conquered by Roman might, once the soldiers had taken their plunder and the garrison set up (which continued such plunder), the conquered area had to be made profitable for Rome. Roads needed to be built, irrigation improved, and rivers bridged. All this made it possible for goods to flow easily from the provinces to Rome.

Klaus Wengst describes this dynamic in a way that makes the parallels with our times clear:

> So what Rome needed in order to exploit a province economically was above all the provision of an infrastructure, though this was tailored to its own needs. If the term "development aid" had already been in existence it would have been just as much a euphemism for exploitation as it is today.[24]

A steady stream of taxes, tolls, offerings, tributes and levies, along with grain, produce, cloth and natural resources, found its way to Rome. As people in the provinces became more impoverished and were unable to pay their taxes, they were forced to sell their land. This enabled those with power to expand their land base.[25]

Even more than military control, the economic policies of Rome were designed to ensure that the lands they controlled would have no resources for resistance to the empire. Such control was on the one hand more lucrative, and on the other cheaper, than maintaining power through military control.

Wengst's comments about development aid hint at the parallels between Rome's economic policies and those of a globalized economy. Through mechanisms such as

---

[24]Klaus Wengst, *Pax Romana and the Peace of Jesus Christ,* trans. John Bowden (London: SCM Press, 1987), p. 28.

[25]Ramsey MacMullen, *Roman Social Relations: 50 B.C. to A.D. 285* (New Haven, Conn.: Yale University Press, 1974), pp. 20, 37-39, 48-52.

the World Bank and the International Monetary Fund, powerful nations in the North are able to dictate the economic terms by which the South is kept firmly ensconced in the cycle of international debt and development aid. By means of such economic control, these structures dictate the social policy of dependent countries, ensuring that it favors the corporations of the North to the detriment of local peoples, economies and land.[26]

While these policies have by and large ensured that the flow of wealth and resources continues to move from the South to the North, on occasion military control must be used to enforce the system. It is no secret that the North, particularly the United States, has been heavily involved in overthrows of legitimate governments and in creation of puppet governments in Africa and Latin America.[27] And while the 2003 war against Iraq was fought in the name of national security and the liberation of the Iraqi people, widespread suspicion that this was a military intervention prompted by larger concerns of the Pax Americana have been validated as more evidence emerges concerning untruths surrounding the call to go to war.

In the face of an empire that rules through military and economic control, what is the shape of a community that serves a ruler who brings reconciliation and peace by sacrificial death rather than military might? If the empire elevates economic greed and avarice into civic virtues, while Paul dismisses such a way of life as idolatrous, then how does a Christian community shaped by Paul's gospel live its life in the empire?

Powerful Myths: The Pax Romana

Everyone loves a good story. And the story that legitimated the economic and military power of Rome was very good. It can be summed up in two words, *Pax Romana*. Ironically, the Roman legitimation for continued military oppression was rooted in a story of peace, proclaiming that Rome was the bearer of cosmic peace, fertility and prosperity.[28] With the coming of the Roman empire a new age had dawned upon which rested the blessings of the gods. And in conquering the barbarian peoples who populated the whole of the known world, Rome was ensuring that its story would become the story of the whole world.

This story shaped the rhythm of life in the empire. Feasts and festivals celebrated Rome's victory over the barbarian hordes (which included, of course, the recalcitrant people of Judea and Galilee). Festivals in honor of the birthday of the emperor and in

---

[26]A vivid picture of such dynamics is found in Bula, "Jubilee Call for African Women," pp. 68-71. See also Joseph E. Stiglitz, *Globalization and Its Discontents* (New York: W. W. Norton, 2003).

[27]For a fictional wrestling with a real overthrow in the Congo in 1960, see Barbara Kingsolver, *The Poisonwood Bible* (New York: HarperCollins, 1998). Other examples include, of course, U.S. subversion of legitimate governments in Chile (September 11, 1973) and the White House-supported Contra rebellion in Nicaragua during the mid-1980s.

[28]Zanker, *Power of Images*, pp. 167-83.

thanksgiving for Rome, its ruler and its power included sacrifices that reinforced the centralization of power by emphasizing the places of nobility, plebeians and slaves in the hierarchy of the empire.[29]

Such myths, of course, drive contemporary globalization as well. Most powerful is the progress myth, which has been the driving force behind Western capitalism since the Enlightenment.[30] The myth that we are moving as a culture toward increasing wealth and technological control, and that this is invariably good, provides the justification for all the economic and military policies of the North. Countries in the South are called "developing countries"; that is, they are not different from us, they are simply behind us, trying to catch up to where we are now. According to the progress myth, this "development" can only be good, and it is defined in terms of increasing industrialization and increasing technology, which will result in increased wealth. In spite of the evidence that increased industrialization and technology lower the standard of life rather than raise it, the progress myth provides powerful legitimation for the lifestyle of Europe and North America.[31]

This myth has come to expression most powerfully, however, in the rhetoric of the United States. If the Pax Romana summarized the Roman imperial mythology, then the Pax Americana, with its clear distinction between good and evil and its self-righteous and aggressive foreign policy, encapsulates the dominant mythology of our day. Like Rome, the United States describes itself as a nation chosen by God to bring democracy and freedom to those parts of the world "backward" enough to endorse a different system of government and different economic priorities from those of global capitalism.[32]

In Colossians Paul is telling a story that is an alternative to the mythology of empire. Mythology is always about salvation, peace and prosperity. Rome found salvation in the universal peace of the age after Augustus. The "American Empire" finds salvation in economic progress and global control. Paul tells a story about a salvation

---

[29]Stanley K. Stowers, "Greeks Who Sacrifice and Those Who Do Not: Toward an Anthropology of Greek Religion," in *The Social World of the First Christians: Essays in Honor of Wayne A. Meeks,* ed. L. Michael White and O. Larry Yarbrough (Minneapolis: Fortress, 1995), pp. 319-29; Gordon, "Veil of Power," pp. 134-37.

[30]Bob Goudzwaard, *Capitalism and Progress: A Diagnosis of Western Society,* trans. Josina Van Nuis Zylstra (Toronto: Wedge/Grand Rapids, Mich.: Eerdmans, 1979).

[31]An ever-increasing gap between the rich and poor, rampant health problems (like cancer, obesity, heart disease), environmental degradation, racial tensions, divorce rates, urban uglification and psychological stress all are indicators of a low standard of living amidst "economic growth." For more nuanced understandings of economic well-being, see Bob Goudzwaard and Harry deLange, *Beyond Poverty and Affluence: Towards an Economy of Care,* trans. and ed. Mark R. Vander Vennen (Grand Rapids, Mich.: Eerdmans, 1994), and Herman Daly and John Cobb Jr., *For the Common Good* (Boston: Beacon, 1990).

[32]For instance, U.S. Attorney General John Ashcroft told an audience in Nashville in February 2002 that "American 'freedoms' are made in Heaven: 'not the grant of any government or document, but our endowment from God.'" Quoted in "Worldbeaters," *New Internationalist* 347 (July 2002): 29.

rooted in Christ, historical sovereignty located in a victim of the empire, and prosperity that bears fruit in the whole world.

Imperial Images That Capture the People's Imagination
In a fascinating book, Paul Zanker describes the way imperial images dominated both public and private space in the Roman empire. Images of Caesar were found in the market, the city square, the public baths, and the theater, at the gymnasium and in the temples. Images of the empire were also found on every imaginable object for private use.[33] The symbolism of the empire became part of daily furnishings, permeating the visual landscape and therefore the imaginations of the subjects of the empire.[34]

It isn't difficult to see how the powerful myths of our own culture are evident in the images that surround us in daily life. Corporate logos and corporate advertising not only shape the public space in our culture but also permeate our private lives. The grocery store, the mall, billboards, buses, television, computers, even our clothing, towels and toothbrushes: all may be marked by corporate logos.[35] The entertainment giant Disney Corporation, whose movies and cartoons reinforce the corporate myth of our culture, markets toothbrushes, towels, pajamas, lunchboxes, backpacks, pens, pencil cases, cuddly toys, coloring books, picture books, encyclopedias, swimming pools, balls and other toys, all emblazoned with Disney images.

These images all tell a story of consumer affluence, Western superiority and the ineluctable march of economic progress. But it isn't just the imagination of the North that is shaped. These images of North American culture are exported via television and the international advertising of corporations such as Coca-Cola and McDonald's, portraying our society as one of prosperity, safety, equality and happiness.

Just as in the ancient world the images of peace and prosperity masked the reality of inequality and violence, so the contemporary images projected by advertising mask the reality of sweatshops, inequality, and domestic and international violence created by our lifestyles. And in the face of the ubiquitous imagery of the empire, Paul proclaims Jesus as the true image of God (Col 1:15) and calls the Colossian Christians to bear the image of Jesus in shaping an alternative to the empire.

---

[33]Seal rings were engraved with Capricorn (the astrological sign under which Augustus was born) or a kneeling Parthian (a symbol of Rome's victory over the barbarians who now kneel before it). Silver cups would portray a battle and triumphal procession; clay lamps depicted the goddess Victoria seated on a globe, signifying Rome's victory over the whole earth. Silver was decorated with sacrificial scenes, and the sphinx, a symbol of hope which Augustus used on his seal ring, appeared on candelabra, bronze utensils, wall paintings, coins and table feet. When the sphinx appeared with the vine, they together symbolized the new age of growth and prosperity. All examples are from Zanker, *Power of Images,* pp. 228-29, 266-67, 270-71.

[34]"Whatever the case with a particular object—whether the owner sought to proclaim his political loyalty or wanted only to enjoy the latest in artistic fashion—the cumulative effect of the new political imagery, echoed in Roman houses on every level of society, must have been inescapable" (ibid., p. 273).

[35]See Klein, *No Logo,* chaps. 1-5.

An Alternative Imagination

The story of Rome was not the only story that would have been competing for the imagination of the Colossian Christian community. This community had heard the story of Israel. In fact, the early Christian communities told the story of Jesus as the story of Israel. From Abraham to Moses, exodus to exile, the writings of the early church refer again and again to the fundamental story of Israel and the God who called her.

This was the story of Abraham, who left the gods of the empire to follow the living God. This was the story of Moses, whom God used to rescue his people from the empire and to lead them into a land where they would live in an alternative covenant community. This was the story of Jesus, who was crucified by the empire and rose to proclaim God's new rule, manifest in communities that sold all they had so that none would have need. This was the alternative imagination that energized and gave life to the early Christian community. As we saw, these stories gripped the imaginations of followers of Jesus such as Lydia and Nympha, who began to see that the stories of Israel and Jesus offered a compelling critique of life in the empire.

Such a critique will form the core of our reading of Colossians, but first we need to explore the alternative story that gave life to the church in Colossae and the way it breathed through the language and imagery of Paul.

—4—

CONTESTED FRUITFULNESS IN
THE SHADOW OF EMPIRE

W hen we ask our students to tell us the biblical story in its briefest outline, we are always struck by the different overarching themes that are used to structure that telling. It may be that the theme of forgiveness dominates, or God as all-powerful, or redemption, or God's concern for the oppressed. Sometimes the role of women in moving the story forward is emphasized, or the theme of life in the midst of barrenness. All of these are legitimate ways to structure a telling of the events we find in the Bible; each of them gives a special insight into God and how God interacts with humanity and creation.

In this chapter we want to explore one particular way of telling the story that we believe to be central for an understanding of Colossians: that is, the biblical story in the face of the empire. Such a telling gives us insight into both how Paul would have understood this story and what this story says to us in the disquieted empire of global capitalism.[1]

Telling the Story

The very shape of the Scriptures roots Israel's story deeply in the context of empire. The creation account of Genesis 1 was written in the face of an empire that sought to relegate its captive people to the role of slaves, forced to do menial tasks of service that were beneath the status of the gods.[2] And Israel finds its most ancient roots as a

---

[1]On Paul's use of imperial language throughout his writing, see Sylvia C. Keesmaat's two articles, "The Psalms in Romans and Galatians," in *The Psalms in the New Testament,* ed. Steve Moyise and Maarten Menkes (Edinburgh: T & T Clark, 2004), and "In the Face of Empire: Paul's Use of the Scriptures in the Shorter Epistles," in *The Use of the Old Testament in the New Testament,* ed. Stanley Porter (Grand Rapids, Mich.: Eerdmans, 2004).

[2]See J. Richard Middleton, "The Liberating Image? Interpreting the *Imago Dei* in Context," *Christian Scholar's Review* 24 (1994): 8-25; and J. Richard Middleton and Brian J. Walsh, *Truth Is Stranger Than It Used to Be: Biblical Faith in a Postmodern Age* (Downers Grove, Ill.: InterVarsity Press, 1995), especially chap. 6.

nation in a context of slavery to one of the greatest empires of all time: Egypt. Israel's God hears the cry of those who are ground down by the empire and acts not only to free this oppressed people from the imperial oppression but also to defeat the empire: "horse and rider he has thrown into the sea" (Ex 15:1)! Who is Yahweh? The One who overthrows empire, that's who!

On these accounts of creation and exodus rest the twin pillars of Israel's belief: monotheism and election. In the face of the gods of Babylon, the empire that would hold the peoples of the world in bondage, there is only one God, ruler of heaven and earth, who has created humanity in God's own image. This one God, true ruler of all, is the heart of monotheistic belief. But alongside that is election: this one, true God has chosen Israel, rescued it from the belly of Egypt, the empire that would stamp out God's people by killing Israel's children. God has called this people Israel to be a light for the nations, a blessing to the whole world. On these two pillars rest the whole of the biblical story.

As the story unfolds, concerns of empire are never far from Israelite consciousness. On Mount Sinai, Israel is given the law and called to be a people whose collective life is antithetical to that of any empire. If the empire is a place of slavery and death, then Israel is called to be a people of jubilee, where slaves are released and life renewed. The laws that God gives point to such an end: laws regarding care for the foreigner, orphans, widows and the poor; laws of gleaning; laws forbidding the charging of interest, the keeping of a collateral pledge and the withholding of wages overnight; laws for seeing that one's kin do not fall into slavery; and laws of redemption for slaves and for the land.[3] All of these things are counter to the ideology of empire, which relegates foreigners, orphans, widows, the poor and slaves to particularly demeaned positions in the midst of an already demeaned humanity.

While the empire is preoccupied with images that represent its own power and hegemony, Israel is called to image a counterreality in a countercommunity. While the empire is frantically caught up in the management of production and consumption, Israel is called to a sabbath keeping that acknowledges the gift character of its life in the land. And while the empire is sustained on the backs of slaves and an economics of oppression, a sabbath-keeping Israel images its God by caring for the poor, the stranger and sojourner, the widow and orphan. The care of the marginalized—those who have no standing ground in the community—is antithetical to the constant striv-

---

[3]Caring for aliens, orphans, widows and poor: Exodus 22:21-27; 23:9; Leviticus 19:9-13, 33-34; Deuteronomy 14:28-29; 15:2-11; 24:10-21; 26:12-13; 27:19; Jeremiah 7:5-7; also Proverbs 14:21, 31; 22:9; 28:27; 31:9, 20; Isaiah 1:16-17; 58:7; Ezekiel 18:5-13. Laws of gleaning: Leviticus 19:9-10; Deuteronomy 24:19-21; cf. Exodus 23:10-11. Laws forbidding the charging of interest: Exodus 22:25; Leviticus 25:35-38; Ezekiel 18:5-13; cf. Ezekiel 22:7. Laws forbidding the keeping of a collateral pledge, or withholding of wages, overnight: Exodus 22:25-26; Deuteronomy 24:12-15. Laws for seeing that one's kin do not fall into slavery: Leviticus 25:35-38. Laws of redemption for slaves and for the land: Leviticus 25; Deuteronomy 15.

ing for power, dominance and hierarchy that characterizes the empire. Israel is called to be an alternative socioeconomic witness to the empire.

When Israel enters the Promised Land, it faces its greatest challenge not to become like the empire it left behind. As the story unfolds, it becomes clear that such an empire is very seductive. When the Israelites ask for a king "like the other nations," God warns them that when they have such a king to rule over them they will indeed become "like the other nations," a people enslaved to the will of the ruler and his concern for empire. Such a king will rule Israel in the same acquisitive way as the emperors of the day. He will take their sons for soldiers, he will take their daughters as royal servants and to keep the harem well stocked, he will take their wealth for his treasury, and he will take their produce for his imperial household (1 Sam 8:5-18). He will take, take, take. In the land of gift, the king, "like the nations," will take. Under such a king Israel will mimic the empire in which sons and daughters are commodities to be used for the glory and feeding of the ruler, where land is a commodity for the satisfaction of the elite, where animals and slaves are property to be expropriated and made productive. And when Israel becomes an empire like the nations, its people will become like the people of the nations: slaves for the imperial good, crying out to their God, just as they did in Egypt (1 Sam 8:18; cf. Ex 2:23).

As the story unfolds, this is precisely what happens. The story of the monarchy is a tension-filled testimony to how even the kings chosen by God find it hard not to behave like the imperial powers around them. From David's rape of Bathsheba, to the rape of Tamar, to Solomon's slave labor for the building of the temple and his palace, to Jezebel's framing of Naboth in order to seize his land, the kings of Israel demonstrate that imperial ethics have now come to characterize Israel (2 Sam 11; 13; 1 Kings 5:13-16; 21).

It is the prophets who most tellingly deconstruct the imperial distortions of Israel. The covenant people do not care for aliens, widows and orphans, or the weak and injured (Is 1:23; 10:2; Jer 5:27-29; 7:5-7; 22:3-6; Ezek 22:7; 34:1-6; Zech 7:8-14; Mal 3:5). Failing to practice mercy and justice (Is 5:7; Jer 22:13-17; Hos 12:7-8; Amos 5:7; 6:12; Mic 6:1-12), Israel grinds down the poor and needy (Is 3:14-15; 10:2; 32:7; 58:3; Jer 2:34; Ezek 22:29; Amos 2:6-7; 4:1; 5:11; 8:4-8; cf. Job 24:9-14; Ps 37:14; 109:16). The people have been engaged in the consumptive practices of empire, filling their land with silver and gold, horses and chariots, buying up neighbors' fields until nothing is left but industrial farms-as-business that kill community (Is 2:7; 5:8). Moreover, they consistently engage in business deals that exploit the poor (Amos 8:5-6).

Exile is God's answer to Israel's imperial ways. If Israel is going to live out of an imperial imagination, then it may as well be taken fully into captivity by the empire. And so it is that in 587 B.C. Israel's leaders and merchants are taken to the heart of Babylon and its temple and land are left desolate.

Then, as enslaved people once again, Israel begins to dream anew what it means to be followers of Yahweh, counter to the empire. Jeremiah contains one of the first words to this people in exile about how to live in the shadow of the empire:

> Build houses and live in them; plant gardens and eat what they produce. Take wives and have sons and daughters; take wives for your sons, and give your daughters in marriage, that they may bear sons and daughters; multiply there, and do not decrease. But seek the welfare of the city where I have sent you into exile, and pray to the LORD on its behalf, for in its welfare you will find your welfare. (Jer 29:5-7)

In the face of an empire that would deny your humanity, the prophet says, do those things that God called you to at the beginning of the story, those things that are linked to bearing the image of this God. Plant gardens, eat the good fruit they produce, be fruitful and multiply. Even in exile Israel is called to fulfill the creational mandate of Genesis 1:28-29. This is, of course, profoundly ironic, because the whole reason these people are in exile is that they were unable to fulfill that calling when they lived in their own land.

So in a sense Jeremiah is saying, "You were unable to fulfill this calling in your own land. Now your task is to fulfill your creational calling in the midst of exile. This is no place to capitulate, to become like the empire that has enslaved you." In the face of hopeless bondage, Jeremiah is calling the people to live lives of hopeful obedience, fruitful lives of building and planting, tending and keeping.

But Jeremiah doesn't stop there. He doesn't stop with a call to live lives of wholeness that upbuild only the community of exiles. He extends this call outward. In the midst of an oppressive empire, in slavery, the exiles have a mission. "Seek the welfare of the city where I have sent you into exile," he says, "and pray to the LORD on its behalf" (Jer 29:7).

You've got to admit that this is a bit of a tall order. The exiles might say, "Okay, I'll build and plant and multiply and carry on an obedient life. But seek the welfare of the empire, of Babylon? Seek the welfare of my oppressors? How on earth can that be expected?" But that is exactly what they are called to do. This small, vulnerable group of refugees has a responsibility for the larger community in which they find themselves. They are to work for its welfare.

This call is profoundly subversive—right up there with "Pray for those who persecute you" (Mt 5:44)—precisely because it is completely antithetical to all the empire could ask or imagine. The empire wants nothing more than to break the spirit and the will of the foreigner in its midst. But with the call to seek the welfare of the empire, the exiles are living out of the vision and hope of Genesis, for the good of the empire itself. This is a call to be God's people by bringing shalom and healing in places of brokenness and despair. And what could be more broken and more in need of healing than the place of oppression, the heart of the empire?

But these are more than words of courageous hope for the exiles: they also contain an element of judgment. Israel had always been called to be a blessing to the nations, to bring light to the Gentiles, a healing covenant for the peoples. Israel had not fulfilled this call in its own land. So it is required to fulfill the calling in exile: to work for the welfare, the blessing, of the Gentiles in Babylon. Israel may have been unfaithful all along, but God is determined that somewhere, somehow, God's people will begin to live as they are called. In the heart of the empire they are called to live a life of community that is paradoxically in direct challenge to all that the empire stands for, while seeking the welfare of the empire itself.

In the face of empire, Jeremiah proclaims a subversive word of the Lord that completely counters Israel's imperial experience. Under the oppressive rule of Babylon and Assyria, the Israelites are still called to build a faithful community and to live subject to a different kind of rule and kingship, one where imperial might and power is used for feeding the hunger of the people and binding up their wounds.

These visions of an alternative kingdom and a different kind of ruler fueled Jewish expectation for the next few centuries. Although the Persian empire permitted the Jews to return to their land, the return was tinged with disappointment. Israel was still a client state, and it remained so, first under Persia, then under the Greeks, then under Rome. One empire after another, and brief periods of independence, served only to give hope to dreams of one day being a free people with no king but God. That the experience of empire cast a shadow over Israel's self-understanding can be seen starkly in many of the intertestamental writings.[4] Under that shadow Israel longed for a true return from exile, a new exodus from under the oppressive weight of empire.[5]

That such hopes were alive in the hearts of the early Christian community can be seen in the Gospel of Luke, which takes pains to situate Jesus very firmly in the setting of the empire of his day. Three times at the beginning of the Gospel we are told very precisely who are the imperial rulers over Israel (Lk 1:5; 2:1-4; 3:1-2). Jesus is born into a world of violent, all-encompassing imperial control, where Emperor Augustus is registering the whole world for the purposes of taxation. Those taxes would then fund his military and building projects, in service of Roman "peace" maintained by an army quick enough to stamp out any dissension or discord. In the face of many levels of imperial control—the divinely sanctioned sovereignty of the emperor, the military power of the empire, together with an economics of oppression managed by client kings and priestly collaborators—a Mes-

---

[4]For examples, see 4 Ezra 4:23-25; Tobias 4:5-7; Baruch 3:6-8; 2 Maccabees 1:27-29; 1 Enoch 85-90.
[5]For a reading of first-century Judaism in terms of a story still waiting for resolution, a story of exile still longing for return, see N. T. Wright, *The New Testament and the People of God* (Minneapolis: Fortress, 1992), esp. pp. 268-72; these themes are further developed in Wright's *Jesus and the Victory of God* (Minneapolis: Fortress, 1996).

siah is born and an alternative peace is announced.[6]

Luke doesn't situate his story so clearly in an imperial context just because he is a historian and delights in the details of historical accuracy. There is more at stake here: Luke tells us about rulers and empire because he is concerned with setting the context of power. Such a context is evident throughout the gospel story as Luke highlights the way the kingdom of Jesus subverts and overthrows the kingdom of Rome. So the song of Mary audaciously proclaims a God who throws down the rich and powerful and raises up the poor and lowly (Lk 1:46-55). And Luke makes sure that we understand John the Baptist's Isaiah-style proclamation of a return from exile in the context of the reign of Emperor Tiberius, when Pontius Pilate was governor of Judea and Herod was the ruler of Galilee (Lk 3:1-6; cf. Is 40:3-5). No one would miss the subversive overtones to this proclamation.

As Luke tells the story, almost everything Jesus did or said was an implicit challenge to the empire and its way of working in the world. Jesus begins his "Nazareth manifesto" in Luke 4 by placing himself in the tradition of Isaiah, announcing good news to the poor, freedom for the prisoner and enslaved, and sight for the blind (Lk 4:18-20; cf. Is 61:2). Then Jesus goes on to indicate that in the kingdom he proclaims there will be welcome and healing even for the despised Gentiles (Lk 4:21-30). And this word of good news to the poor is enacted in strange ways: banquets that include both the rich and the poor, and food multiplied for the peasants who follow him.[7] The rich are welcome if they are willing to sell all that they have, become as lilies of the field and little children, worship God rather than mammon, and become poor.

In this new social order everything is redefined from the bottom up; but the bottom does not then participate in the power grabs that have characterized the top. No, those who are the greatest in Jesus' kingdom are to be like those who serve (Lk 22:24-27). This is a kingdom in which the master comes home from a banquet and serves the waiting slaves (Lk 12:35-38). This is a kingdom where the ruler is enthroned on a cross—the Roman empire's instrument of torture—and in such an enthronement wins freedom and life for his people. And then he calls his followers to do likewise.

In Luke, Jesus' whole life is framed by questions of whether to submit to the empire in the paying of taxes. His birth to two peasant parents is in the midst of a trek to be enrolled for taxation (Lk 2:1-7); his ending is in the midst of questions of whether it is lawful to pay taxes to the emperor (Lk 20:20-26); and the charge against him at his trial is that he forbade the people to pay imperial taxes and set himself up as a king over against the emperor (Lk 23:2).

These themes were central to the stories that first-century Christians learned about

---

[6]"And suddenly there was with the angel a multitude of the heavenly host, praising God and saying, 'Glory to God in the highest heaven, and on earth peace among those whom he favors!'" (Lk 2:13-14).

[7]The account of the feeding of the five thousand ends with the statement "And all ate and were filled" (Lk 9:17), an echo, we are sure, of "He has filled the hungry with good things" (Lk 1:53).

Jesus and the history of Israel. We have focused largely on Luke's telling of the Jesus story, although the proclamation of a kingdom antithetical to the empire is present throughout all the tellings in the Synoptic Gospels.[8] It is the Jesus met in these stories that the early Christian community followed. It is this Jesus who enamored Nympha and revolutionized her life.

We have focused on Luke's version of the tale because it is likely that his story would have been known to the Colossian church. At the end of the letter to them, Paul conveys greetings from "Luke, the beloved physician" (Col 4:14).[9] It is therefore reasonable to assume that either through Tychicus or previously, the Colossians have heard Luke-shaped stories of Jesus.

Now, it could be contested that the Colossians were not completely immersed in the story of Israel, especially since they were primarily pagan converts to Christianity. Two points need to be made here. In the first place, converts bring with them to their new faith the passion and zeal of conversion. They invariably throw themselves into their new faith and learn everything they can about its beliefs and story. In the second place, Paul's immersion in the story would have shaped his writing and articulation whether or not the community to which he was writing would have understood all his allusions and references. As we shall see as we look at Colossians, however, it seems evident that the story of Israel was a foundational story for the writer of the epistle.

Fruitfulness in the Face of Empire

Although Colossians contains no overt quotations of Israel's Scriptures, it is rich in allusions that not only appeal to Israel's story but also deepen the critique of empire that we have been exploring so far in this letter. This critique begins in the first ten verses of Colossians 1, which contain two provocative references to bearing fruit:

> You have heard of this hope before in the word of the truth, the gospel that has come to you. Just as it is bearing fruit and growing in the whole world, so it has been bearing fruit among yourselves from the day you heard it and truly comprehended the grace of God. (1:5-6)
>
> For this reason, since the day we heard it, we have not ceased praying for you and asking that you may be filled with the knowledge of God's will in all spiritual wisdom and understanding, so that you may lead lives worthy of the Lord, fully pleasing to him,

---

[8]For example, as Richard A. Horsley notes, "Mark's Gospel was an alternative way of conceiving history. History was not running only or primarily through Rome and her empire, but God, who acted previously to deliver, establish and renew a people, is active again now in Jesus delivering and renewing people" ("Submerged Biblical Histories and Imperial Biblical Studies," in *The Postcolonial Bible,* ed. R. S. Sugirtharajah [Sheffield, U.K.: Sheffield Academic Press, 1998], p. 161). See also Warren Carter, *Matthew and Empire* (Harrisburg, Penn.: Trinity Press International, 2001), and Richard Horsley, *The Politics of Plot in Mark's Gospel* (Louisville, Ky.: Westminster John Knox, 2001).

[9]That the Luke referred to here is the same as the author of Luke-Acts is an ancient tradition that can be found in Eusebius *Historia Ecclesiastica* 3.4.1-7; 3.14.14-15; 5.8.3; 6.25.6.

as you bear fruit in every good work and as you grow in the knowledge of God. (1:9-10)

The Colossian community was surrounded by a claim of fruitfulness and fertility, a claim rooted in the oppressive military might of the empire, in the controlling social structures of the empire, and in evocative images of lush fertility found on the buildings, statues and household items that shaped their visual imagination.[10] It was a claim that incessantly called everyone to acknowledge that Rome was the source of fruitful abundance. In the midst of scarce resources, one could share in that abundance and partake of that fruitfulness only if one remained faithful to the empire and the structures, oppressive or not, that made the empire powerful.

This was no new claim. Throughout its history, Israel not only lived in the shadow of empire but also constantly grappled with the claims of empire to be the source of abundance, security and fertility, whether those claims were made by Egypt, Babylon, Persia, Rome or even its own rulers. In Egypt the abundance of the empire resulted in the captivity of the people; in the wilderness Israel longingly remembered the secure fertility of the empire; and in the land God gave Israel, Solomon demonstrated that even an Israelite king could behave like the ruler of an empire, reveling in the abundance that comes from extensive and oppressive military control.[11] When Israel behaved like an empire, it was not surprising that it embraced imperial gods of guaranteed fertility who sanctioned the expropriation of fruitful land from peasant landowners.[12] Then, under the imperial control of Babylon, Persia, Greece and Rome, Israel painfully discovered that the preferred economics of empire is to enslave the producers of food and resources, so that the fruit of their labor ends up on the table of the elite. By the first century, the people of Israel knew that the promise of abundance within a secure empire was a lie.

Throughout all of Israel's history, however, there had been a countertestimony, a witness to an alternative social vision that challenged the claims of empire. The fruitfulness of Yahweh, and the fruit that Israel was called to bear, was central to that countertestimony. Yahweh is recalled as the Creator who graciously supplies abundance for humanity and the rest of creation (Ps 104; 146). Moreover, according to the psalmist, such fruitfulness is linked to justice and righteousness (Ps 146:5-9). In God's rule, fecund authority is practiced for liberation and shalom.

---

[10]See Paul Zanker, *The Power of Images in the Age of Augustus,* trans. Alan Shapiro (Ann Arbor: University of Michigan Press, 1990), pp. 171-79, for descriptions of the link between fruitfulness and military might, as well as the ubiquity of images of fruitfulness.

[11]See Genesis 47; Exodus 16:3; 1 Kings 4:20-23; 21. On 1 Kings 4:20-23, see Walter Brueggemann, "'Vine and Fig Tree': A Case Study in Imagination and Criticism," in *A Social Reading of the Old Testament: Prophetic Approaches to Israel's Communal Life,* ed. Patrick D. Miller (Minneapolis: Fortress, 1994), pp. 91-110.

[12]While the theme of embracing the worship of Baal permeates the narrative of Ahab and Jezebel (1 Kings 16:29—22:40), the expropriating character of such an imperial ideology is highlighted in the story of Naboth's vineyard in 1 Kings 21.

Such themes of creational fruitfulness and social justice become the grounding rhythm for Israel's life before God. In every period of its history and in every genre of its literature, there is a witness to God's fruitful blessing in creation and the practice of an alternative social ethic that images God in redemption and care for creation and neighbor. The alternative social ethic of the practice of jubilee envisioned in Leviticus 25 will result in fruitfulness and peace:[13]

> If you follow my statutes and keep my commandments and observe them faithfully, I will give you your rains in their season, and the land shall yield its produce, and the trees of the field shall yield their fruit. Your threshing shall overtake the vintage, and the vintage shall overtake the sowing; you shall eat your bread to the full, and live securely in your land. And I will grant peace in the land, and you shall lie down, and no one shall make you afraid; I will remove dangerous animals from the land, and no sword shall go through your land. (Lev 26:3-6)

Again and again the two are linked: fertility and fruitfulness in the land on the one hand, and peace and security on the other, are rooted in rejection of the militaristic consumerism of the empire and the social and economic practices that support it.

Isaiah's parable of the vineyard is perhaps the strongest example of the link between covenantal faithfulness and fruitfulness. Only when Israel is practicing justice and righteousness will she be truly fruitful (Is 5:1-7). The familiar call of Isaiah 58 "to loose the bonds of injustice, . . . let the oppressed go free" (v. 6) moves to this promise of fertility: "You shall be like a watered garden, like a spring of water, whose waters never fail" (v. 11). The chapter ends with a call to observe sabbath rather than pursue consumptive economic practices (Is 58:13-14; see also Ezek 34; Mic 4:1-5; Zech 8:1-16).

Of course, while the promise of fertility is rooted in faithfulness to an alternative covenantal way of life that God outlines in Torah, the story reveals how unfaithfulness and idolatry result in barrenness and drought. For when Israel believes the words of empire rather than the words of Yahweh, when Israel tries to guarantee fertility and abundance by means of promiscuous idolatry and abusive and consumptive economics, it is made desolate (Is 24:4-12; Hos 4:1-3). In the face of such judgment, it is no surprise that the prophets describe Yahweh's coming salvation in terms of fruitfulness and safety for the whole of creation and peace in the land (Is 19:9; 32:14-20; 41:18-19; 43:19-20; 55; Ezek 34:25-31; Zech 8:12-13). While Israel was looking for peace in political alliances, worshiping the gods of the empire, following the fashion of the fertility gods, and engaging in a militaristic economics, Yahweh was shaking his head: "She did not know that it was I who gave her the grain, the wine, and the oil" (Hos 2:8). Nonetheless, God's restoration of the people will still be a matter of fruitfulness in a milieu of peace: "For there shall be a sowing of peace; the vine shall yield its fruit,

---

[13]Sylvia C. Keesmaat, "Sabbath and Jubilee: Radical Alternatives for Being Human," in *Making a New Beginning: Biblical Reflections on Jubilee* (Toronto: Canadian Ecumenical Jubilee Initiative, 1998), pp. 15-23.

the ground shall give its produce, and the skies shall give their dew; and I will cause the remnant of this people to possess all these things" (Zech 8:12).

These counterimperial themes of fruitfulness and peace set in the context of Israel's covenant come to their climax in Jesus. The community that Jesus envisions not only results in fruitfulness but is itself a manifestation of the fruitfulness of Yahweh. At key points in the Gospel narratives we meet metaphors and language of fruitfulness. For instance, the parable of the sower, which sets the stage for all the other parables, reaches its zenith in those who hear the word and understand it and bear fruit and yield a hundredfold, or sixty or thirty (Mt 13:23; Mk 4:20; Lk 8:15). This is fruit that grows out of being rooted in the word of Jesus. Again, at the end of the Sermon on the Mount (or the Sermon on the Plain, in Luke), Jesus uses the metaphor of a tree being known by its fruit (Mt 7:16-20; Lk 6:43-45). This is the summation of a long discourse where Jesus describes the fruit that the people are called to bear: "Love your enemies, do good to those who hate you, bless those who curse you, pray for those who abuse you" (Lk 6:27-28). This was already strange advice to give to people who quite justifiably looked forward to a day of vengeance on their imperial overlords. But Jesus takes it even further by commanding his followers to offer the other cheek when abused, not withholding their shirt when they are oppressed in a court of law, giving to those who beg, lending without expecting in return, withholding judgment, giving and forgiving (Lk 6:29-30, 35-38). Such fruit will indeed result in abundance: "A good measure, pressed down, shaken together, running over, will be put into your lap; for the measure you give will be the measure you get back" (Lk 6:38). This is an image of overflowing abundance growing out of generosity—a generosity of heart as well as possessions. Indeed that is the fundamental link between loving your enemies and giving without expecting in return: a generosity of spirit is needed for both. That is what we call grace.

This is the fruit that the community forming itself around Jesus is called to bear; and it is fruit that refuses to engage the empire on its own terms. It refuses to let enemies be enemies, to let debtors be debtors. As the parallel passage in Matthew shows, reconciliation is the fruit of this kingdom (Mt 5:2-26). This is an ethic in which the generosity of God overcomes the violence and economic exploitation of the empire. And once they are so overcome and undermined, the empire begins to crumble.

Colossians Revisited

So here's the question. When Paul employs the metaphor of fruitfulness in his opening section of this letter, what echoes and overtones does this language carry? Wouldn't this language reverberate with fruitfulness as a dominant metaphor in the conflicting narratives of this community's life? If the empire encodes in the imagery of everyday life—on public arches, statues and buildings—the claim that Rome and its emperor are the beneficent provider and guarantor of all fruitfulness, then can a claim that the "gospel" is bearing fruit "in the whole world" be heard as anything less than a challenge to this imperial fruitfulness? Especially if we remember that the word *gospel (euangelion)* is the very same term that the empire reserves for announcements of military success and pronouncements from the emperor, doesn't it become clear that there is something deeply subversive in what Paul is saying here? Whose gospel is the source of a fruitfulness that will last and sustain the world—the gospel of Caesar or the gospel of Jesus?

And what kind of fruitfulness are we talking about? Paul tells the Colossians that the gospel of Jesus bears a fruit in their lives that is fundamentally different from the fruit of the empire. The fruit of this gospel is rooted not in military might and economic oppression but in the practice of justice and sacrificial faithfulness. This is a gospel that bears fruit "in every good work" of forgiving generosity and therefore undermines the hoarding abundance touted by the empire.

But it is not just Roman narratives of fruitfulness that reverberate with Paul's language here. For those with ears to hear, Paul is evoking a larger narrative counter to that of empire: Israel's story as it comes to its fulfillment in the story of Jesus.[14] When Paul says that the gospel is bearing fruit and growing in the whole world and that the knowledge of God in Christ results in a life worthy of the Lord, bearing fruit in all kinds of good works, his language echoes the stories of Jesus, the prophets' promises of restored fruitfulness, the Torah's connection of fruitfulness to justice and obedience, and the very foundational calling for humanity to bear fruit and multiply. Remember our hermeneutical advice earlier in this book: always hear the New Testament with Old Testament ears. Paul, as a convert rooted in the best traditions of pharisaic Judaism, could do nothing other than to think and write in the metaphors and images of that tradition. When he uses a metaphor as seemingly common as "bearing fruit," the whole scriptural tradition of Israel is informing its meaning.

And what a powerful and liberating meaning this is! Just as Israel was called to be a fruit-bearing community in the shadow of various empires making arrogant claims to provide fertility and abundance to their people, so also does this small Christian community in Colossae struggle to bear the fruit of a gospel that is counter to the dominant ideology all around them.

For those in the community who had learned the history of Israel vis-à-vis other empires, together with the countertestimony of the law and the prophets, Paul's language would have evoked a whole other way of political and economic being in community, rooted in Torah and God's calls to justice and care for the disfranchised. This path of covenant faithfulness leads to a fruitfulness for the whole earth that God alone can provide. For those who knew the story of Jesus, Paul's language sug-

---

[14]Sylvia Keesmaat has explored these themes in greater depth in "Scripture, Law and Fruit: Paul and the Biblical Story," *Pro Rege* 27, no. 4 (June 1999): 10-19.

gested a call to an alternative ethic in the face of the empire, an ethic rooted in Jesus and his act of reconciliation on the cross. For those in Colossae with ears to hear, Paul's scriptural allusions evoke a whole new world and way of life. And as we shall see, that alternative world and liberating way of life form the heart of Paul's teaching in Colossians.

PART TWO

TRUTH REMIXED

CONTESTED IMAGINATIONS

— 5 —

SUBVERSIVE POETRY
AND CONTESTED IMAGINATION

*H*ello there, can we talk?

Yes, of course. It's good to hear from you again. You've been rather quiet for a while now.

Yes, well, it has been a little hard to get a word in edgewise.

We do apologize. Have we been a little long-winded?

Maybe a little, but I do understand that you had a lot of ground to cover to introduce the rather complex context for this letter of Paul.

But you are still with us?

Yes, but I just want to make sure that I've understood what's going on. You began, in chapter three by offering us a fictional account of Nympha as a way to introduce us to the first-century context. Then you went on to give us a description of the imperial reality of these early Christians in terms of captured imaginations, powerful myths, social and economic control, and the ways power was centralized in slave-owning male masters.

So far, so good.

Then you went on in the next chapter to argue that the "imagination" of this early Christian community was shaped by another story—the story of Israel as told through the perspective of the story of Jesus.

Yes, but the telling that we offered focused specifically on how this story is shaped by and in response to various imperial regimes.

And your telling focused on the language of fruitfulness in the biblical story. My question is this: Are these echoes of Israel's Scriptures really there? And if they are really there, who are they there for? Who would have caught them? Was Paul even aware of them?

This is an important theoretical question. But before we try to answer it, can we ask why it matters so much to you? What is hanging on this question for you?

Two things. First, the integrity of your interpretation of the text. As you know, the Bible is very important to me, and I want to make sure that any interpretation that suggests that one text is somehow intertextually related to another text is telling us the truth. I want to know that those echoes are really there. And second, the integrity of Christian life today in response to this text. You see, only if those echoes and allusions were really there for Paul and the Colossians can I feel comfortable asking my most important question: Are those echoes still there for the Christian community today, and if so, what does that mean for our life at the beginning of the twenty-first century?

Those are important reasons to pose your question. We will attempt to honor them as we offer at least a partial answer.

When it comes to interpretation, it's often said that there are three important hermeneutical rules: context, context, context. Actually there is more to interpretation than context, but we agree that context is central. In the last two chapters we have attempted to sketch out the context of this letter in terms of both imperial symbolism, with its mythology and socioeconomic-political realities, *and* the narrative memory of Israel as reinterpreted by Paul, the follower of Jesus. In the first two chapters of this book, however, we summarized the twenty-first-century context in which we read this ancient letter.

Now consider this. If a letter written to a Christian community today said something like "Just as the gospel has been investing and growing in the whole world, so also it is producing rich dividends among you," how would we interpret this sentence? And if the author went on to say that he prays that the community will be filled with the knowledge of God's will in all spiritual wisdom and understanding "so that you may lead lives worthy of the Lord, fully pleasing to him, as you reap great profits in all your productive endeavors," what field of discourse is the author clearly appealing to?

If the language is that of investments, dividends, productivity and profits, then the author is clearly appealing to the world of economics, stock markets and industry.

And one would have to say these allusions are "really there." Right?

Right.

Well, in light of everything we have learned about how the imagery and language of "fruitfulness" functioned in the empire, is there any good reason to have reticence about saying that Paul's language here makes *real* allusions to his cultural context? Given the pervasive nature of the iconography of fruitfulness in the empire, it is hard to imagine how it could not have had such allusions. It's like the folks who were saying, "He's the real thing," meaning Jesus, when Coca-Cola was running the "It's the real thing" ad campaign. Christians picked up on the cultural discourse and set their faith directly in the midst of that discourse in a potentially subversive way.

All right, I'll buy your argument that the allusions to the empire are there.

You'll what?

I'll buy it. On this point I'm convinced.

How much?

How much am I convinced?

No, how much will you buy it for?

What? You know full well what I mean when I say that "I buy it." This is a well-known phrase that means, "I am convinced."

Precisely. And what kind of discourse does this well-known phrase come from?

Um, economic discourse, I guess.

Exactly. Do you see our point? First, when you used the metaphor of "buying" an argument, you simply assumed it would be perfectly understandable to us. Second, that metaphor is embedded in a narrative of economic growth and the commodification of all of life so deeply that it can be said that one "buys" an argument, even if it is offered free and was never for sale.

Okay, okay, I understand. But are you saying that we shouldn't talk about "buying arguments" if we are followers of Jesus?

No, we shouldn't. Nor should we talk about "the bottom line" and getting "bang for the buck" when attempting to evaluate the stewardship of resources for ministry, education, health, home life and a whole host of other dimensions of life. This economically loaded language ends up distorting our lives.

Let's get back to Paul. If "fruitfulness" was so overlaid with imperial meaning, and if he intended to subvert the imperial imagination, then why did he use it at all?

Because this language also had a rich meaning and memory in the narrative that so fundamentally shaped his worldview. For Paul, both the meaning of "fruitfulness" and the way to achieve it were always contested in the context of empire. And that's why we will argue that the allusions to both the Roman empire and the stories of Israel and Jesus are "really there" for Paul in the first chapter of Colossians. This language has, if you will, a multiple referentiality—empire, Torah, prophets, wisdom, Jesus, Paul. All of those multiple discourses come together in Paul's letter to the Colossians.

Did they get it?

Did they hear with complete hermeneutical clarity all of these discourses echoing through Paul's use of the metaphor of fruitfulness? We don't know. Maybe not. But you have already agreed that they would have heard the imperial echoes, that when Paul talked about fruitfulness that metaphor's imperial use would have come to mind. And since they had begun to immerse themselves in the Scriptures of Israel—it is clear that the early church did precisely this—at least some of the echoes of Israel's Scriptures would have been heard.

Who knows, perhaps even language that is not fully understood still manages to shape us. Perhaps even if the Colossian believers did not quite get all the allusions, their communal life would still have been transformed so that they bore fruit that was radically different from the fruit of the empire.

That brings me to another question—and this is really the question I've had all along in this conversation. How does the Christian community today "bear fruit in every good work"? What does that look like? If the early Christian context was the empire and its preoccupation with its own fruitfulness, what is our context?

Didn't we address that question at the end of the last chapter?

Yes, you did, but I still don't quite get it. It is clear the fruit of this gospel is evident in a communal life of love, forgiveness, justice, compassion, mercy, peace and care. And the implications that you began to draw of fruitfulness in our economic, political, ecological, social and personal lives are all compelling. But there is still a problem somewhere. And the problem isn't just "out there"—it's deep within me as well. It is all so—well, so unimaginable. Not only do I find it almost impossible to get the people in my church to think about this stuff, I find it hard to think it through myself. Or maybe the issue isn't that I can't "think" it through, it is more that I can't "live" it through. Heck, I can't really imagine what a life that is alternative to the dominant culture would look like. And you just pointed out that I can't even "talk" outside of the dominant discourse.

Let's slow it down a little. Just as Rome wasn't built in a day, it also can't be dismantled in a day—not in political reality, nor in our own worldviews. You are right, the question is what we can or cannot imagine. So if you don't mind, we're going to cut off the conversation here for a while and move on to a discussion of perhaps the most remarkable section in Paul's letter to the Colossian believers. There Paul shifts his metaphor from fruitfulness to "image." And in this shift he ups the ante on the conflict with the empire. Perhaps he will also both deepen the struggles you are having and point to a radical way through them. Stay with us for a few pages and come back later if you need to interrupt again.

On Subversive Poetry

We have seen that empires maintain their sovereignty not only by establishing a monopoly of markets, political structures and military might but also by monopolizing the imagination of their subjects. Indeed, vanquished peoples are not really subjects of the empire until their imagination has been taken captive. As long as they continue to have memories of life before exile, and as long as they harbor dreams of a social reality alternative to the empire, they are a threat to the empire. Their liberated imagination keeps them free even in the face of violent military repression. And until that imagination is broken, domesticated and reshaped in the image of the empire, the people are still free.

Israel understood the dynamics of empire and imagination and always had a counterplan. In the shadow of empire, Israel's prophets wrote evocative and subversive poetry that wove together images of homecoming, restoration, dimly burning wicks, free food and a coming Messiah who would do a new thing. These are prophetic images that break the monopoly of the empire.

Of course, the first Christians also knew all about empires. As we have seen, Rome was especially adept at shaping the imagination. Images of the emperor were as ubiquitous in the first century as corporate logos are in the twenty-first century. The image of Caesar and other symbols of Roman power were literally everywhere—in the market, on coins, in the gymnasium, at the gladiatorial games, on jewelry, goblets, lamps and paintings. The sovereign rule of Caesar was simply assumed to be the divine plan for the peace and order of the cosmos. Of course, this is the way the world works. Under such conditions it becomes hard to imagine any life alternative to the empire.

In this context the apostle Paul takes a leaf out of the book of the ancient prophets and counters the imperial imagination with radical and evocative poetry. Here is the poem he inserts into the first chapter of his letter to the Colossians (1:15-20).[1]

> He is the image
>   of the invisible God
> the firstborn of all creation
>   for in him were created all things
>   in heaven and earth
>   things visible and invisible
>   whether thrones or dominions
>   whether rulers or powers
>   all things have been created through him and for him
>
> And he is before all things
>   and in him all things hold together
> And he is the head
>   of the body, the church
>
> He is the beginning
>   the firstborn from the dead
>   so that he might come to have first place in everything
>   for in him all the fullness
>   was pleased to dwell
>   and through him God was pleased to reconcile to himself
>   all things
>   whether on earth or in heaven
>   by making peace through the blood of his cross

In a world populated by images of Caesar, who is taken to be the son of God, a world in which the emperor's preeminence over all things is bolstered by political structures and institutions, an empire that views Rome as the head of the body politic

---

[1] This poetic rendering of the passage is from N. T. Wright, "Poetry and Theology in Colossians 1.15-20," from his book *Climax of the Covenant: Christ and the Law in Pauline Theology* (Edinburgh: T & T Clark, 1991), p. 104.

in which an imperial peace is imposed—sometimes through the capital punishment of crucifixion—this poem is nothing less than treasonous. In the space of a short, well-crafted, three-stanza poem, Paul subverts every major claim of the empire, turning them on their heads, and proclaims Christ to be the Creator, Redeemer and Lord of all of creation, including the empire.

He does all of this in a poem composed with the goal of providing alternative images for a subversive imagination. If the allusions involved in Paul's employment of the metaphor of fruitfulness were subversive to those who had ears to hear, then this poem constitutes a frontal assault on the empire. While rich in echo and allusion—*image, firstborn, creation* and *reconciliation* all have clear echoes in the Torah, the Prophets and wisdom literature—this poem leaves little in doubt as to who is sovereign in creation, who images the invisible God, who holds the cosmos together in peace and who brings about the reconciliation of all things. And it isn't Caesar!

Paul's letter to the Colossians is fundamentally about shaping the imagination of the Christian community. Walter Brueggemann says that "the key pathology of our time, which seduces us all, is the reduction of the imagination so that we are too numbed, satiated and co-opted to do serious imaginative work."[2] If this is true, then the primal responsibility of Christian proclamation is to empower the community to reimagine the world as if Christ, and not the powers, were sovereign. If the image of the emperor that is on every coin serves to ensnare the imagination of a domesticated people, then radical Christian proclamation and cultural practice will seek to demythologize the empire and devalue its currency.[3] Such proclamation, such poetry, will always be a subversion of the dominant version of reality.

But what is that dominant version? Is there an empire in the shadow of which we live? Are there cultural forces that seek to take captive our imaginations? Well, think about it for a moment. The average North American person is confronted every day by somewhere between five and twelve thousand corporate messages, all geared to shaping a consumer imagination. Whether you are running a political campaign for the highest office in the land or selling a particular brand of cigarette, it's all about image! Whether you are designing a new fashion line for the summer, the lines on a new running shoe or the look of a new website, it's all about image! A society directed by the consumerist imperatives of global capitalism is driven by images with a vengeance. And these images—purveyed especially through that quintessential image-producing medium, television—must change constantly in order to create and sustain an insatiable desire for more consumer goods and reach the ultimate goal of economic abundance.[4]

---

[2] Walter Brueggemann, *Interpretation and Obedience* (Minneapolis: Fortress, 1991), p. 199.
[3] This image of devaluing the currency of the empire is an evocative suggestion from Curtis Chang, "Images of Judaism and Empire in Colossians," typescript, Harvard Divinity School (December 13, 1999), p. 12.
[4] See Neil Postman, *Amusing Ourselves to Death: Public Discourse in the Age of Show Business* (New York: Penguin, 1985).

Some of us wear these messages on our shoes, our jackets and our shirts. The messages are all telling the same story: a finite world can sustain infinite growth, economic growth is the driving force of history, consumer choice is what makes us human, and greed is normal. If we live in an empire, it is the empire of global consumerism.

In the first chapter of this book we suggested that a radically consumptive imagination fueled by a cybernetically driven information revolution is what we could call postmodernism. After all, is there really much difference between the multiplicity of perspectives available in a radically postmodern culture and the multiplicity of products and lifestyles available in the global market? If postmodernity celebrates "difference," globalization recognizes that every difference is a marketing opportunity. Many postmodern authors "see perpetual shopping and the consumption of commodities and commodified images as the paradigmatic and defining activities of postmodern experience."[5]

Now here is the question. What is the Christian community to do? How do we speak and live the gospel in this kind of cultural context? How do we shape our collective imagination as followers of Jesus in such a way that we are set free from the constricted imagination of the empire?

Our suggestion is simple. Follow Paul, who was following the prophets. Write and perform evocative and subversive poetry that provides an imagination alternative to the empire's. The point is to so immerse ourselves in the Scriptures, so indwell their narrative, be so permeated by their images, that our imagination is transformed according to the image of Christ.

The question is *how* the discourse of Scripture becomes our first language, our normative discourse. We don't make it so by simply repeating the ancient text over and over again. We need a method that is more creative than simple repetition but that remains faithful to the vision of the Scriptures if we are to be set free from the empire.

So we offer another targum, another extended translation and expansion that attempts to read the world through the eyes of the text, allowing the Scripture to resonate with and confront our changing cultural reality. Since our targum is on the poem found in Colossians 1:15-20, it takes a poetic structure.[6]

In an image-saturated world,
   a world of ubiquitous corporate logos
      permeating your consciousness
   a world of dehydrated and captive imaginations
      in which we are too numbed, satiated and co-opted
      to be able to dream of life otherwise
   a world in which the empire of global economic affluence
      has achieved the monopoly of our imaginations

---

[5]Michael Hardt and Antonio Negri, *Empire* (Cambridge, Mass.: Harvard University Press, 2000), pp. 151-52.
[6]An earlier version of this targum was first published in an article by Brian Walsh, "Subversive Preaching in a Postmodern World," *The Banner* 136, no. 13 (June 18, 2001).

in this world
Christ is the image of the invisible God
   in this world
      driven by images with a vengeance
Christ is the image par excellence
   the image above all other images
   the image that is not a façade
   the image that is not trying to sell you anything
   the image that refuses to co-opt you
Christ is the image of the invisible God
   the image of God
      a flesh-and-blood
      here-and-now
      in time and history
      with joys and sorrows
      image of who God is
   the image of God
      a flesh-and-blood
      here-and-now
      in time and history
      with joys and sorrows
      image of who we are called to be
         image-bearers of this God
He is the source of a liberated imagination
  a subversion of the empire
because it all starts with him
and it all ends with him
      everything
      all things
   whatever you can imagine
      visible and invisible
      mountains and atoms
      outer space, urban space and cyberspace
      whether it be the Pentagon, Disneyland, Microsoft or AT&T
      whether it be the institutionalized power structures
      of the state, the academy or the market
  all things have been created in him and through him
he is their source, their purpose, their goal
      even in their rebellion
      even in their idolatry
   he is the sovereign one
      their power and authority is derived at best
         parasitic at worst

In the face of the empire
  in the face of presumptuous claims to sovereignty
  in the face of the imperial and idolatrous forces in our lives
    Christ is before all things
      he is sovereign in life
      not the pimped dreams of the global market
      not the idolatrous forces of nationalism
      not the insatiable desires of a consumerist culture

In the face of a disconnected world
  where home is a domain in cyberspace
  where neighborhood is a chat room
  where public space is a shopping mall
  where information technology promises
  a tuned-in, reconnected world
    all things hold together in Christ
      the creation is a deeply personal cosmos
      all cohering and interconnected in Jesus

And this sovereignty takes on cultural flesh
And this coherence of all things is socially embodied
  in the church
    against all odds
    against most of the evidence
In a "show me" culture where words alone don't cut it
    the church is
      the flesh-and-blood
      here-and-now
      in time and history
      with joys and sorrows
      embodiment of this Christ
    as a body politic
    around a common meal
    in alternative economic practices
    in radical service to the most vulnerable
    in refusal of the empire
    in love of this creation
      the church reimagines the world
      in the image of the invisible God

In the face of a disappointed world of betrayal
  a world in which all fixed points have proven illusory
  a world in which we are anchorless and adrift
    Christ is the foundation
      the origin

the way
the truth
and the life
In the face of a culture of death
a world of killing fields
a world of the walking dead
Christ is at the head of the resurrection parade
transforming our tears of betrayal into tears of joy
giving us dancing shoes for the resurrection party
And this glittering joker
who has danced in the dragon's jaws of death[7]
now dances with a dance that is full
of nothing less than the fullness of God
this is the dance of the new creation
this is the dance of life out of death
and in this dance all that was broken
all that was estranged
all that was alienated
all that was dislocated and disconnected
what once was hurt
what once was friction
is reconciled
comes home
is healed
and is made whole
because Grace makes beauty out of ugly things[8]
everything
all things
whatever you can imagine
visible and invisible
mountains and atoms
outer space, urban space and cyberspace
every inch of creation
every dimension of our lives
all things are reconciled in him

And it all happens on a cross
it all happens at a state execution
where the governor did not commute the sentence

---

[7]The "glittering joker dancing in the dragon's jaws" is an image found in Bruce Cockburn's song "Hills of Morning," from the album *Dancing in the Dragon's Jaws,* ©Golden Mountain Music, 1979.
[8]Images borrowed here from U2's song "Grace," on the album *All That You Can't Leave Behind,* ©Polygram International Music, 2001.

> it all happens at the hands of the empire
>> that has captured our imagination
> it all happens through blood
>> not through a power grab by the sovereign one
> it all happens in embraced pain
>> for the sake of others
> it all happens on a cross
>> arms outstretched in embrace
> and this is the image of the invisible God
>> this is the body of Christ

The imaginative richness of Paul's poetic proclamation in Colossians 1:15-20 is not a matter of clever wordplay. Rather, it is a matter of life and death. He is struggling for nothing less than the imagination of this young Christian community. That is what biblically shaped subversive poetry has always been about, and that is what exercises in a discerning imagination must still be about in a postmodern culture.

In a culture of captured imaginations, we need a Christian imagination in the arts and in neighborhood activism that will set the captives free, especially when they have become comfortable in captivity. In a culture of ubiquitous graven images and rampant consumerist idolatry, we need Christian practices in business, environmental protection and politics that will topple the idols and energize an alternative economics of God's kingdom. In a culture of disconnection, we need Christian scholarship in the academy and psychological practices in the community that see things whole, cohering in Christ. In a culture of power as truth, we need servant communities ministering to the most vulnerable to demonstrate that truth is on a cross. In a culture of radical uncertainty, we need preaching and liturgy that build the body of Christ, where truth takes on flesh.

On Naming Names

But is truth always so in your face when it takes on flesh?

No, not always. But it is certainly in your face in Paul's poem in Colossians.

And that is why your poem takes such an aggressive stance?

Basically, that's right. Unfortunately, it may well be that what we achieve in clarity by being so aggressive we lose in aesthetic quality.

Well, my question is, are you more aggressive than Paul? After all, you name names. He doesn't.

He didn't have to name names. As soon as he made references to "image of God," "firstborn" and "first place," everyone with ears to hear would know that he was contrasting Jesus with Caesar. Remember, in the imperial cult and throughout the empire it was proclaimed that Caesar was "equal to the Beginning of all things." It was the emperor who "restored order" and was the "beginning of life and vitality." Moreover, Caesar was the "savior" who had "put an end to war and . . . set all things in order" and therefore was proclaimed as "god-manifest."[9] And putting together "head" and "body" would immediately conjure up both Hellenistic ideas of Zeus as the sovereign head of the body of the cosmos[10] and images of Caesar (or Rome) as the head (the sovereign source) of the body politic of the empire.[11]

So what does Paul do with these cultural myths? He turns them on their head and replaces Zeus, Caesar, Rome and any other pretender to sovereignty with Christ. Then he takes it a step further and replaces the body—whether it be the cosmos or the empire—with the church.

Imagine the shock on the faces of this little group of Christians meeting in a house church in Colossae when they heard that! Doesn't all that sound just a tad aggressive, given the circumstances?

When you put it that way, I guess it does. And I guess it could also sound aggressive when Paul writes of peace coming on the cross in the context of the Pax Romana, where crucifixion was capital punishment for those who had committed crimes against the empire. But he still didn't name names as you did.

Making in-your-face allusions to Caesar isn't naming names?

He didn't identify particular people in the Roman hierarchy. He didn't go after the military per se. He didn't name any particular institutions of the empire or any particular businesses that profited from the empire. You did. While you more generally referred to "institutionalized power structures of the state, the academy or the market" you also named particular institutions like the Pentagon, Disneyland, Microsoft and AT&T. Why them?

Why these institutions in particular, or why did we particularize at all?

Well, both. But I guess I want to ask why you had to name such names at all.

Again, because Paul names names. You're right, he doesn't refer to any particular people in the imperial hierarchy. Nor does he refer to specific farmers who have expropriated land and enslaved the inhabitants or specific merchants who profited from the oppression of the empire. But he does get specific when he is talking about the creative and sovereign rule of Christ in creation. Remember how he put it?

For in him were created all things

---

[9]All of these references to Caesar are found in *Orientis Graeci Inscriptiones Selectae,* vol. 2, ed. Wilhelm Dittenberger (Leipzig, 1903-1905), no. 405; quoted by Richard A. Horsley, "The Gospel of the Savior's Birth," in *Christmas Unwrapped: Consumerism, Christ and Culture,* ed. Richard A. Horsley and James Tracy (Harrisburg, Penn.: Trinity Press International, 2001), p. 116.

[10]Andrew T. Lincoln, "The Letter to the Colossians," in *The New Interpreter's Bible,* ed. Leander Keck (Nashville: Abingdon, 2000), 11:598-99, 603-5.

[11]Richard Gordon, "The Veil of Power," in *Paul and Empire: Religion and Power in Roman Imperial Society,* ed. Richard A. Horsley (Harrisburg, Penn.: Trinity Press International, 1997), p. 129.

in heaven and earth
things visible and invisible
whether thrones or dominions
whether rulers or powers

What's he talking about here? He wants to convey in no uncertain terms that "all things" are created in Christ. This phrase, "all things," recurs throughout the poem. And to make clear the sheer comprehensive and universal scope of what he is talking about, Paul invites his hearers to imagine all things "in heaven and earth." Then he adds to that "visible and invisible."

Now try to imagine everything in heaven and on earth, and everything visible and invisible. What's left?

Nothing is left. That covers everything.

Yes, but just in case, Paul will push our imagination even further. All things, he says—whether in heaven or on earth, visible or invisible—are created in Christ. Then he adds, "Whether thrones or dominions, whether rulers or powers." In case you thought there were some high-level structures, institutions, powers or authorities that might be exempt from this radical claim, Paul wants to make sure that they too are included in the "all things" created in, through and for Christ.

Isn't all of that a reference to ancient beliefs about heavenly forces, astral deities and the like?

But Paul insists that he is talking about all things in heaven and *on earth, visible* and invisible. That would suggest to us that "thrones, dominions, rulers and powers" cannot simply be a reference to "invisible" or "heavenly" realities—they must also have a visible and earthly reference. Indeed, the parallelism of the text would seem to indicate that these powers are *both* earthly and heavenly, visible and invisible.[12] Throughout the Greek translation of the Hebrew Scriptures (the Septuagint), the word *throne* (*thronos*) "is used 123 times of kings and dynasties, emphasizing the continuity and legitimacy of royal office."[13] Thrones are centralized structures of political, economic and military authority. *Dominions* (*kyriotētes*) refers to actual realms over which a ruler exercises sovereignty. The empire was a dominion. While *rulers* (*archai*) could refer to spiritual entities, this was an extension of the normal political, military and other uses of power in daily sociocultural life. And the main use of *powers* (*exousia*) is not in reference to spiritual beings but to what Walter Wink calls the "legitimations, sanctions, and permissions that undergird the everyday exercise of power."[14]

So it isn't a stretch to say that in the Roman empire, "thrones, dominions, rulers and powers" referred to Rome—to its *ruler,* Caesar, on the *throne* established by the

---

[12]Walter Wink, *Naming the Powers: The Language of Power in the New Testament* (Philadelphia: Fortress, 1984), p. 11.
[13]Ibid., p. 18.
[14]Ibid., p. 17.

gods, to his *dominion* over all of the known world, established and maintained by the *power* and might of the empire.

Are you saying that all of this language is in reference to politics?

Well, not just politics, but the very shape of life in the empire. For example, the "powers" that legitimate and sanction the way power is exercised in the empire are not just military regiments or threats of capital punishment but the very structure of life, including relationships of client and patron, slaves and masters. The imperial calendar (beginning as it did with the birth of Augustus and marked by dates of importance to the empire), imperial architecture and images of the emperor that were in your face wherever you turned—all of this functioned as a "power" in the life of subjects to the empire. Paul is addressing these dynamics of daily life in his use of this language. It would be impossible for his listeners to hear this list—thrones, dominions, rulers, powers—and *not* have thought of imperial thrones, imperial rule, the emperor and his court, and imperial sanctions and legitimations.

None of this has to do with spiritual forces?

That is not quite our point. *All* of this has to do with "spiritual forces"—the spiritual force of the empire.

But what about spiritual beings? Isn't Paul referring to spiritual forces like fallen angels, demons and the like?

To begin with, remember that Paul has said visible and invisible, earthly and heavenly. So there is a clear reference to something that goes beyond socioeconomic structures of political and military power. We believe in demons, and if we had the eyes to see we would discern their destructive power in both personal and structural dimensions of life. Having said that, it is important not to make a division in our thinking between so-called spiritual forces and earthly structures. You see, it seems to us that the text wants to say that all thrones, dominions, rulers and powers are, at root, spiritual in character. The question is, which spirit is directing these structures of the cosmos?

So rather than entering the debate regarding whether Paul is talking about angels or about economic structures, we suggest that there is a spiritual dimension to all socioeconomic and political structures. That spiritual dimension has to do with whether these structures of our life are directed by an idolatrous spirit of empire or the Spirit of God in Christ, who created all of these structures of life and before whom they are subject.[15]

So the point of insisting that all things—even thrones and rulers—are created "through him and for him" is to say that even though the empire structures and organizes life in idol-

---

[15]The debate about the nature of these thrones, dominions, rulers and powers is judiciously mediated by Andrew T. Lincoln, "Liberation from the Powers: Supernatural Spirits or Societal Structures?" in *The Bible in Human Society,* ed. M. D. Carroll, David Clines and Philip R. Davies (Sheffield, U.K.: Sheffield Academic, 1995), pp. 350-54.

atrous self-promotion and self-preservation, the Christian community knows that really they are themselves subject to Christ. Is that it?

Sure looks that way, doesn't it? Now just think how liberating, and how subversive, this would have been for the early Christian community. All around them the thrones, dominions, rulers and powers exert their imperial control, and along comes Paul and deconstructs them all in the name of Christ! Their sovereignty is false, and that means the Christian community need not render to them the absolute obedience they demand. We are subject to another ruler, bow before a messianic throne, live in the dominion known as the kingdom of God, and are shaped through the power manifest in Christ, who is the image of God, not Caesar.

This still doesn't quite explain to me why you had to name names.

We have already argued that Paul's language was, in effect, naming names. He didn't have to say "Caesar" or "the imperial cult" or explicitly refer to the images of the emperor and empire that were everywhere. The listening community would have filled in the blanks for themselves.

So why not let the contemporary listening community fill in the blanks too? Why get so explicit by identifying certain corporations or cultural systems as these thrones and dominions today?

Maybe because we aren't so sure that the church would get it.

If Paul was pretty convinced that his community—made up of new Christians—would get it, why don't you have faith that the church today would get it too?

Because the church today is more enculturated, more taken captive by the dominant culture, more comfortable in the empire, than that radical group of young converts in the first century.

Okay, say that today's church needs a targum that is more explicit than the church needed in Paul's day. But still, why these names? Why these institutions and power structures rather than others?

Of course other institutions could have been used. There is nothing more problematic with AT&T or Microsoft than with IBM. And we could have just as easily referred to General Electric or Boeing as to the Pentagon, because these are two significant players in the military-industrial complex. Nor is there any particular reason why Disney should get pride of place over any other expression of the American entertainment industry. Any of these—and other—institutions and corporate structures could have been named.

The point was simply to name some names in order to suggest that we are not dealing with simply abstract principles. When Paul says that Christ is the image of the invisible God, contemporary readers of his poem have to ask both, what are the images that he is confronting in his imperial context, and what are the images that we confront? What is it that seeks to captivate our imagination? What are the imperial forces of our existence in the twenty-first century? So we referred to the centralizing of military power in the Pentagon, the imagination industry symbolized by Disney, and a couple of corporations that in their advertising and corporate images seem to epitomize the dynamics of a cybernetically driven corporate capitalism.

The trick to reading a text like this, then, is to pay close attention to its first context, so that we can then make the appropriate jump to our context?

Yes, that is part of it. But the church doesn't hear this text in all of its power because there is a deeper problem than just a lack of historical background. We have also lost the comprehensive vision of the text. Because we have been so preoccupied with "incanting anemic souls into heaven," as Wendell Berry puts it,[16] we have missed the fact that this poem envisions nothing less than the reconciliation of all of creation. If "all things" are created in, through and for Christ—even the thrones, dominions, rulers and powers—and "all things" are reconciled through the blood of the cross, then the power of this good news must permeate all of life.

The problem with narrowly spiritualistic interpretations of these thrones and dominions is that they leave the temporal structures of oppression alone.

The church hasn't necessarily found that to be problematic. Aren't you playing into a kind of Marxist liberation theology when you begin to talk of the temporal structures of oppression?

Not all discussions of oppressive social structures are Marxist.[17] Some are deeply rooted in the biblical story, especially the prophetic texts and the Gospels. And, we have argued, precisely such a critique is central to Paul's letter here—a critique rooted in the Scriptures of Israel.

You see, when the Christian community abandons discussion of oppressive social structures, there are consequences. In the first instance, if the Christian voice is absent, then the discussion necessarily goes on without a Christian perspective. It is not surprising that other worldviews and categories of analysis fill in the void. And if Christians don't like those worldviews—whether they be Marxist, anarchist, "green" or whatever—then they really have no right to complain. After all, these same upset Christians had left the world of oppressive social and economic structures for someone else to worry about.

A lack of attention to the temporal structures of oppression is devastating for the community that follows Jesus. Berry describes a dualistic church in an imperial context:

> [The church] has, for the most part, stood silently by while a predatory economy has ravaged the world, destroyed its natural beauty and health, divided and plundered its human communities and households. It has flown the flag and chanted the slogans of empire. It has assumed with the economists that "economic forces" automatically work

---

[16]Wendell Berry, "Christianity and the Survival of Creation," in *Sex, Economy, Freedom and Community* (New York: Pantheon, 1993), p. 114.

[17]Indeed, the nineteenth-century Dutch theologian Abraham Kuyper offered profoundly biblical structural analysis of the dynamics of poverty in a capitalist society in his 1891 address *The Problem of Poverty*, ed. James W. Skillen (Grand Rapids, Mich.: Baker/Washington, D.C.: Center for Public Justice, 1991).

for good and has assumed with the industrialists and militarists that technology determines history. It has assumed with almost everybody that "progress" is good, that it is good to be modern and up with the times. It has admired Caesar and comforted him in his depredations and defaults. But in its de facto alliance with Caesar, Christianity connives directly in the murder of Creation.[18]

That's a pretty negative assessment of the church.

It sure is! And it is a far cry from Paul's vision of the Christian community. For Paul, rather than "flying the flag of empire," the church is a community in refusal of the empire which bears the image of another Lord in its daily life. The church reimagines the world in the image of the invisible God. Because this is a body (*soma*) subject to a head (*kephale*) whose lordship overrules Caesar's, the church replaces the body politic of the empire.[19]

This is an incredibly audacious way for a vulnerable little community to view itself!

Yes, but given the cosmic vision of creation and redemption Paul's poem proclaims, audacity is nothing new to this community. That's why we had to name names and spell things out the way we did. In the face of the domestication of the church and its accommodation to empire, our language is forced to be over the top. The poem of Colossians 1:15-20 has the potential not only to set our imagination free from the captivity of empire but also to shatter the way our dualism has restricted our faith. A split-vision worldview that divides faith from life, church from culture, theology from economics, prayer from politics and worship from everyday work will always render Christian faith irrelevant to broad sociocultural forces. And that is exactly what the empire wants—a robust, piously engaging private faith that will never transgress the public square. Allow religion to shape private imagination, but leave the rest of life, the public and dominant imagination, to the empire. Only as we break through this dualism can the poem be given enough space in our lives to liberate our imagination. Failing to see that this poem proclaims a vision of cosmic redemption and failing to see that all of life is created and redeemed in Christ, we fail to even ask how this redemption is made visible in our daily, earthly existence. So yes, in the face of empire, this is an audacious vision of life.

But can it fly in a postmodern world?

Good question. Let's try it out in the next chapter.

---

[18]Berry, "Christianity and the Survival," p. 115.

[19]N. T. Wright, "Paul's Gospel and Caesar's Empire," *Reflections* 2 (Spring 1999): 61.

REGIMES OF TRUTH
AND THE WORD OF TRUTH

The Colossian Christians had trouble on both sides. To many Jews they were heretics, and to the empire they were seditious. Think about it for a moment. Here they were, a group primarily composed of Gentile converts to the way of Jesus. They had believed the good news of Jesus that Epaphras had proclaimed to them (1:6). They knew that this Jesus was embraced by his followers, and now embraced by them, as the Messiah of Israel. Believing the gospel and becoming followers of Jesus meant that these Gentiles now had also accepted the story of Israel as somehow their own. Like all converts, they began to passionately investigate that story. That is why Paul can write a letter to them that will assume they know both the overall shape of Israel's story and certain very important details.

But there is an immediate problem. Followers of "the Way"—that is, people like Nympha and Lydia, Onesimus and Tychicus who embrace Jesus of Nazareth as the Messiah of Israel—are a controversial and sometimes despised group in the eyes of Judaism of the first century. "You may, in your pagan foolishness, accept Jesus as Messiah," say their Jewish detractors, "but we know that he was yet another failed messiah who uttered blasphemy, and his followers are heretics within Israel." It had to be painful and confusing to these early Christians to be rejected by the faith tradition and community that gave birth to their faith in Jesus.

That was only half of their problem, though. It is one thing to be heretics within a community that is itself a minority within the Roman empire. It is quite another thing to hold a faith that is seditious to the empire. How do you go about confessing Christ as Lord when everything all around you—all the power structures, the images that dominate your daily life and even the very temporal rhythms of that life—declare the sovereignty, lordship, honor and glory of the empire and its emperor?

This was as vexing a problem for first-century Christians as it is for twenty-first-century Christians. How do you confess with integrity that Christ is Lord of the cosmos when global economics and the cybernetic revolution seem to demonstrate decisively that economic determinism fueled by information technology is sovereign over the affairs of the world? And if you could find a way to make this confession in the face of such conflicting evidence, then how do you have the audacity to claim that the Christian gospel is true when the violent history of Christendom seems to demonstrate that such "truth" has often made common cause with violence and repression?

But we are getting ahead of ourselves. Back to Colossians.

Paul's Preoccupation with Truth

Given the tenuous relationship the early Christian movement had to both its Jewish forebears and the imperial regime of Rome, it is not surprising that the epistle to the Colossians seems to be preoccupied with questions of truth and knowledge. After all, the question of heresy is fundamentally a question of truth. Is this a true fulfillment of the promises and hopes of Israel? Is the Christian reinterpretation of the story of Israel in light of the story of Jesus true? Is the gospel proclaimed by Epaphras, and now articulated by Paul, true? And if we recognize that those with the power get to say what counts as truth and legitimate knowledge, then how does this small, struggling community manage to embrace and embody an alternative truth in an empire that can afford to have a monopoly on truth? Here we have a problem that the Jewish and Christian communities had in common. How do you sustain profound commitments and truth claims that tend to be rather exclusive ("there is no Lord but God," for first-century Jews, and "there is no Lord but Christ," for first-century Christians) in the face of a monolithic empire that subsumes all spiritualities and religious options under one imperial cult?

Upon even a cursory reading, it is clear that Paul knows that truth and knowledge are central issues for this young Christian community. He first describes the gospel they have received as a "word of truth" that has come to this community (1:5). He then goes on to pray that the community might be filled with "the knowledge of God's will in *all* spiritual wisdom and understanding" (1:9). Such a knowledge, like all true knowledge, will engender a praxis ("bear fruit in *every* good work") that itself results in further growth "in the knowledge of God" (1:10). Moreover, the author invites the community to understand their life prior to their conversion as a hostility of "mind" (1:21). And he says his deepest hope for this community is that the word of God be "fully known" (1:25) in their midst. He teaches "everyone in *all* wisdom" so that *everyone* in the community will come to maturity in Christ (1:28).

When Paul begins to describe what that maturity will look like, he remains focused on matters of wisdom and knowledge. He says that he longs for this community to have "assured understanding" and sure and secure "knowledge of God's mystery, that is, Christ himself, in whom are hidden *all* the treasures of wisdom and knowledge" (2:2-3). Such secure knowledge is necessary lest the community be taken "captive through philosophy and empty deceit, according to human tradition" (2:8). While such deceitful philosophy is dismissed as a mere "appearance of wisdom" (2:23), he counsels the community to have a mind set on the risen and ascended Christ. This is a mind rooted in the narrative of Christ died, risen, ascended and coming again (3:1-4). Moreover, this is the mind of the new self, "which is being renewed in knowledge according to the image of its creator" (3:10). To conclude this quick survey of themes of knowledge and truth in this epistle, note that the "word of truth" we met in chapter one is said to "dwell . . . richly" in the lives of the Colossian believers as they "teach and admonish one another in *all* wisdom" (3:16) and seek to speak to outsiders with wisdom and grace (4:5-6).

We have highlighted the repetition of words like *all* and *everyone* because we must remember that Paul is writing this letter in the face of the all-encompassing claims of the empire. It would seem that he adopts a rhetorical strategy of matching comprehensive claims with comprehensive claims. Do you think that riches of wisdom and knowledge are to be found in Rome, in its plurality of cults subsumed under the imperial cult? Are you impressed with the scope of the empire which encompasses everyone? Then, says Paul, let me tell you that true wisdom is found in Christ alone and that just as the empire is growing and taking claim of the whole world, so also is the word of truth growing and bearing fruit in "the whole world" (1:6).

Of course, all of this is as seditious in the first century as it is heard as totalitarian absolutism in the twenty-first century. Remember that William's immediate problem with Colossians was the huge claims it makes for itself—its preoccupation with totality as evidenced in the language of "all" and its pretentious statements about wisdom and knowledge. Again, it would appear that the absolute is hitting us in the face. Let's try to look at this more closely.

Colossians as a Worldview Book

It is clear that Paul is preoccupied with knowledge writ large. He is concerned to ground this community in a knowing, a truth that is as all-encompassing and as broad in its scope as anything that either Judaism or the empire has to offer. At stake here are foundational questions about the story of the world, the nature of humanity, the source of salvation and the locus of truth. If you will, this epistle answers ultimate questions like "where are we? who are we? what's wrong? and what's the remedy?"[1] Such questions are the stuff that worldviews are made of. In its few pages, this letter offers its readers a foundational understanding of the nature of the cosmos, an anthropology, an understanding of evil, and a clear proclamation of the

---

[1]Brian J. Walsh and J. Richard Middleton, *The Transforming Vision: Shaping a Christian World View* (Downers Grove, Ill.: InterVarsity Press, 1984), pt. 1.

way evil is overcome and resolution is offered to the cosmos. The epistle to the Colossians unpacks the contours of its worldview in terms of the story of Israel and of
Jesus, the implications of this story for the daily lives of the believing community,
and it does so in the face of a struggle between the dominant symbols of Israel,
Rome and the church.[2]

As a worldview text, Colossians weaves for its readers and hearers a vision of life.
It tells us who rules the world, where the world has come from and where it is going,
where wisdom is ultimately to be found, and even which community of people holds
the promise and destiny of the world in its hearts and lives. The worldview on offer
here seeks to provide this young Christian community with a fundamental orientation in life. Orientation is a matter of navigation, a matter of getting the "lay of the
land" in order to go somewhere. Therefore worldviews are not simply visions *of* life
but always also visions *for* life. "They are both descriptive *of* the world, providing their
adherents with the lens through which they can understand and interpret the world,
and prescriptive *for* the world, providing the community with its most foundational
values and norms."[3]

But as soon as we say that Colossians is an ancient writing preoccupied with something like what we today describe as a worldview, we find ourselves in some tension
with the postmodern cultural and intellectual climate. The problem with worldviews
is they are *world*views. In other words, they are by definition comprehensive in scope,
seeking to present an integrating vision that encompasses everything. In this respect
they bear some uncomfortable likeness to empires. Or, in more postmodern terms,
they are inherently totalizing. Michel Foucault puts it this way: "A total description
draws all phenomena around a single center—a principle of meaning, a spirit, a
world-view, an overall shape."[4] Such total descriptions depend on a singular way of
describing the world, a singular narrative. But singular views of the world come at a
price. To maintain their own singular superiority, they must negate all other visions,
all other narratives. That is to say, worldviews have a tendency to become absolutistic
ideologies which forget that they are particular ways of conceiving life that have been
constructed by particular traditions, religions or communities in particular times and
places. Worldviews-turned-ideologies present their view of the world as simply the
way the world is. They are *world*views that function so well that it is forgotten that
they are "views."

---

[2]N. T. Wright, *The New Testament and the People of God* (London: SPCK/Minneapolis: Fortress, 1992), pp.
109-12, 122-26.
[3]Brian J. Walsh, "Worldviews," in *The Complete Book of Everyday Christianity*, ed. Robert Banks and R. Paul
Stevens (Downers Grove, Ill.: InterVarsity Press, 1997), p. 1137. See also James H. Olthuis, "On Worldviews," *Christian Scholar's Review* 14, no. 2 (1985): 153-64.
[4]Michel Foucault, *An Archeology of Knowledge,* trans. A. M. Sheridan Smith (New York: Pantheon, 1972),
p. 10.

In light of the postmodern suspicion of worldviews, it is not surprising that a young man like William, raised within a Christian tradition that uses such language, ducks when he hears talk of worldviews. Worldview discourse and being "punched in the face" by the absolute go hand in hand. Worldview language tends to take on the role of the protector of an ideologically shaped orthodoxy that will fence you in, inhibit creativity, close you down to other perspectives and impose uniformity and sameness.[5] In a postmodern world we become aware of the constructed character of our worldviews and recognize (so the argument goes) that no story, no vision, no orientation or worldview can be absolute. And "once we let go of absolutes, nobody gets to have a position that is anything other than a position. Nobody gets to speak for God, nobody gets to speak for American values, nobody gets to speak for nature."[6]

So we come back to Colossians. If this is a worldview text that presents a comprehensive vision of and for life, rooted in the narratives of Israel and Jesus, then how might we be able to hear it and make it our own in a postmodern age? To help us get at this question, we will look for a moment at another scholar who has taken to reading Colossians as a worldview text.[7] Things are about to get a little technical for a few pages, but there is an important problem here that we need to address. And it will all come back to "truth."

In his book *The Hope of Glory: Education and Exhortation in the Epistle to the Colossians,* Walter Wilson describes a worldview as "a person's *comprehensive* and pre-reflective understanding of reality, an *integrating* framework of fundamental considerations which gives context, direction, and meaning to life in light of one's ultimate commitments." As such, worldviews integrate "knowledge and experience into a *symbolic totality*" that "serves as a *map* of fact and value for a person, *legitimating* all roles, priorities, and institutions by situating them in the context of the *broadest horizon of reference* conceivable, bestowing meaning on *all domains* of life."[8]

Using this understanding of worldviews, Wilson argues that the purpose of the epistle to the Colossians is to lead this young community to so internalize their new worldview that its understanding of "the broader structures that order society and the powers and priorities that govern those structures are [recognized to be] inevitable or 'natural.'"[9] This internalization will then serve to profoundly legitimate Paul's gospel

---

[5]Brian Walsh has discussed the relation of worldview and ideology further in "Transformation: Dynamic Worldview or Repressive Ideology," *Journal of Education and Christian Belief* 4, no. 2 (Autumn 2000): 101-14.
[6]Walter Truett Anderson, *Reality Isn't What It Used to Be* (San Francisco: Harper & Row, 1990), p. 183.
[7]Much of the material in this chapter was first published in an article by Brian Walsh, "Regimes of Truth and the Rhetoric of Deceit: Colossians 2 in Postmodern Context," *Interface: A Forum for Theology in the World* 2, no. 1 (May 1999): 23-37. This article also appeared in *Pro Rege* 28, no. 3 (March 2000): 10-17.
[8]Walter T. Wilson, *The Hope of Glory: Education and Exhortation in the Epistle to the Colossians,* Supplements to *Novum Testamentum* 88 (New York: Brill, 1997), p. 100. Italics added.
[9]Ibid., pp. 102-3.

while delegitimating any variant perspective as *"deviant* and *disruptive."*[10]

There is something appealing about this worldview analysis of the epistle to the Colossians. It is hard to read this text as doing anything less than promoting the validity and ultimate truth of a particular "cosmic-social-anthropological order."[11] New Testament scholar John Barclay says that Colossians offers "an integrated view of reality" and "a comprehensive vision of truth."[12] This is the stock and trade of worldviews. Colossians is indeed a worldview text.

But that creates a problem for us. As we have already begun to see, within a postmodern context some dimensions of such an analysis are immediately problematic. Postmodern discourse is deeply suspicious of all talk of totality. Systems of *symbolic totality* are subjected to a radical hermeneutic of suspicion precisely because they hide their constructed character behind reifications of that which is viewed simply as "natural" in order to *legitimate conformity* to their own *horizon of reference.*[13] Such self-legitimation is achieved only by violently delegitimating all other worldviews, which are dismissed as *deviant.* But if modernity, with its penchant for totality and its concomitant marginalization, totalitarian control and violence, "has given us as much terror as we can take,"[14] then it might well be arguable that what postmodern people need is not a *map* that *naturalizes* the world in terms of our totality constructs but a moral instruction that will "de-naturalize some of the dominant features of our way of life; to point out that those entities that we unthinkingly experience as 'natural' are in fact 'cultural'; made by us not given to us."[15]

The issue here isn't whether Wilson's analysis of Colossians as a worldview text is fruitful for understanding this ancient epistle in its historical context. The problem comes when we attempt to appropriate this text as our own in a postmodern context. Colossians may well be a worldview text par excellence, but worldviews do not fare well in a postmodern climate. What are we to make of a text that claims to be rooted in a Christ "in whom are hidden all the treasures of wisdom and understanding" (2:3) and who is encountered in a "word of the truth" (1:5) that imparts assured understanding and knowledge of the very divine will (cf. 1:6, 9-10; 2:2-3; 3:10, 16)? Can this word of truth, as articulated in this letter, together with its comprehensive truth claims, be believable—indeed livable—in a postmodern cultural context?

---

[10]Ibid., p. 104.

[11]Ibid.

[12]John M. G. Barclay, *Colossians and Philemon,* New Testament Guides (Sheffield, U.K.: Sheffield Academic, 1997), p. 77.

[13]A worldview is reified when we forget that it is itself a cultural product. See Peter Berger, *The Sacred Canopy: Elements of a Sociological Theory of Religion* (Garden City, N.Y.: Doubleday, 1967).

[14]Jean-François Lyotard, *The Postmodern Condition,* trans. Geoff Bennington and Brian Massumi (Minneapolis: University of Minnesota Press, 1984), p. 81.

[15]Linda Hutcheon, *The Politics of Postmodernism* (New York: Routledge, 1989), p. 2.

Regimes of Truth

Foucault both heightens our problem and sharpens it. Remember that Colossians is preoccupied with "truth." In a rather famous statement, here is Foucault's take on truth:

> Truth is a thing of this world: it is produced only by virtue of multiple forms of constraint. And it induces regular effects of power. Each society has its regime of truth, its "general politics" of truth: that is, the types of discourse which it accepts and makes function as true; the mechanism and instances which enable one to distinguish true and false statements; the means by which each is sanctioned; the techniques and procedures accorded value in the acquisition of truth; the status of those who are charged with saying what counts as true.[16]

This quote wonderfully sums up a postmodern antirealist, constructivist epistemology. Let's pay attention to what Foucault is saying. Truth is not found, nor does it "come" to us from any place beyond our worldly realities. Truth is made, it is produced, and such production (like all production) requires the imposition of power, of constraint. Once such a constructed vision of things is taken to be true, it becomes a regime, a structure of political control that will determine what kind of discourse might function as true, how one will establish and sanction truth within such a discourse, which techniques will be authorized as legitimate paths to truth, and how the truth-tellers within the regime will be regarded. If Foucault's devaluation of truth as simply power grabs of various regimes is at all on target, then religious faith in general, and any quick appropriation of the faith on offer in Colossians in particular, is in deep trouble.

Let's take a look at Colossians 2:8-23 and read it, for a moment, through postmodern—Foucauldian—eyes.

> See to it that no one takes you captive through philosophy and empty deceit, according to human tradition, according to the elemental spirits of the universe, and not according to Christ. For in him the whole fullness of deity dwells bodily, and you have come to fullness in him, who is the head of every ruler and authority. In him also you were circumcised with a spiritual circumcision, by putting off the body of the flesh in the circumcision of Christ; when you were buried with him in baptism, you were also raised with him through faith in the power of God, who raised him from the dead. And when you were dead in trespasses and the uncircumcision of your flesh, God made you alive together with him, when he forgave us all our trespasses, erasing the record that stood against us with its legal demands. He set this aside, nailing it to the cross. He disarmed the rulers and authorities and made a public example of them, triumphing over them in it.
> Therefore do not let anyone condemn you in matters of food and drink or of observ-

---

[16]Michel Foucault, *Power/Knowledge: Selected Interviews and other Writings, 1972-1977,* ed. Colin Gordon (New York: Pantheon, 1980), p. 131.

ing festivals, new moons, or sabbaths. These are only a shadow of what is to come, but the substance belongs to Christ. Do not let anyone disqualify you, insisting on self-abasement and worship of angels, dwelling on visions, puffed up without cause by a human way of thinking, and not holding fast to the head, from whom the whole body, nourished and held together by its ligaments and sinews, grows with a growth that is from God.

If with Christ you died to the elemental spirits of the universe, why do you live as if you still belonged to the world? Why do you submit to regulations, "Do not handle, Do not taste, Do not touch"? All these regulations refer to things that perish with use; they are simply human commands and teachings. These have indeed an appearance of wisdom in promoting self-imposed piety, humility, and severe treatment of the body, but they are of no value in checking self-indulgence.

In this passage Paul is warning the Colossian converts to be careful lest they be taken captive by "philosophy" and "empty deceit." He then, as in the rest of Colossians, continues to make claims that are deemed incredible from a postmodern perspective. Consistent with the cosmic claims made in the Christ poem of 1:15-20, Paul claims in 2:9 that in Christ the fullness of deity dwells bodily. Here is an affirmation of universal presence manifest in the embodied particularity of one historical person. The totalizing tone continues when Christ is confessed to be the "head of every ruler and authority" (2:10) because he has disarmed and made public examples of such rulers and authorities (2:15). Totality systems are regimes of truth, and regimes defeat their enemies.

Beyond the content of Paul's attack on the opposing philosophy, we can recognize all the telltale characteristics of a regime of truth in his rhetoric. Isn't Paul engaging in a rather clear act of "constraint" here? "Don't be taken in by this other voice, this dissenting perspective!" And doesn't the passage seem to presuppose some clear "mechanisms" by which Paul distinguishes the truth from falsehood—namely, the final authority of the Christ story and his interpretation of that story? Does not his depiction of the "philosophy" as a "human tradition," a "human way of thinking" that imposes "human commands and teachings," assume a certain kind of discourse—apostolic discourse—that has an exclusive claim on truth? Isn't it a rather clear implication that while his opponents have a human tradition, Paul's own apostolic tradition comes with divine sanction and authority?

Doesn't all of this suggest that Paul's rhetoric reflects an inherently totalizing regime of truth designed to wipe out alterity, delegitimate difference and allow only for the univocal discourse of orthodoxy? Isn't this rhetoric precisely the kind of privileging of a single narrative, a single vision of life, that postmodernity has taught us to suspect? If postmodernity could be described as "a way of attending to the world that finds itself without the authority to dismiss other ways" because these other ways, other visions, "all remain equally present and equally capable of engendering persuasive accounts of things,"[17] then this text is decidedly alien to a postmodern culture and can be read only as fundamentally repressive in its attempt to silence the voice of any other perspective.

This would be one way of reading this text—and it is a way that is becoming common among postmodern biblical critics. These scholars would argue that just as modern technologies of power are based on claims to self-evidence and truth, so also Paul's discourse is intended to control power relations in the early Christian communities, and this control is given ultimate legitimacy by claims to apostolic authority and truth.[18]

But what about the adherents of the philosophy under attack in this passage? What about those who are advocating the "philosophy" that is challenged in Colossians 2? Would a postmodern sensitivity to marginalization and the way totality thinking creates deviance lead us to ask different questions regarding the censored voice in this text? In this light, the authors of *The Postmodern Bible* raise a number of questions:

> To what extent have the echoes of other voices in these letters been drowned out simply by being labeled *the opponents,* the biblical scholar's equivalent of the term *other?* To what extent does the term *opponents* connote the normativity of Paul's own discourse? And to what extent does such Pauline commentary become an extension of Paul's own discourse, a testament to its cooptive power, and a repetition of its gesture of exclusion? A Foucauldian reading would attempt a different rendering of the multiple voices within the Pauline corpus. It would attempt to rearticulate competing interpretations of truth in terms other than those of norm and aberration.[19]

Here we meet a distinctively postmodern reading strategy. Unmask the power grab involved in the text, deconstruct the normativity of the author's voice and give back legitimate voice to that which has been silenced and marginalized.

But while at first glance this seems to be an ethically motivated hermeneutic, in the end it is, we suggest, a facile strategy. It has, if you will, an "appearance of wisdom," but it is of no profit for really hearing the voice of the marginalized. You see, telling us that the term *opponents* "connotes the normativity" of the writer's discourse isn't all that insightful or creative. *Of course* such language connotes normativity! So what? And we certainly shouldn't be duped into thinking that such a strategy is in the service of hermeneutical peace, respect for the other and abandonment of the rhetoric of deviance and opponents. What such "reading against the grain"[20] of the text actually accomplishes is a new kind of violence with a new opponent who is deemed to

---

[17]Joseph Natoli, *A Primer to Postmodernity* (Oxford: Blackwell, 1997), p. 16.

[18]Elizabeth Castelli, *Imitating Paul: A Discourse of Power* (Louisville, Ky.: Westminster John Knox, 1991).

[19]Bible and Culture Collective, *The Postmodern Bible* (New Haven, Conn.: Yale University Press, 1995), p. 143. Similar sentiments are found in Stephen D. Moore's *Poststructuralism and the New Testament: Derrida and Foucault at the Foot of the Cross* (Minneapolis: Fortress, 1994).

[20]Ibid., p. 275.

have deviated from another assumed normative stance. The new deviant, the new opponent, is the power-grabbing Paul (and the Scriptures attributed to Paul), imposing a totalizing vision on the early Christian community. The poststructuralist critic will employ all the same rhetorical techniques, assuming the ethical normativity of her own postmodern stance, against Paul as the apostle did against his opponents.

If deconstruction is fascinated with the marginal, the repressed and the borderline—with the way in which "deviant modes of thought are excluded"[21]—then we are not sure that we have made any progress simply by judging Paul's thought to be deviant, requiring exclusion from our biblical scholarship and Christian lives. Indeed such readings, we contend, perpetuate the violence.

Whose Regime Is It?

Perhaps there is a more creative way forward. Rather than myopically applying a hermeneutic of trust to the marginal voice of the "philosophy" under attack in Colossians 2 and a hermeneutic of suspicion to the orthodoxy by which this philosophy is judged, what happens if we apply a Foucauldian critique to both the author of Colossians 2 and the philosophy itself?[22] Of course, the first part of this proposal is easier to execute. We actually have the text of Colossians 2 to deconstruct. We do not have a text of the philosophy under question. Indeed there is considerable debate as to the exact identity of this "philosophy." While there have been various interpretive reconstructions, it is fair to say that "precision and clarity is really an impossible task" when attempting to identify this "philosophy."[23] We will not attempt to offer any particular reconstruction of this philosophy. Rather, we are concerned with the nature of Paul's attack on it. What happens if we apply Foucault's description of regimes of truth to the philosophy as we find it here depicted, just as we have applied it to Paul's rhetoric? The results are amazingly similar.

Like all regimes, this philosophy is preoccupied with captivity. Hence Paul warns the Colossians to not be taken captive by any deceitful and oppressive regime of truth that parades itself as something other than a mere human tradition (2:8). As a regime of truth, the philosophy depends on deceit for its power. It has to hide the fact that it is a mere human construction, a human tradition. Therefore it "imposes multiple

---

[21] Ibid., p. 121.

[22] In contrast to a binary opposition between "trust" and "suspicion," we propose a more dialectical approach. Suspicion always presupposes a stance of trust that has entered into a time of crisis. But suspicion is not an end in itself. Rather, the moment of suspicion is always on the way to renewed trust. Paul Ricoeur would describe this as a movement from the first naiveté of trust through the critical fires of suspicion and on to a postcritical second naiveté. See *The Symbolism of Evil,* trans. Emerson Buchanan (Boston: Beacon, 1967), pp. 347-57. See also Walter Brueggemann, *The Message of the Psalms: A Theological Commentary* (Minneapolis: Augsburg, 1984), chap. 1.

[23] Clinton Arnold, *The Colossian Syncretism: The Interface Between Christianity and Folk Belief at Colossae* (Grand Rapids, Mich.: Baker, 1996), p. 228.

forms of constraint"—do not handle, do not taste, don't even touch (2:21). This philosophy not only "induces regular effects of power," it is preoccupied with powers,
rulers and authorities and employs such power precisely for the purposes of exclusion. The status of those who are "charged with saying what counts as true" is such
that they function in the life of the community as self-appointed umpires whose central role seems to be exercising condemnation, ruling people out (2:16)! And this philosophy, this regime of truth, has clear "techniques and procedures which are ac-
corded value in the acquisition of truth"; these are procedures of ascetic self-
abasement (for the creation of docile bodies),[24] fasting and ecstatic visions (2:18). The
point of all of this is to achieve a sharing in the worship of angels, a transcendence
beyond the situatedness of material reality, in order to somehow enter into a heavenly
realm that relegates all temporal, bodily existence to mere shadow or appearance
compared to the essential reality of a disembodied higher realm (v. 18).

Hmm. It looks like a regime of truth, it acts like a regime of truth, it has all the
telltale characteristics of a regime of truth. Therefore, upon this reading of the philosophy at Colossae, Paul has good Foucauldian grounds for dismissing this particular
"philosophy" as the regime of truth that it is.

But now we have a new problem. It would appear that we are faced with two competing, mutually exclusive regimes of truth—Paul's and the one he here dismisses. If
this is the case, and if the ethical force of Foucault's critique of such regimes at all rings
true to us, then it would seem that a hermeneutic of trust—to say nothing of
retrieval—is impossible for us.

Perhaps we can formulate another way of putting the question. Is Paul's gospel a
regime of truth in ideological combat with another regime of truth? Or is there a
marked difference between a Foucauldian regime of truth and the "kingdom of [the]
beloved Son" (1:13) proclaimed in this letter?

Is the Bible a Regime of Truth?

This question, asked of this particular text, must also be asked of the whole Bible. Is
the biblical metanarrative, together with its large-scale truth claims about the whole
cosmos, inherently totalizing, violent and oppressive, or are there counterideological,
antitotalizing dimensions of this grand story that militate against, delegitimate and
subvert any ideological, violent, totalizing uses of this narrative? Note carefully how
we have put this question. We are not contesting the fact that the biblical metanarrative
—and Paul's epistles—have been used in totalizing and oppressive ways. The weight
of Christian history is too great to attempt any such cover-up. What we are asking is
whether we might discern counterideological tendencies in the biblical tradition that

---

[24]The rendering of bodies as docile is another Foucauldian theme. See Foucault's *Discipline and Punish: The
Birth of the Prison*, trans. Alan Sheridan (New York: Vintage, 1979). See Elizabeth Castelli, "Interpretations of Power in 1 Corinthians," *Semeia* 54 (1992): 197-202.

undermine such oppressive readings and praxis. Is there anything in the Bible itself that, if taken seriously, would prevent or inhibit us from using the Bible as an absolute with which to punch people in the face? Our answer is yes!

We discern two such antitotalizing dimensions or trajectories in the biblical meta-narrative. The first consists in a radical sensitivity to suffering which pervades the biblical narrative, from the introduction of "covenant" in Genesis 6 to the cross and the ongoing expectation that the church must share in Christ's suffering as part of its redemptive presence in the world. The second consists in the rooting of the story in God's overarching creational intent, which delegitimates any narrow, partisan use of the story. These two dimensions, we suggest, are intrinsic to the biblical metanarrative.[25]

From God's decision to make covenant with a creature that had nothing but violence in its heart (Gen 8—9), to the story of God's *knowing* the Israelites' pain in Egyptian bondage and the divine commitment to set the people free (Ex 3:7), to the abrasive tradition of the psalms of lament (Ps 44 and 88, among others) and the weeping prophets (especially Jeremiah, Amos and Hosea), an "embrace of pain" has characterized the biblical story from the beginning.[26] Old Testament scholar Terence Fretheim notes that "grief has been characteristic of the history of God almost from the beginning of things."[27] It is important to note that within this overarching biblical narrative it is not just that God empathizes with the pain of the people and creation but that God, in God's self, suffers. "By deciding to endure a wicked world, while continuing to open up the heart to that world . . . God has decided to take personal suffering upon God's own self."[28]

This biblical trajectory is kept alive in the prophets, who tell a story not only of a liberating God who hears the cries of a suffering people but of a suffering God, pained by the brokenness and infidelity of precisely those people. This is a servant God who is burdened by the people's sins (Is 43:24). Indeed Isaiah speaks of a servant who has "borne our infirmities" and is "wounded for our transgressions, crushed for our iniquities" (Is 53:4-5). If Genesis recognizes that "every inclination of the thoughts" of the human heart is continually captivated by evil, such that "the earth is filled with violence" (Gen 6:5, 13), then Isaiah realizes that such evil and violence will ultimately be let loose on God's very self. In the voice of the prophets this is a pathos-filled God, brokenhearted by the violence that has wreaked havoc in creation.[29]

The biblical embrace of pain refuses to cover up or deny suffering. To use a post-

---

[25]J. Richard Middleton and Brian J. Walsh, *Truth Is Stranger Than It Used to Be: Biblical Faith in a Postmodern Age* (Downers Grove, Ill.: InterVarsity Press/London: SPCK, 1995), esp. chap. 5.

[26]Walter Brueggemann, "A Shape for Old Testament Theology II: Embrace of Pain," *Catholic Biblical Quarterly* 47, no. 3 (July 1995): 395-415.

[27]Terence Fretheim, *The Suffering of God,* Overtures to Biblical Theology (Philadelphia: Fortress, 1984), p. 112.

[28]Ibid.

[29]See also Jeremiah 3:19; 4:14; 13:27; Hosea 8:5; 11:1-2.

modern metaphor, this biblical trajectory does not make false claims to "presence" but instead highlights "absence"—the absence of justice and shalom, and in the lament tradition even the absence of God. Biblical texts in this trajectory critique the unjust status quo that legitimates itself on the basis of a false presence (notably that of the temple and monarchy), in the name of a God of justice and liberation.[30]

This trajectory of pain and suffering, we suggest, functions as a counterideological dimension of the biblical witness. The admitted tendency of worldviews to become rigid, exclusivist ideologies, painfully illustrated in much church history, finds a counterforce here. The centrality of suffering in the biblical narrative serves to delegitimate any ideological use of the biblical story that will cause violence within exclusionary us-them polarities.[31] A story that has God intimately involved with suffering and that sees violence to be the root of the human predicament should engender a worldview that eschews all violence, including violence to those who radically disagree with us.

This leads to the second antitotalizing dimension of the biblical story. If there is a biblical trajectory that refuses to legitimate violent us-them polarities, then why does the Bible tell us a story of an elect people, chosen out of the rest of humanity as the particular object of God's redemptive concern? Why elect Israel? The answer that rings through the biblical witness is that Israel is chosen to be a light to the nations, the agent of God's reconciliation of all creation and all peoples. In this story Israel is called to be "a priestly kingdom and a holy nation" (Ex 19:6) not so it could be a regime of truth that exists for the exclusion of others but in order to play a role in the restoration of the whole human race.

And it is not just humans that are the object of God's love. If we look closely at the biblical narrative, it is clear that all of creation is to be brought back into covenantal relationship with the Creator. In Genesis 9, where we have the establishment of a covenant after the flood narrative, the narrator is at pains to make it clear that the covenant is not just with Noah and his descendants but with "every living creature" (9:10, 12-13, 15-17). Because all of creation is party to the covenant, it is not surprising that stones can bear witness to covenant renewal ceremonies (Josh 24:27), donkeys can speak the word of the Lord (Num 22:22-30), the land can grieve and vomit out its inhabitants (Lev 18:28; Jer 4:23-28; 14:2-6; Rom 8:22-23), trees and hills can sing

---

[30]On the traditions of temple and monarchy as ideological legitimations of false presence, see Middleton and Walsh, *Truth Is Stranger*, pp. 94-95, 104, 158; and Walter Brueggemann, *The Prophetic Imagination* (Philadelphia: Fortress, 1978), chap. 2.

[31]That such a statement suggests tension within the biblical witness between traditions of exclusion and embrace is simply noted here. Further explication of the meaning of this for inner-biblical interpretation will have to be left for another time. Obviously the most telling counterevidence to the tradition of embrace is the conquest of Canaan recorded in Joshua. Suffice it to say at this point that whatever we might make of the conquest narrative, such violence in the name of the kingdom of God could never be justified in the light of the gospel.

for joy (Ps 96:12; 98:8), mountains can hear words of prophecy directed only to them (Ezek 36:1-15), and even roadside rocks recognize their Redeemer (Lk 19:40).[32]

There is a wonderful paradox here. It is precisely the creationwide intent of Israel's God that functions as a counterideological, antitotalizing dimension of the biblical story. It is precisely its comprehensive, even universal, scope that militates against its being co-opted by a totalizing ideology. If this drama has the redemption of all of creation as its focus, then any violent, ideological, self-justifying ownership of the story—either by nationalistic Jews or by sectarian and self-righteous Christians—brings the story to a dramatic dead end that has missed the creationally redemptive point.

To summarize these counterideological dimensions of the biblical metanarrative, we need to see, first, that a story rooted in and radically attentive to suffering is a story of liberation from violently imposed regimes of truth, not a story that legitimates newly imposed slavery. Second, a story with the redemption of all of creation as its focus subverts any partisan, self-justifying co-option of its message.

Regime of Truth or Kingdom of the Beloved Son?

The question that remains, however, is whether Paul's interpretation of the story in the letter to the Colossians and in the conflict with the so-called Colossian philosophy remains faithful to these counterideological trajectories or imposes an exclusionary ideology on the overall biblical story. Is the "kingdom of [the] beloved Son" (Col 1:13) markedly different from Foucault's regimes of truth? We suggest that there is a profound difference between the two precisely because the very counterideological and antitotalizing dimensions of the rest of the biblical narrative are at work in this epistle to the Colossians.

We can begin by recalling that the phrase "the kingdom of [God's] beloved Son" occurs in a context in which the apostle is making a direct allusion to the exodus tradition—the very tradition that is foundational to Israel's memory of suffering and pain. Paul encourages his readers/hearers to give thanks to the Father, "who has enabled you to share in the inheritance of the saints in the light. He has rescued us from the power of darkness and transferred us into the kingdom of his beloved Son, in whom we have redemption, the forgiveness of sins" (1:12-14). This language of inheritance, forgiveness and rescue from one empire in order to be freed in another kingdom harks back to the exodus narrative. It was Israel who was rescued from the imperial captivity of Egypt. It was Israel who received the promised land as an inheritance. And it was to rebellious Israel that God revealed himself as a God of forgiveness (see Ex 32:7—34:10). Now, says Paul, we experience an exodus liberation in Jesus.

---

[32]Brian J. Walsh, Marianne Karsh and Nik Ansell, "Trees, Forestry and the Responsiveness of Creation," *Cross Currents* 44, no. 2 (Summer 1994): 149-62. This article is also included in *This Sacred Earth: Religion, Nature, Environment,* ed. Roger S. Gottlieb (New York: Routledge, 1995), pp. 423-35.

Interpreting the Jesus story in light of the exodus tradition, Paul is saying that in Jesus the final exodus from slavery to freedom, from darkness to light, from empire to kingdom is accomplished. In postmodern terms, this liberation is not in order to enslave us in yet another regime that would violently imposes its ideology on us. Indeed while regimes of truth invariably trade on the sense of guilt and unworthiness of their subjects, this kingdom is rooted in forgiveness. In place of the exclusionary constraints of self-imposed umpires who would rule us out, who would pound us with an absolute standard before which we could not stand, the kingdom of the beloved Son is a reign of forgiving and welcoming inclusion.

A kingdom of loving inclusion must be established in a radically different way from regimes of truth. It is not surprising therefore that, in profound contrast to regimes of truth with their multiple forms of constraint, the kingdom of the beloved Son is a kingdom won not through violence imposed on others but through violence imposed upon the Son. Notice that the cross is at the very heart of our text:

> And when you were dead in trespasses and the uncircumcision of your flesh, God made you alive together with him, when he forgave us all our trespasses, erasing the record that stood against us with its legal demands. He set this aside, nailing it to the cross. He disarmed the rulers and authorities and made a public example of them, triumphing over them in it.

Again, the foundation of this kingdom is not in self-righteous exclusion but in the inclusion of forgiveness.

There is in this text a profound sense of an oppressive force that must be defeated. This is a force of death because it strips human life of its vitality and joy in the face of a damning absolute. But if the rulers and authorities, regimes and empires that so oppress us are to be defeated, they must be defeated not by further violence but by sacrificial love. That is precisely how Paul describes the victory of the kingdom of the beloved Son over the regimes of truth in this passage. Andrew Lincoln notes, "The powers of evil are defeated not by some overwhelming display of divine power but by the weakness of Christ's death." Moreover, when viewed in the light of Jesus' resurrection, "the death of the victim, who has absorbed the destructive forces of the powers, becomes precisely the point at which their domination is decisively brought to an end. Their claims, their accusations, their oppressive and divisive influence have all been subverted by a very different power: the power of the victim on the cross."[33]

Is there a life-and-death struggle between two worldviews here? Yes. Does Paul's gospel make large, universalizing, even *total* claims? Yes. Is there a power struggle going on here? Indeed! From the author's point of view this is *the* power struggle of the cosmos.

---

[33]Andrew T. Lincoln, "The Letter to the Colossians," in *The New Interpreter's Bible,* ed. Leander Keck (Nashville: Abingdon, 2000), 11:628.

But note how the struggle is won. Not by might versus might, not by regime overtaking regime, but by sacrificial love absorbing the violence and fury of the powers. N. T. Wright puts it this way: "The cross was not the defeat of *Christ* at the hands of the *powers*: it was the defeat of the powers at the hands—yes, the bleeding hands—of Christ."[34]

Paul is convinced that evil is devastatingly real and that it is oppressing the Colossian community both from without (the sheer imaginative, political and economic force of the empire) and from within (the "philosophy" that runs the risk of tearing the community apart, stripping them of their hope and enslaving them in a system of ascetic discipline). If they are to be liberated, then this evil must be defeated. But it cannot be defeated on its own terms. Evil expects to engage in a battle of strength against strength, enmity against enmity. And as long as those are the terms, it remains victorious. The whole biblical drama, however, the whole tradition of the embrace of pain—from the initiation of covenant to the devastating events of Passion Week—declares that evil is defeated when it is allowed to expend itself in demonic fury on that which it hates the most, the Source of all good. On the servant of the Lord, in the Messiah's death on the cross, that demonic fury is let loose. The cross was "the victory of weakness over strength, the victory of love over hatred. It was the victory that consisted in Jesus' allowing evil to do its worst to him, and never attempting to fight it on its own terms. When the power of evil had made its last possible move, Jesus had still not been beaten by it. He bore the weight of the world's evil to the end, and outlasted it."[35]

Paul uses deliberately provocative language in Colossians to make this point. What happens at the cross is that both the "record that stood against us with its legal demands" is erased ("nailed to the cross") and the "rulers and authorities" that violently oppress us and arrogantly lead their captives in the kind of triumphal processions that characterized Roman imperial display are themselves "disarmed," "made a public example of" and triumphed over. The irony should not be lost on us. Paul is saying both that the legal demands of the philosophy are erased at the cross and that the imperial rulers and authorities who put him on that cross were defeated in the very act that seemed like their victory. Turning the empire on its head, the cross becomes the site of the victory march of the victim.

This upside-down understanding of how the embracing power of love defeats and disarms exclusionary rulers and authorities is as radically new today as it was in the context of the Roman empire. In a postmodern world where truth claims are reduced to little more than power struggles between competing interests, Paul seems to be tell-

---

[34]N. T. Wright, *Following Jesus: Biblical Reflections on Discipleship* (Grand Rapids, Mich.: Eerdmans, 1994), p. 19.

[35]N. T. Wright, *New Tasks for a Renewed Church* (London: Hodder & Stoughton, 1992), p. 72. This is what C. S. Lewis calls "deeper magic from the dawn of time" in *The Lion, the Witch and the Wardrobe* (London: Fontana, 1950), chap. 15.

ing us that such power games are simply not worth playing. Jesus is up to something profoundly different.[36]

In a world suffused with hostility, all of this is scandalous. In *The Anti-Christ* Friedrich Nietzsche sees only weakness in the cross—Christ's "inability for enmity."[37] Miroslav Volf, however, responds to Nietzsche's provocation by evocatively suggesting that the cross bespeaks "the kind of enmity toward all enmity which rejects all enmity's services. Instead of aping the enemy's act of violence and rejection, Christ, the victim who refuses to be defined by the perpetrator, forgives and makes space in himself for the enemy."[38] Herein is the radical distinction between regimes of truth and the kingdom of the beloved Son.

But there is a second counterideological dimension to the gospel—its creational scope. The language of this epistle makes it clear that Paul works with as comprehensive an understanding of God's love for all of creation as we have already seen characterizes the Old Testament understanding of covenant. We have already suggested that Paul's greeting of "grace . . . and peace" at the beginning of the letter evokes the Hebrew understanding of shalom, including Ezekiel's notion of a covenant of shalom that encompasses all of creation. And in the last chapter we discussed Paul's anti-imperial poetic vision, which is as comprehensive as the creation itself.

Remember how explicit Paul's language is. The "word of the truth" that has come to the Colossians, not unlike the Wisdom of Israel's writings, is bearing good creational (or new creational) fruit "in the whole world" (Col 1:6). That is why it ought not be surprising that Paul will later say that this gospel "has been proclaimed to every creature under heaven" (1:23). "The whole world"! "Every creature under heaven"! This gospel comes not just as good news to the nation of Israel, nor even to all human beings. This is good news for *every* creature under heaven. Paul's creationwide understanding of the gospel could not be clearer. But as we have seen, it *does* get clearer.

In the subversive poem we find in 1:15-20, we see that it is precisely Paul's understanding of the comprehensiveness of the kingdom of the beloved Son that serves to undermine the deceitful philosophy of chapter 2. What is wrong with that philosophy? Its dualistic devaluation of the body and imposition of strict ascetic regulations in order to transcend to a heavenly realm of spirit miss the creational point of redemption. *All things* have been created through Christ and for Christ. He is before *all things,* and in him *all things* hold together. Therefore through him God is pleased to

---

[36]Commenting on the trial scene before Pilate in John's Gospel, Miroslav Volf says that Jesus shifts the discourse from the "truth of power" (Pilate's preoccupation and, it would seem, Foucault's) to the "power of truth" (*Exclusion and Embrace: A Theological Exploration of Identity, Otherness and Reconciliation* [Nashville: Abingdon, 1996], p. 266).

[37]Friedrich Nietzsche, *Twilight of the Idols and the Anti-Christ,* trans. R. J. Hollingdale (London: Penguin, 1990), p. 153.

[38]Volf, *Exclusion and Embrace,* p. 126.

reconcile *all things*. That the empire would find all of this seditious is clear enough. Paul insists that to embrace a philosophy or spiritual practice that would be anti-creational in any way is to misunderstand not only the meaning of the gospel but the whole creational inclusiveness of the tradition of Israel. And once you have embraced such a philosophy, it is not surprising that you would find yourself again subject to oppressive regimes or authorities, because you have forgotten that even these rulers and authorities are created in, through and for Christ and that they too are subject to his redemptive rule.

We therefore suggest that in the Colossian poem we meet one of the most eloquent articulations of the second counterideological trajectory of the biblical metanarrative. But notice again how the poem culminates precisely by bringing together these two counterideological dimensions. "And through him God was pleased to reconcile all things, whether on earth or in heaven [creational scope], making peace through the blood of his cross [embrace of pain]" (1:20). Here is a vision of radical, creationwide inclusiveness of the kingdom, in contrast to the dismissive exclusiveness of the regime. All things are to be reconciled—*even* the thrones, dominions, rulers and authorities that put Christ on the cross and continue to wreak havoc in countless human lives. But that redemptive inclusion comes via the path of the cross, the embrace of pain.

Universal Claims, Redemptive Inclusion and Truth

While the Colossian regime is characterized by exclusion and disqualification, the gospel engenders embrace and forgiveness in which there is no longer Gentile and Jew, circumcised and uncircumcised, barbarian, Scythian, slave and free (Col 3:11). All ethnic, religious, social and economic barriers are broken down. The universal claim "Christ is all and in all" is in the service not of violent marginalization but of redemptive inclusion.

It is the universality of a worldview's claim—its appeal to the broadest horizon of reference conceivable—that makes it applicable to all domains of life. Consequently, a worldview is only as good as the praxis or way of life that it engenders. That is why, in the rhetoric of this epistle, Paul's critique of the Colossian philosophy is concerned less with matters of theory and doctrine than with praxis. Rather than debating the ontological nature of "the powers," Paul addresses the tyrannical hold that these forces have over the life of the community. How does he know that this philosophy is deceitful (2:8), a mere human tradition (2:8, 18, 22), a sham of wisdom (2:23), and does not hold fast to the head who is Christ (2:19)? Because it imposes an ascetic re-gime of exclusion that is inconsistent with everything we know about Christ, the story of redemption and a biblical understanding of creation. But this means that the proof of the truth of the gospel that Paul proclaims is not in the power of his rhetoric against the competition but in the "fruit" that such truth bears in the community (1:6, 10). Therefore the apologetic of Colossians 2 is incomplete without the moral exhortation of Colossians 3. The "philosophy" will always be a plausible alternative (2:4) so long as the truth of the gospel is not manifest in the life of the community.

What was true of an ancient community of Christian believers struggling with a powerful and appealing philosophy is also true for Christians in a postmodern context. Arguments that deconstruct the regimes of truth at work in the late modern culture of global capitalism are indispensable. So also is a deeper understanding of the counterideological force of the biblical tradition. But such arguments are no guarantee that the biblical metanarrative will not be co-opted for ideological purposes of violent exclusion, nor do arguments prove the truth of the gospel. Only the nonideological, embracing, forgiving and shalom-filled life of a dynamic Christian community formed by the story of Jesus will prove the gospel to be true and render the idolatrous alternatives fundamentally implausible.

WHAT IS TRUTH?

*D*o you mind if I interrupt?

No, go ahead.

I'm glad to see we've finally come back to truth. You started the last chapter by rehearsing how Paul is preoccupied with truth and knowledge in this epistle, and you ended by talking about "proving the gospel to be true" through the historical and cultural life of the Christian community. But in the middle, as you were talking about Foucault's "regimes of truth," I am not so sure we didn't kind of abandon truth and slip into rhetoric.

You might be on to something there. Can you explain this a little more for us?

Well, it seems to me that once you concede Foucault's point that truth is "produced only by virtue of multiple forms of constraint," aren't you saying that truth is simply a power game? If there is no more to truth than this kind of imposition of power, then the only argument for the truth of any particular position would be a rhetorical argument. The person or group with the best persuasive skills, and maybe the most social and economic power behind them, wins all contests for truth. Isn't this what you are left with?

If that is what we were left with, then Paul would certainly want to disown us.

What do you mean?

Think for a moment about Paul's social location and the location of the Christian community. If truth was simply a matter of rhetoric backed up by power, then it is pretty clear that the "word of the truth" that Paul proclaims is going to be on the losing side in the battle over truth in the world. It is, after all, the empire that has the power, and just to prove it, Paul is writing this letter from an imperial prison cell. Empires love to have a monopoly on truth. So Paul wants to appeal to a truth that is beyond rhetoric and not reducible to power—or at least power as the world understands it.

Why then did you walk down that Foucauldian path and subject both Paul and the "philosophy" to such a rhetorical analysis? You focused on the nature of their discourse—whether it was exclusionary, whether it engaged in power grabs, whether it sanctioned certain ways to ascertain truth and censored others—rather than on whether the content of their discourse was true or not.

In the first place, we walked the Foucauldian path because it seems to us that there is ample evidence in the history of the church, and in our own lives, that truth claims do often function as violently ideological regimes. There is something therapeutic about such a deconstructive exercise, because it forces us to take a good look at what is really going on in our discourse and in our lives. It forces us to ask difficult and potentially embarrassing questions of ourselves, our tradition, and even the biblical text and its authors.

I can see the usefulness of asking such questions of ourselves and even of our various Christian traditions, but isn't subjecting the text to such a hermeneutic of suspicion inherently problematic—even spiritually dangerous? And doesn't the very posing of such questions arrogantly place us over the text? Isn't this really a modernist kind of attitude?

On one level, we agree with you. Much suspicion of the biblical text is a modernist power game. And insofar as the kind of suspicion we investigated in the chapter was postmodern, we also attempted to say in what ways we think this kind of textual criticism can amount to little more than facile, cheap critique. But we have another, more compelling reason to walk down this Foucauldian path.

What is that?

Well, it's William. You see, folks like William ask these kinds of questions of this text. As we said, William and countless others duck when they hear worldview talk and experience little more than revulsion when they engage a text that speaks with the kind of authority of Colossians 2. That allergic reaction to Paul's kind of rhetoric needs to be taken seriously. And it needs to be addressed if we are ever to hear Paul anew.

But when we hear Paul anew, we still need to address the question of whether what he is saying is true.

Sure we do.

Do you think your counterideological dimensions of the biblical metanarrative—even in the ways they are present in Colossians—prove the truth of Paul's gospel?

No. They don't "prove" anything at all. What we attempt to suggest by pointing out these counterideological dimensions is that the postmodern suspicion of all metanarratives as metanarratives is an overreaction. There is at least *this* metanarrative that contains the resources within itself to undermine its ideological distortion. Not all worldviews are regimes of truth, we are saying. The worldview on offer in Colossians is the kingdom of God's beloved Son.

But is it true?

Well, what do you mean by that?

Is the gospel that Paul proclaims true in and of itself? Is it an accurate reflection of the Truth that stands outside of what he says about it, outside of his interpretation of it? Is the truth "out there," or is it, as Foucault puts it, something we produce?

Why is it important for you that the truth is "out there"?

Because if it isn't "out there," if truth isn't objectively verifiable in some way, then we end up with relativism. My worry here is that you are so concerned about the postmodern reaction to absolutes that you end up watering down the gospel and providing a text with no absolutes at all. In fact, if I read you rightly, you identified a belief in absolutes with the philosophy under attack, as if the message Paul is preaching isn't itself a presentation of absolute truth.

This is a very deep-rooted concern for you, isn't it?

Yes. I raised similar issues in our first dialogue. At that time you held off on talking further about the postmodern critique of objective truth. I'm putting the issue back on the table because the last chapter didn't resolve the issue for me.

Before we try to respond to your concerns, we have one question for you. In our first conversation we focused on various dimensions of the biblical understanding of truth as fidelity, as relational and covenantal. Does that approach to truth mitigate any of your concerns here?

Yes and no. I have to admit that was a new way of thinking about truth for me. And I have to admit that what you were saying certainly appeared to be biblical and struck all kinds of intuitive chords in me. But I am still uneasy. If truth is as relational as you are suggesting, then isn't that just one small step away from a thorough-going relativism? Isn't the conviction that the truth is "out there" absolutely essential to the claims of Christian faith?

This is very interesting. You recognize that this way of speaking about truth is biblical, and such an understanding of truth actually strikes intuitive chords, but still you are uneasy. What we are talking about has both exegetical and experiential warrant, but still it makes you anxious. You identify the source of that anxiety as fear of relativism and a need for truth to be "out there." You know, there is a name for this kind of anxiety. It is "Cartesian anxiety,"[1] and in response to it we want to offer you this word of pastoral advice: Fear not.

Easy to say, not so easy to live. I think relativism and subjectivism should strike fear into our hearts. Surely Allan Bloom was right when he wrote, "There is one thing a professor can be absolutely certain of: almost every student entering the university believes, or says he believes, that truth is relative."[2]

Well, the first question we need to ask here is, relative to what? If truth is relative, what is it relative to in the minds of these students who so offended Professor Bloom? Of course, the answers are legion: truth is relative to your gender, your social standing, your relative power in society, your time in history, your religious tradition, your race, et cetera, et cetera.

All of this relativity spells the closing, not the opening, of the American mind, says

---

[1] Richard J. Bernstein, *Beyond Objectivism and Relativism: Science, Hermeneutics and Praxis* (Philadelphia: University of Pennsylvania Press, 1983), pp. 16-17.

[2] Allan Bloom, *The Closing of the American Mind* (New York: Simon & Schuster, 1987), p. 25.

Bloom. But there is an interesting twist to all of this. You see, while Bloom's statement is offered as both an "objective statement" and a lament, the statement itself can actually be seen to prove the point of relativity—much to Bloom's chagrin.

Note, for example, that Bloom writes as a tenured professor who did not have a very good experience of teaching at Cornell in the 1960s. Indeed he is a white male professor who has no difficulty with using the male pronoun as generic for all students in his statement. It's as if he hasn't noticed that something called feminism has begun to reshape the face of American culture and scholarship. He is a professor with classical training and a classicist understanding of the world who is deeply disappointed that the discipline of reading the great books of the Western tradition has come into bad times during his career.

Our point is that Bloom's lament about relativistic students needs to be heard, understood and evaluated in terms that are relative to Professor Bloom himself. He makes his statement, indeed he writes his apologia for a classicist understanding of the world and the academy, not as a neutral observation from nowhere but as a lament uttered from a particular social, intellectual, professional, historical, political, racial and gendered perspective. His statement about relativism is, if you will, a relative statement.

I am not going to debate the details of Bloom's book with you—it is actually a little before my time—but surely your critique doesn't totally eliminate the concern he has raised about relativism. Even if it could be established that his own views are rather biased, that doesn't mean bias is okay. Rather, it means we need to be even more diligent in our attempts to be objective.

How do you know when you are being objective?

When you are submitting your ideas, beliefs and truth claims to rational evaluation.

That is precisely Bloom's position. He insists that reason has a "special claim" on us, that we need to submit to the "primacy of reason" because where the "rule of reason" holds sway the "voice of reason is not drowned out by the loud voices of . . . various 'commitments.'"[3] But despite all this commitment to reason, it takes only a little scratching at the surface of the rhetoric to discern all kinds of special interests at work in Bloom's book.

So is Bloom just inconsistent, or is the problem deeper?

The problem is much deeper. The problem has to do with commitment. Note that he says that the voice of reason must not be drowned out by the loud voices of various "commitments." Let us give you a postmodern translation of that: the hegemonic, absolute and finally authoritative commitment to reason trumps all other commitments.

Come again? How are you reconfiguring the relationship of reason and commitment?

It's really quite simple. All that we are saying is that the commitment to reason is

---

[3]Ibid., pp. 39, 259, 266, 261.

just that—a commitment. And this commitment has no more rational foundation to it than any other commitment.

Are you saying that we shouldn't be committed to rationality?

Yes, that is exactly what we are saying. We shouldn't be "committed" to rationality for two reasons. First, we should be committed to Jesus, not to rationality. And second, once we become committed to rationality we are engaging in idolatry, and promiscuous copulation with idols bears bad fruit in our lives.

Hold it for a second there. Surely the way we are "committed" to rationality is very different from what a commitment to Christ is like. And surely a commitment to being rational is not in itself any more idolatrous than being committed to being ecologically friendly in the ways I dispose of my waste.

Well, we think it is even possible to make an idol out of ecological concerns if they become the ultimate and final criteria by which all decisions in life are made. But this hasn't been the characteristic idolatry of Western culture, nor is it a very powerful temptation to most Christians. The commitment to reason, however, is the most insidious idolatry to capture the imagination of the church in its history. What is so insidious and ingenious about this commitment is that it has for so long managed to disguise the fact that it is a commitment.

Think about it for a moment. Seldom is the commitment to rationality ever recognized to be a commitment.[4] It is just being rational! But the heart of the postmodern deconstruction of this tradition of rationality has been to uncover how this commitment to rationality is a commitment, how this tradition of rationality is a tradition. This has been a central feature of the modernist commitment to reason; it has attempted to eschew all tradition, all historically situated perspective, in favor of a universal stance that leaves the religious wars and conflict of traditions behind. But this has been achieved only at the cost of elevating one tradition—the particular, historically situated tradition of the Enlightenment itself—over all other traditions.[5] We have not avoided tradition, we have not risen above historical particularity or the limitations of temporally and spatially bounded perspective; we have simply granted final and imperial hegemony to one tradition over all others.

And from a Christian perspective, the greatest tragedy is that the church has mostly bought into this lie.

I am still worried that this amounts to relativism. Is the truth "out there" or not? And can we know the truth objectively?

We understand your dilemma, and we recognize that there is a valid problem you

---

[4]For a powerful critique of the belief that reason is religiously neutral, see Roy Clouser, *The Myth of Religious Neutrality: An Essay on the Hidden Role of Religious Belief in Theories* (South Bend, Ind.: University of Notre Dame Press, 1992).

[5]Alasdair MacIntyre, *After Virtue: A Study in Moral Theory,* 2nd ed. (Notre Dame, Ind.: University of Notre Dame Press, 1984).

are addressing. Truth cannot be reduced to "what your peers will let you get away with."[6] This rather famous, though flippant, remark by Richard Rorty may cynically reflect much of what goes on in the academy, but it's much too reductionistic to satisfy a reflective Christian.

More than that. Christians believe that the truth is the truth even if your peers won't let you get away with it. Jesus died at the hands of his peers in the contest over truth.

Great point. Truth is, in the end, not reduced to a matter of agreement. After all, oppressive regimes love to manipulate agreement.[7] Truth is always contested. And if truth really does set us free, as Jesus said, then truth participates in a life-and-death conflict with oppression.

Then don't we need "objectivity" to avoid such oppressive paths?

Well, it hasn't worked so far; why should it start to work now?

What do you mean?

We mean that the twentieth century was the most violent century in history and that the most oppressive regimes we have seen have all claimed to be basing their power on nothing less than an objectively and scientifically based ideology. We need only think of the three holocausts of the 1940s and 1950s to see the point. Germany was at the pinnacle of Enlightenment civilization, and the gas chambers were seen as a scientifically sound and efficient way to bring a solution to the problem of the "genetically deficient" Jews. It was scientific objectivity and American know-how that produced and justified Hiroshima and Nagasaki. And it was in the name of scientific dialectical materialism that Stalin sent all dissenters to the gulags.

Our point is that "objectivity" does not set us free from oppressive regimes. In fact, every modern ideology has hidden behind the façade of scientific objectivity. To be postmodern is to say, enough! Enough of this kind of objectivity. Indeed, to be postmodern is to not be able to "get over" these holocausts, but rather to allow these events of radical evil to bring into question the whole Enlightenment ideology of objectivity.

Let's say that I can "get over it." Let's say that I can write off these admittedly terrible events as aberrations. It wasn't objectivity that brought the holocausts but the sinfulness of the human heart. If you will grant me that (even if we will still disagree), then again, what's the problem with objectivity?

The issue isn't objectivity as a particular kind of intellectual discipline used to perform certain kinds of intellectual exercises. In this sense, attempting to be "objective" when sitting on a jury or performing a physics experiment or trying to understand a complex argument is an important and necessary stance to take. Our problem is not with objectivity per se but with an *objectivism* that privileges a certain kind of objec-

---

[6]Richard Rorty, *Philosophy and the Mirror of Nature* (New York: Princeton University Press, 1979), p. 176.
[7]Noam Chomsky, *Manufacturing Consent: Noam Chomsky and the Media,* ed. Mark Achbar (New York: Black Rose, 1994).

tivity in the quest for something called "truth."

Objectivism makes the truth into a passive entity "out there" that is best discovered and grasped by means of the detached observation of knowing subjects who adopt a stance of neutrality. Objectivism posits that truth is achieved when we make propositions, statements and reports about the objects "out there" in the world that accurately *mirror* the way things are. These propositions must conform to the "canons of reason" and be reproducible "by other knowers operating by the same rules."[8] The rules, however, dictate that human subjectivity, historical context, religious beliefs and so on must not be allowed to influence the quest for truth. Objectivism, then, is an approach to knowledge that attempts to eschew all perspective rooted in particular times, places and traditions, in order to aspire to the "view from nowhere."

The problem is, there is no view from nowhere! There is no neutral standpoint. There is no detached objectivity. Knowing the world is not a matter of simply mirroring reality "as it really is," because we have no access to reality "as it really is" apart from the place in which we stand and the view or views of the world afforded to us from that place.[9]

Rorty's remark about truth being what your peers will let you get away with is flippant, but we think he is right when he insists that we have no access to something called "reality" apart from the way we represent that reality in our language. Since we never encounter reality *"except under a chosen description,"* we are denied the luxury or pretense of claiming any immediate access to the world.[10]

Note the problem here isn't whether there is a world that in some important respects is "out there." Postmodernists do not, as a rule, step out into moving traffic under the illusion that the world is just a matter of their perspective. The world may well be "out there"; the only question here is one of access. Do we have access to the world apart from perspective? The answer, we suggest, is no.

So are you saying that the whole modernist enterprise of objectivism is bankrupt?

That pretty much sums it up. And we are not alone in our judgment. We agree with Miroslav Volf when he writes:

---

[8]Parker Palmer, *To Know As We Are Known* (San Francisco: HarperSanFrancisco, 1983), p. 27.

[9]Rodney Clapp argues that "there is no such thing as safely and absolutely secured knowledge. Knowledge is particular and perspectival and as such is always contestable" (*Border Crossings: Christian Trespasses on Popular Culture and Public Affairs* [Grand Rapids: Brazos, 2000], p. 28).

Now we can already hear the Christian objectivist retort: "Are you sure that there is no such thing as safely and absolutely secured knowledge?" The implication, of course, will be that Clapp's statement is self-contradictory: he demonstrates precisely what he seeks to deny by making such a seemingly secure statement against the possibility of epistemological security. So let us reply to that rhetorical ploy right now. Even the statement that there is "no such thing as safely and absolutely secured knowledge" is itself "particular and perspectival, and as such . . . always contestable."

[10]Richard Rorty, "Pragmatism and Philosophy," in *After Philosophy: End or Transformation?* ed. Kenneth Baynes, James Bohman and Thomas A. McCarthy (Cambridge, Mass.: MIT Press, 1987), p. 57. Italics in original.

The agenda of modernity has overreached itself. Its optimism about human capacities is misplaced and its assumption that there is a neutral standpoint wrong. There can be no indubitable foundation of knowledge, no uninterpreted experience, no completely transparent reading of the world. A cosmic or a divine language to express "what was the case" is not available to us; all our languages are human languages, plural dialects growing on the soil of diverse cultural traditions and social conditions.[11]

We concur totally. If modernity overreached itself, then objectivism is an expression of intellectual pride. The problem is that we abandoned all epistemological humility.

What do you mean by "intellectual pride"?

Well, it takes a fair bit of pride to believe that autonomous human reasoning will bring about a sort of secular utopia. But there is more. You see, modernity is a cultural movement rooted in a reaction against Christian faith. Two things that Christian faith has a high regard for are finitude and fallibility. Modernity attempts to erase the limitations of finitude by means of a scientific method that seeks near-infallibility. That is the path of idolatry.

A Christian view of knowledge, however, has good reasons to be humble precisely because of finitude and fallibility. Finite knowing is always limited. We know the world only from a particular perspective or worldview that can function both to open up and to close down the world to us. Since we are fallen creatures, distortion and the tendency to close down knowledge are never far from our attempts to know the world. Postmodern suspicions of totality claims are well founded. Recognizing the situated particularity of all finite knowing and the universal brokenness of all knowers should engender a deep humility in our knowing that runs counter to the aggressive arrogance of objectivism.[12]

Then wouldn't the path to truth be just a more chastened, more humble objectivity?

That's a start, but it doesn't go far enough. You see, the issue of how we know something depends on what it is we are attempting to know. Philosophically, this is to say that ontology precedes epistemology; that is, our understanding of being precedes our understanding of knowing. For example, if the world is viewed in fundamentally materialist terms (the whole world is matter in motion governed by unbending laws), then certain kinds of techniques for knowing such a world will be given the status of orthodoxy, in the academy and in society at large. In a mechanistic world, scientific processes that are preoccupied with measurement, repeatability and law-

---

[11]Miroslav Volf, *Exclusion and Embrace: A Theological Exploration of Identity, Otherness and Reconciliation* (Nashville: Abingdon, 1996), p. 243.

[12]Richard Mouw has wisely argued that while we must be "actively working to discern God's complex designs in the midst of our deeply wounded world," that discernment must be rooted in an appropriate sense of "modesty and humility" (*He Shines in All That's Fair: Culture and Common Grace* [Grand Rapids, Mich.: Eerdmans, 2001], p. 50).

determined behavior are privileged over such things as intuition, myth and feeling. How you understand the nature of the world shapes how you go about knowing it.

So the question is, what kind of world is best known "objectively," and is that the world Christians inhabit if their imagination and worldview are biblically shaped? Let's try to get at this from the opposite direction. Instead of talking about the objectivists, listen to what Foucault has to say:

> We must not imagine that the world turns toward us a legible face which we would have only to decipher; the world is not the accomplice of our knowledge; there is no prediscursive providence which predisposes the world in our favor. We must conceive discourse as a violence we do to things, or, in any case as a practice which we impose on them.[13]

On one level this is a postmodern unmasking of the violence that is part of any aggressive knowing of the world, such as objectivism. But Foucault isn't simply engaging in a critique of modernity here. He is also saying something about the world. If the world does not turn a legible face toward us, if it is not something we can know and if there is nothing that helps us know the world, then knowledge is always a matter of violence and imposition.

However, in stark contrast to the anthropocentric preoccupations of both modernity and postmodernity, biblical faith affirms that creation is an eloquent gift of extravagant love. This is not a world of objects that sit mutely waiting for the human subject to master them. Rather, this a world of created fellow subjects, all called into being by the same Creator, all born of the Creator's love, all included in the Creator's covenant of creational restoration, and all responsive agents in the kingdom of the beloved Son. Philosopher Albert Borgmann describes biblical faith wonderfully when he speaks of "the eloquence of reality."[14] A creation called into being by the Word of God, created in, through and for Christ in whom all creation coheres, is not a mechanistic system but a dynamic, personal, living creation that has a voice. This eloquence is manifest in the witness of the stars (Ps 19), the groaning of creation (Rom 8:22), the joyful singing of the trees of the field (Ps 96:12), the vomiting and mourning of the land (Lev 18:24-28; Jer 12:4; Hos 4:1-3) and the hosannas of the rocks on the side of the road (Lk 19:40).

But surely the biblical language about creation singing, groaning and the like is all metaphorical.

Of course it is metaphorical! But the metaphors that one employs both bear witness to and give shape to one's view of the world. A materialist worldview that talks about the world in mechanistic terms also necessarily has to revert to metaphors— the metaphors of machines. So also do all worldviews.

---

[13]Michel Foucault, *The Order of Things* (London: Travistock, 1970), p. 316.
[14]Albert Borgmann, *Crossing the Postmodern Divide* (Chicago: University of Chicago Press, 1992), p. 117.

Could you give another example?

Well, consider the language used for forests. Whether we see trees as crops, or products, or habitats, or parks, or responsive agents in God's creation that have a capacity both to sing for joy and weep in travail will have profound effects on how we will go about getting to know trees. If biblical metaphors shape your understanding of creation, then something like a tree is no longer "merely an object in our world of experience but also a subject of relations in its own right. It is acted upon and it acts."[15] If this is true, then the categories of objectivism, with their penchant for distance and detachment from the "object" under investigation, become hopelessly inadequate.

Okay, let's say that our view of the world is profoundly shaped by these biblical metaphors of a responsive creation. I still don't understand what this means for how we know the world.

It means that we attempt to engender a listening epistemology. If the world is eloquent, if it speaks and if we share a profound kinship with all other creatures, then we need to develop the skills to listen more attentively to creation and to interpret what one author has described as "creational glossolalia."[16] This means we need a science that functions as "an invitation to engagement with nature."[17] That engagement calls for nothing less than a love for the subject.[18]

Remember that the Hebrew word for knowing (*yada*) doubles as the word used for sexual intercourse. It is this kind of knowing Paul is talking about when he prays that the Colossian Christians would be filled with all wisdom and understanding and the knowledge of God's will. Well, if our imaginations are biblically shaped, if we know the world, and know God, with this kind of holistic intimacy, and if we believe that all of creation is so known by God and is invited to know God in this way, then shouldn't that inform how we know the world? Why would we settle for the abstract coldness of detached objectivity when we had already tasted the tangible warmth of intimacy? Why would we think that disinterestedness is an epistemological virtue in a world suffused with intimate relatedness?

This is a relational epistemology rooted in a relational ontology. Since we confess that this relationship is rooted in the love of God, knowing this world is always at

---

[15]Charles Birch and John B. Cobb Jr., *The Liberation of Life: From the Cell to the Community* (Cambridge: Cambridge University Press, 1981), p. 123. See also Brian J. Walsh, Marianne Karsh and Nik Ansell, "Trees, Forestry and the Responsiveness of Creation," *Cross Currents* 44, no. 2 (Summer 1994): 149-62.

[16]Calvin G. Seerveld, *Rainbows for the Fallen World* (Toronto: Tuppance, 1980), p. 11. Scott Hoezee cites John Calvin's insistence that when we are contemplating the vast array of creatures in God's world, "we should not merely run over them cursorily and, so to speak, with a fleeting glance; but should ponder them at length, turn them over in our minds seriously and faithfully, and recollect them repeatedly" (*Remember Creation: God's World of Wonder and Delight* [Grand Rapids, Mich.: Eerdmans, 1998], p. 29). Such a "pondering" is at the heart of a listening epistemology.

[17]Evelyn Fox Keller, *Reflections on Gender and Science* (New Haven, Conn.: Yale University Press, 1985), p. 163.

[18]John Stott insists that the works of creation are to be the "subjects," although not the "object," of our worship ("The Works of the Lord," in *The Best Preaching on Earth: Sermons on Caring for Creation,* ed. Stan L. LeQuire [Valley Forge, Penn.: Judson, 1996]).

heart a matter of love. Such an epistemology of love is described beautifully by N. T. Wright: "The lover affirms the reality and the otherness of the beloved. Love does not seek to collapse the beloved in terms of itself."[19] And Parker Palmer writes that "the act of knowing is an act of love, the act of entering and embracing the reality of the other, of allowing the other to enter and embrace our own."[20]

Again, what does this look like in practice?

It's difficult to really say, because our imaginations have been so captivated by modernist objectivism that we have few role models. But there have been some. Think of John Muir, the father of the national parks system in the United States. Muir would sit down beside unfamiliar plants every day to "listen" to what they had to say. He combined the analytical scrutiny of his botanical training with an empathic sensitivity that attended to the particularity of the plant within its web of environmental relationships. Of trees he said, "I could distinctly hear the varying tones of individual trees—Spruce, and Fir, and Pine, and leafless Oak. Each was expressing itself in its own way—singing its own song, and making its own particular gestures."[21]

A similar perspective characterized the work of Nobel laureate Barbara McClintock. Her genetic analysis of corn plants was informed by a view of each plant as "a unique individual," a "mysterious other" and a "kindred subject."[22] For McClintock the complex intricacies and detailed analysis of plant genetics required the intimacy of a listening epistemology in order for her to "know" her subject in truth.

Or consider economists like Bob Goudzwaard and Harry de Lange, who listen to the groaning of creation in the form of ecological despoilation, the voices of the most indebted nations of the Two-Thirds World, and the complaints of the unemployed, homeless and working poor. These economists have developed an economics of care in the face of an economic orthodoxy that has made gods out of efficiency and growth.[23] This too requires a listening epistemology—hearing the voices drowned out by the dominant paradigm.

All of this hangs on commitment. McClintock, Muir, Goudzwaard and de Lange do their science from a committed place, from a particular perspective that they hold with something like faith.

And Christians know the world from a committed place, a place of faith.

---

[19]N. T. Wright, *The New Testament and the People of God* (London: SPCK/Minneapolis: Fortress, 1992), p. 64. For a similar attempt at a more holistic epistemology see Esther Meeks, *Longing to Know* (Grand Rapids, Mich.: Brazos, 2004).

[20]Palmer, *To Know As We Are Known*, p. 8.

[21]Quoted by Richard Austin in *Baptized into Wilderness: A Christian Perspective on John Muir* (Atlanta: John Knox, 1987), p. 29.

[22]Quoted by Jay McDaniel in *Of God and Pelicans: A Theology of Reverence for Life* (Louisville, Ky.: Westminster John Knox, 1989), pp. 86-87.

[23]Bob Goudzwaard and Harry de Lange, *Beyond Poverty and Affluence: Towards an Economy of Care,* trans. and ed. Mark R. Vander Vennen (Grand Rapids, Mich.: Eerdmans, 1994).

Yes, that's right.

But not everyone holds the same beliefs. People have different commitments. So they'll "know" the world differently.

If you keep going down this path you'll be a postmodernist.

Not so long as I am afraid of relativism. And isn't that where all of this leads if our knowing is rooted in faith without any court of appeal beyond it?

Well, if there is any court of appeal, it is God who sits as the judge. The deep blasphemy of modernity is that it made "reason" the judge. Now if you submit your faith claims to the adjudication of reason and you justify your belief in the sovereignty of God or the authority of the Bible on the basis of reason, take a close look to see what is *really* sovereign and where real authority lies. Reason ends up being the sovereign authority. The Bible has a word for this kind of thing: idolatry. We have taken a good dimension of human life—cognitive reasoning abilities—and made a god out of it, subjecting all else to its authority.

Again, what then is the alternative?

Recognize that all reasoning is rooted in what Nicholas Wolterstorff calls "control beliefs." In a revolutionary work in Christian epistemology, Wolterstorff took Immanuel Kant's enlightenment belief that religion should always be within the bounds of reason and put it on its head by claiming that the opposite was the case and reason was always within the bounds of religion. Reasoning is an activity done by real, honest-to-goodness alive human beings, not detached brains objectively crunching data like a computer. And these embodied human beings are, at their core, religious creatures who necessarily place ultimate faith and trust somewhere. It is from this place of faith and trust that people reason. Wolterstorff argues that "in weighing a theory one always brings along the whole complex of one's beliefs." The most foundational of these beliefs are "control beliefs."[24]

While modernists are "embarrassed" about such talk of beliefs and faith, postmodernists should have a more sympathetic view of the role of faith and belief in all knowing, since they have been so adept at uncovering precisely such beliefs where, by modernist standards, they were not supposed to be. This is what Richard Rorty calls a "final vocabulary."

> All human beings carry about a set of words which they employ to justify their actions, their beliefs, and their lives. . . . These are the words in which we tell, sometimes prospectively and sometimes retrospectively, the story of our lives. I shall call these words a person's "final vocabulary." It is final in the sense that if doubt is cast on the worth of these words, their user has no noncircular argumentative recourse.[25]

---

[24]Nicholas Wolterstorff, *Reason Within the Bounds of Religion* (Grand Rapids, Mich.: Eerdmans, 1976), pp. 62-63.

[25]Richard Rorty, "Ironists and Metaphysicians," in *The Truth About the Truth: De-confusing and Re-constructing the Postmodern World,* ed. Walter Truett Anderson (New York: G. P. Putnam's Sons, 1995), p. 100.

For Rorty, a final vocabulary is not something one acquires by means of objective metaphysical reflection. Rather, a final vocabulary is a poetic achievement—it is a way we learn to use certain kinds of metaphors to engage and describe the world. In this light we think it is no accident that Paul writes a poem as the heart of his letter to the Colossians. To say that Paul writes this epistle to shape and form the worldview of the young Christian community in Colossae is to say that he is trying to provide them with a final vocabulary that is alternative to the empire's.

Is there an appeal to anything beyond a final vocabulary—like maybe to the world?

If you are asking, are there any external criteria by which final vocabularies are evaluated, then Rorty would answer no. And we would agree with him. In other words, we do not believe that there are any metaworldview criteria by which all worldviews can be fairly evaluated. You see, whatever criteria one would propose would themselves be worldview dependent.

So we are left with relativism after all.

Only if relativism is the only option available when the so-called religious neutrality of objectivism has been unmasked for the particular worldview and particular final vocabulary it is. We don't believe this. In fact, to believe this is to grant an epistemological primacy to objectivism that we have been resisting throughout this whole dialogue. To use biblical language, don't allow the idol to set the terms of the conversation.

So what criteria are there to evaluate worldviews, and where do they come from?

To begin with, any criteria are worldview dependent, so the criteria for the truthfulness of a worldview we propose would not necessarily convince everyone. That said, we suggest the following. Any worldview, any final vocabulary or set of control beliefs, needs to

1. be comprehensive in scope. Is it truly a *world*view? Does it open up all of life, or are there serious blind spots, places where the worldview in fact seems to put blinkers on its adherents?

2. be coherent. By this we do not mean that the worldview must manifest the theoretical coherence of a system of thought (worldviews are not systems, nor are they theoretical in character) but that the vision of life hangs together and is not at war within itself.

3. sensitize its adherents to justice. Perhaps this is a very clearly Christian criterion, but it is, interestingly, shared by many worldviews, including postmodern takes on these issues. Does the worldview legitimate oppression of the other, or does it open us up to the needs, cries and pain of the other?

4. be humble about its own claims and therefore open to correction. If a worldview is held with a sense of universal finality, then it has been distorted into a totalizing ideology. Recognizing the fallibility and finitude of all human knowing should entail a humility in the manner in which we hold our final vocabularies and a will-

ingness to have our worldviews opened up and expanded (even corrected) through hearing the voices of other people who live out of other visions of life.[26]

5. be able to generate a praxis that puts into action the vision of life that is at the heart of the worldview.[27] A worldview that does not take on flesh in a particular way of life is no worldview at all.

Is this list offered in order of priority? Is comprehensiveness most important, then coherence, and on down the line?

No, it is not a matter of saying that if these five criteria are all fulfilled, in the order in which they are here presented, that then one has "justified" the truthfulness of the worldview. That would itself, be too mechanistic for us. And it isn't that each criterion is more important than the next. In fact, we think that given the way things usually function in human life, praxis is most important. When people are first attracted to another worldview it is usually because of the lived lives, the praxis, of the community that holds it. The truth of the worldview must be embodied if it is to be known.

In a provocative essay entitled "There's No Such Thing as Objective Truth, and It's a Good Thing Too," Phillip Kenneson argues that part and parcel of the objectivist's view from nowhere was detachment from any particular community in order to adopt a more universal standpoint. We have already seen this to be an impossible and bankrupt epistemology. Kenneson, however, pushes the point further and says that when Christian objectivists claim that the gospel is "objectively" true, they are also abandoning the church as the locus of the truth claims of the gospel.

> Too often appeals to the objective truth of the gospel have served as a means for the church to evade its responsibility to live faithfully before the world. In short, Christians insisted that the gospel was objectively true regardless of how we lived. The paradigm I am advocating frankly admits that all truth claims require for their widespread acceptance the testimony of trusted and thereby authorized witnesses. . . . What our world is waiting for, and what the church seems reluctant to offer, is not more incessant talk about objective truth, but an embodied witness that clearly demonstrates why anyone should care about any of this in the first place.[28]

Embodied witness—that is what we've been talking about all along.
Then it all hangs on us?
Well, an awful lot more hangs on us than we have been willing to admit.
And you are saying that this is the epistemology of Colossians?

---

[26]It needs to be added that this "other" could be the other of any other worldview or the "otherness" of the voice of God, Scripture and creation.

[27]Brian J. Walsh and J. Richard Middleton, *The Transforming Vision: Shaping a Christian World View* (Downers Grove, Ill.: InterVarsity Press, 1984), pp. 36-40.

[28]Phillip D. Kenneson, "There's No Such Thing as Objective Truth, and It's a Good Thing Too," in *Christian Apologetics in the Postmodern World,* ed. Timothy R. Phillips and Dennis L. Okholm (Downers Grove, Ill.: InterVarsity Press, 1995), p. 166.

Paul isn't writing a letter about epistemology, and the kinds of struggles we are having around objectivism would be quite alien to him. Nonetheless, we think that this embodied, relational epistemology of love is pretty close to what Paul is getting at.

I'd like to see some evidence from the letter.

Okay, look at this section from 2:1-4:

> For I want you to know how much I am struggling for you, and for those in Laodicea, and for all who have not seen me face to face. I want their hearts to be encouraged and united in love, so that they may have all the riches of assured understanding and have the knowledge of God's mystery, that is, Christ himself, in whom are hidden all the treasures of wisdom and knowledge. I am saying this so that no one may deceive you with plausible arguments.[29]

Paul is concerned with plausible arguments, so we can say that epistemology isn't all that far from what he is talking about. What makes an argument plausible? In this passage Paul has made plain the purpose of his letter to the Colossian Christians and their friends down the road in Laodicea. He is worried that they might be deceived by plausible arguments. Our question is, what would make an argument in favor of a worldview alternative to the gospel seem plausible to these young Christians?

Perhaps an answer to this question can be discerned in what Paul says more positively about his purpose in writing. He says that he wants "their hearts to be encouraged" and for their community to be "united in love, *so that* they may have all the riches of assured understanding." This is really quite remarkable when you think about it for a moment. Something like assured understanding—that is, a settled firmness in one's faith and a deep confidence in the truth of the gospel—is rooted, most foundationally, in encouraged hearts and the unity of love in the Christian community.

I'm not sure I'm getting it.

Well, it seems that Paul thinks that personal and communal despair and enmity within the community have the greatest power to rob us of assured understanding. It is hard to be sure about your faith when you are discouraged of heart and experience the Christian community as a place of bitterness and enmity.

Paul cuts through much of the intellectualism of contemporary Christian thought here. We tend to think that if we can help Christians get their theology right—even form a biblical worldview—then they will have a firm foundation for their knowledge of Christ. Now obviously we don't want to knock the importance of such reflection—we are writing this book as an exercise in worldview formation—but we want to make sure we have our priorities straight and a clear sense of how things work in human life. The lived experience of deep-rooted encouragement and communal love is foundational for assured understanding.

---

[29]Much of the exegesis that follows first appeared as a "Commentary" column by Brian J. Walsh in *Third Way* 24, no. 4 (June 2001).

I still don't quite get it. Why should such assured knowledge be so integrally tied to the quality of life in the Christian community?

Who is this knowledge about?

Christ.

Precisely. And who is this Christ but the incarnate Word of God, full of grace and truth? Remember, from a biblical perspective truth is not a correspondence between ideas and facts. Truth is embodied in a person. If incarnate truth is to be known in its fullness, then it must be met in the flesh. If this truth is not enfleshed in our lives and in the community that claims to bear witness to it, then it quite literally becomes unknowable to us. We cannot know this truth, we are stripped of assured understanding, because—well, we can't *see* it. In this respect, seeing—experiencing, touching and feeling—is indeed believing. Maybe that's why Paul is so concerned about people who have not seen him "face to face." They have not had the opportunity to see how he embodies the truth.[30]

When you put it that way, I can begin to see your point. Of the friends of mine who have abandoned Christian faith, very few of them stopped believing in Christ because of intellectual problems with the Bible or because they were seduced by some other worldview or belief system. Rather, they tend to abandon Christian faith because of the irrelevance, judgmentalism, internal dissension and lack of compassion they experience within the Christian community. Rather than finding the church to be the community that most deeply encouraged them in their struggles, they lost heart in their discouragement and lost their faith in the process. Rather than experiencing the church as the site of the most profound hospitality, love and acceptance, they felt excluded because of their doubts and struggles.

This is our point. What makes an argument that is alternative to the gospel plausible? Is it the internal consistency of the argument? Is it its scientific verifiability? Its political and economic power? No, what makes an argument that is alternative to the gospel plausible is the implausibility of the Christian community itself.

When the church fails to be a listening community, attentive to the cries of the poor, then the gospel is implausible and alternative social philosophies take on an air of plausibility. When the church becomes a site of bitter enmity while the world is spinning ever more quickly into war and violence, then the gospel is not only implausible, it is an embarrassment. In the face of such failures to be a community that embodies the truth that came to save the world, it is no wonder that alternative visions become more plausible to us.

The knowledge that Paul is talking about in this passage is "Christ himself, in whom are hidden all the treasures of wisdom and knowledge." One would think that once we have met in this Christ all the treasures of wisdom and knowledge, no mere imitation of wisdom, no false claims to knowledge, could ever be plausible to us

---

[30]We are indebted to Nik Ansell of the Institute for Christian Studies in Toronto for this insight.

again. But the implausibility of the opposition is dependent on the plausibility of the gospel as it is enfleshed in the historical and cultural life of the church.

So the church needs to put up or shut up.

That pretty well sums up a biblical epistemology. We need to struggle to discern Christian paths in politics, the arts, ecology, economics and all the rest of our life because the very plausibility of the gospel hangs on it. That's why Paul must move beyond his attack on the false philosophy in Colossians 2 to sketch out what Christian life looks like on the ground. The false philosophy will remain plausible as long as the Christian community is immature in its Christian character. So it is to further character formation that Paul turns.

But before we follow him into that discussion, let's return one more time to Paul's rhetorical attack on the "philosophy" in the rest of chapter 2 and ask how we might hear this text address the twenty-first century.

—8—

FAITHFUL IMPROVISATION
AND IDOLATROUS LIES

E arlier in this book we offered a targum on Colossians 1:1-14 in the face of what we
have called "disquieted globalization." At that time our imaginary reader interrupted
us with questions about exactly what we were up to in that rather odd genre. Our
discussion quickly focused on questions of exegesis. What is going on when we write
a targum that criticizes a view of truth as a "detached set of verities"? Why do we take
Paul's language of wisdom, knowledge and understanding in that text to be in conflict
with a modernist understanding of truth and knowledge? After our second targum,
on the Colossian poem, other questions arose. Why do we name names? Why do we
interpret language of "thrones, dominions, rulers and powers" as having sociocultural
reference? And our discussion of Colossians 2 in the face of what Foucault calls "regimes of truth" gave rise to more questions in the last chapter concerning truth. Can
we offer exegetical support for the rhetorical moves we are making when we contrast
regimes of truth with the kingdom of God's beloved Son? And what are the broader
implications of these moves for a Christian epistemology and ethic?

In a few pages we are going to offer another targum—this time on Colossians
2:8—3:4. While we certainly do not want to foreclose on any further discussion of
that targum, we want to anticipate a question we think may have been lying behind
our reader's concerns from the beginning. What kind of a hermeneutical method is
being employed when one writes a targum? How do we move from an ancient text
addressing a very different socioeconomic and cultural context to the contemporary
situation? Or to put it concretely in terms of our study of Colossians, what is going
on when, in our targums and throughout the book thus far, we make a jump from the
dynamics of the Roman empire in the first century to problematics of globalization
and postmodernity in the twenty-first century? What justifies these kinds of interpretive moves?

In response to these questions we need to describe the model of biblical authority we are employing, and then we need to indicate the principles that guide the actual writing of a targum.

An Unfinished Drama

It should be rather clear by now that we read a text like Colossians in the context of a broader narrative understanding of Scripture and the life of the church. Paul's thought, we have argued, is deeply rooted in the metanarrative of Israel. This meta-narrative provides the matrix of meaning within which Paul understands the story of Jesus and the life of the body of Christ. But this raises an important hermeneutical question. How does a narrative, indeed a metanarrative, function authoritatively in the life of the community that adopts this grand story as its own?

Borrowing from N. T. Wright, we find it helpful to understand the task of reading and living out of the biblical story in terms of an unfinished six-act drama.[1] If Act I consists of *creation,* where the Author's plot intentions are initially revealed and the scene is set, then Act II is the *crime* or the *break in the relationship,* the garden revolt in which we meet the first major incursion of plot tension or conflict in the story. The remainder of the narrative, which consists of the often tortuous route to the resolution of this tension, could be divided into four further acts. If Act III is the story of *Israel* and Act IV the story of *Jesus* (the decisive, pivotal act that begins to unravel the plot conflict at its deepest roots), then Act V is the story of the *church* beginning on the day of Pentecost, and the sixth and final Act is the *eschaton* or consummation in which the Author's narrative purposes are finally realized.

What is unusual about the biblical drama, however, is that the script breaks off in the midst of Act V, resulting in a sizable gap between Act V, scene 1 (the story of Pentecost and the early church), and the climactic finale of the drama in Act VI. While there are many clear indications of the shape that Act VI will take (the restoration of all of creation and the establishment of the kingdom of God on earth), there is no canonically established script that gets us from the beginning of Act V to the final Act VI. We are now living in Act V and are on the stage as actors in this divine love story that seeks to restore the covenantal bond between the Creator and his beloved cre-

---

[1] N. T. Wright first developed this approach to biblical authority in "How Can the Bible Be Authoritative?" *Vox Evangelica* 21 (1991), and employed it further in *The New Testament and the People of God* (London: SPCK/Minneapolis: Fortress, 1992), pp. 139-43. Following J. Richard Middleton and Brian J. Walsh, *Truth Is Stranger Than It Used to Be: Biblical Faith in a Postmodern Age* (Downers Grove, Ill.: InterVarsity Press, 1995), chap. 8, we modify Wright's five-act model into six acts. Recognizing that we compromise the Shakespearean overtones in so doing, we think it is theologically necessary to create a little more discontinuity between the history of the church and the consummation of all things in the second coming. Hence our distinction between act 5 and act 6 below. Beyond this, our position is essentially the same as Wright's. See also Brian J. Walsh, "Reimaging Biblical Authority," *Christian Scholar's Review* 26, no. 2 (Winter 1996): 206-20.

ation. Our task is to keep the drama alive and move it toward Act VI, recognizing that in this final Act God becomes the central actor again and finishes the play. But how do we move the drama forward? We turn to the Author and ask for more script. And the Author says, "Sorry, but that is all that's written—*you* have to finish Act V. But I have given you a very good Director who will comfort you and lead you."

So here we are, with an unfinished script, at least some indication of the final Act and a promise that we have the Holy Spirit as our Director (though not a new writer!), and we have to improvise. If we are to faithfully live out the biblical drama, then we will need to develop the imaginative skills necessary to improvise on this cosmic stage of creational redemption. Indeed, it would be the height of infidelity and interpretive cowardice to simply repeat verbatim, over and over again, the earlier passages of the play. The task is not so much a matter of being able to quote the earlier script as it is to be able to continue it, to imaginatively discern what shape this story now must take in our changing cultural context.

It is important to note, however, that such imaginative improvisation must be so deeply immersed in the text, and so completely absorbed in the story, that our imaginations are transformed and liberated by the vision the story sets before us. Deuteronomy 6:6-9 gives us a sense of how such an imagination would be shaped. According to Deuteronomy, every moment of every day is supposed to be filled with Torah, with the story of who God is and what God has done. We should so indwell this story that it permeates our very being, so that it is constantly on our tongue and at the heart of our daily discourse. The cadences of this tale should become our native tongue. The Deuteronomy text doesn't limit the impact of this story just to our waking hours—even when we are asleep we dream in its symbols and metaphors! This story is on our hands so that we see it enacted in all that we do, and on our forehead so that others see the story in all that we think and say. Our homes and our life in the public square are to be shaped by this story.

This story has come from somewhere and is going somewhere, and we can truly know where we are going only if we know where we have come from. In order to have vision we must have memory.[2] Indeed forgetfulness or amnesia is precisely what strips us of vision—without the past there can be no future. So our contemporary improvisation must be informed and directed by both a profound indwelling of the biblical vision of life and a discerning attentiveness to the postbiblical scenes that have already been acted out in the history of the church.

There is a certain dynamic in this approach to biblical authority that could be described as a dance between innovation and consistency. Our serious reading of Scripture must be characterized by fidelity to the thrust of the narrative and thus provide our life with a consistency and stability, a rootedness. At the same time, however, the

---

[2]Walter Brueggemann, *Hopeful Imagination: Prophetic Voices in Exile* (Philadelphia: Fortress, 1986).

Bible as an unfinished drama gives us freedom for historical innovation and thus a creative and imaginative flexibility in our historical responses. It is only by maintaining the essential relationship between stability and flexibility that we "may avoid the hazards" of both a rigid fossilization of our faith and a "deeper *relativizing* which gives up everything for a moment of [contemporary] relevance."[3]

As we read through the biblical story, it is clear that the Israelites themselves retold their stories with such fidelity and innovation. As the ancient Israelites encountered new situations, they remembered and interpreted their traditions in such a way that they engaged contemporary problems and concerns. Indeed without such dynamic interpretation, the texts and the traditions contained within them were seen to be incomplete.[4] There is therefore a dynamic of "inner-biblical exegesis" wherein various biblical traditions are creatively reworked in Israel's Scriptures. As the biblical story unfolds, the received traditions were "adapted, transformed, or reinterpreted."[5]

James Sanders describes this biblical dynamic as both stable and adaptable. This text tells the true story that provides the very identity of the believing community. Herein is stability. But that community can be sustained through time and changing circumstances only if the story is adaptable to those circumstances. Herein is flexibility. Sanders discerns in the constant telling, retelling, reciting of the story within the Bible itself precisely such an adaptability.[6]

Stability and flexibility, fidelity and creativity, consistency and innovation—these are key if a narrative text is to have any current authority in our lives. It seems that Paul himself understood something of these dynamics in Christian life and discipleship. Recall the wonderful mixed metaphors he strings together in Colossians 2:6-7: "As you therefore have received Christ Jesus the Lord, continue to live your lives in him, rooted and built up in him and established in the faith, just as you were taught, abounding in thanksgiving." Paul frames metaphors of solidity and stability (rooted, built, established) with metaphors of growth and dynamic change (live, or "walk," and abounding, or "overflowing"). Roots that do not bring forth dynamic growth and change are taking in no new sustenance and result in a stultifying conservatism that grinds the biblical narrative to a halt. Growth and change, however, if divorced from firm foundations and deep roots are tossed by every new cultural wind and lack identity and consistency.

What is true of Christian life in general is true of the task of reading and interpret-

---

[3]Walter Brueggemann, *The Creative Word* (Philadelphia: Fortress, 1982), p. 7.

[4]See Sylvia C. Keesmaat, *Paul and His Story: (Re)interpreting the Exodus Tradition* (Sheffield, U.K.: Sheffield Academic, 1999), chap. 1, and Michael Fishbane, "Inner-biblical Exegesis: Types and Strategies of Interpretation in Ancient Israel," in *The Garments of Torah: Essays in Biblical Hermeneutics* (Bloomington: Indiana University Press, 1989), pp. 4-5.

[5]Michael Fishbane, *Biblical Interpretation in Ancient Israel* (Oxford: Clarendon, 1985), p. 6.

[6]James Sanders, "Adaptable for Life: The Nature and Function of Canon," in *From Sacred Story to Sacred Text* (Philadelphia: Fortress, 1987), p. 19.

ing Scripture. Fidelity to the Scriptures, attempting to indwell this story and embody it in our lives, requires creative improvisation, and that improvisation, if it is to be Christian, requires fidelity.

Dynamic Analogy

So here is the question.[7] If we are called to faithful improvisation, how can we read a text like Colossians in such a way that its ancient character and historical distance from us is honored and not erased, yet it is as fresh and current as if it had been written this morning? Can the text have that kind of currency for us? How do we read this text and make it integral to our lives so that it can continue to speak anew to us?

If Christian life is a matter of living in an unfinished drama, then the improvisatory discipleship to which we are called requires something of a double immersion. We must be immersed in the biblical story—in this case Colossians—and we must be immersed in the world. Only through such a double immersion will we have any ability to discern faithful improvisations from missteps and dead ends. Rooted in a biblical vision of life, being formed in our very identity and character by this narrative, we attempt (in fear and trembling) to discern a path ahead. Such discernment requires something like the cultural analysis we have been engaged in throughout this book.

But how do we move from the issues addressed in a particular biblical text to particular contemporary issues? We propose that we adopt a stance of *dynamic analogy,* seeking to discern dynamic equivalents in our own cultural context to that which is addressed in the text.[8] Developing a similar approach with specific reference to Colossians 2:8-15, Andrew T. Lincoln says what is needed is that "we determine the analogies that underlie the metaphors [of the text] and then in an act of imagination . . . explore whether there might be striking contemporary images that will make graphic how Christ's death deals with whatever has a hold over people's lives in our world."[9] If Paul's concern in the text under consideration was to address practices and forces that had a hold on people's lives in Colossae, then our interpretation of the text must identify similar forces and practices in the late/post modern world. Our interpretation must be carefully attentive to the particularities of the text (not too quickly moralizing or generalizing without attending to the internal dynamics and tensions of the text) and must be rooted in the overall plot, tensions and resolutions of the biblical narrative. This is how the interpretation seeks to maintain the deep roots of fidelity and stability. But if the interpretation is to be serviceable to the listening community today, it must engage in the always risky business of identifying and naming

---

[7]Much of what follows first appeared in Brian Walsh's article "Late/Post Modernity and Idolatry: A Contextual Reading of Colossians 2.8-3.4," *Ex Auditu* 15 (1999): 1-17.

[8]On "dynamic analogy" see Sanders, "Adaptable for Life," p. 70.

[9]Andrew T. Lincoln, "The Letter to the Colossians," in *The New Interpreter's Bible,* ed. Leander Keck (Nashville: Abingdon, 2000), 11:627.

the rulers, authorities, principalities and powers of our own cultural context, thus addressing real temptations facing the contemporary Christian community. This creative improvisation requires serious cultural discernment.

The analogies we make in such an interpretation are always dynamic in at least two ways. First, no analogy, no imaginative connection, made between this ancient text and what we discern to be the principalities and powers of our own time is final. These are dynamic analogies—imaginative hunches that we hope are suggested by reading the world through biblical eyes and maybe even inspired by the Holy Spirit. Second, the analogies are dynamic in the sense that we are not suggesting to have found clear, strict one-to-one parallels between the concerns addressed in the text and the contemporary context. Our intentions are more humble than that and more tentative.

With this kind of interpretive approach, what might this ancient text have to say to postmodern cultural sensitivities in a context of global consumerism? We offer you another targum, extending our reading from Colossians 2:8 to 3:4.

(Re)citing Paul: Colossians 2:8—3:4 Meets Postmodernity

Make sure that no one takes your imaginations captive through a vacuous vision of life rooted in an oppressive regime of truth that parades itself as something other than a mere human tradition, as if it somehow had privileged access to final and universal truth about the world apart from Christ. You see, in Christ there is a radical presence of Deity, fully instantiated and situated in the particularities of history. And you have come to partake in that presence; that fullness is yours in Christ, who is the very source of every rule and authority that purports to have sovereignty over your lives.

In him you find your legitimacy, your entrance into the covenantal community, because in relation to him your real problem—a deeply rooted sinfulness manifest in violence and self-protective exclusion—is addressed and healed. The symbol of legitimacy is not the size of your stock portfolio or the number of hits your website gets daily, but that ancient rite of baptism in which you die with Christ to all these pretentious symbols of self-aggrandizement and are raised with him through a trusting and believing faith in the power of God, who raised Jesus from the dead.

Don't forget that you were once dead too—dead in the dead-end way of life that characterizes our cannibalistic and predatory culture. But now you are dead to that way of life, and God has made you alive with Christ by dealing with the real problem through radical forgiveness. You see, when the idolatrous power structures that bolster this oppressive regime of truth nailed Jesus to the cross and poured out all their fury on him, all of your debts were nailed there too. All of the ways the empire of death held you captive and robbed you of your life—the exhausting and insatiable imperative to consume, the bewildering cacophony of voices calling out to us in the postmodern carnival, the disorientation and moral paralysis of radical pluralism, the loss of self in a multiphrenic culture, the masturbatory self-indulgence of linguistic and societal games, the struggle to not become roadkill on the information highway—all of this is nailed to the cross, and you are set free. Let's not beat around the bush here. What is at stake in this conflict at the cross is indeed a power struggle. And Jesus takes precisely the principalities and powers that placed him on the cross—the idols of militarism, nationalism, racism, technicism, economism—and on that very cross disarms, dethrones, conquers and makes public example of them. In this power struggle, sacrificial love is victorious precisely by being poured out on a cross, a symbol of imperial violence and control.

If all of this is true, then don't allow the front-men of these vanquished powers to tell you what to eat and drink. Don't buy into the simulated grocery stores made to remind shoppers of an era in which shopping was more integral to community life. Don't be duped by advertising that tells you that various products are indispensable to constructing certain images and personas. This is all crap. They are still trying to captivate your imagination, to suck you into a globalistic regime of homogeneous consumption. Resist this Mc-World nightmare with all the strength you have! Avoid the Disneyization of your consciousness! This stuff has no substance to it, no depth. It suffers from the unbearable lightness of being. But in Christ we find substance, something of weight and power.

And don't get sucked into consumerist ideology when it comes dressed up in the clothes of Christian faith. A "new manly piety" just might be more of the same old patriarchal power-grabbing, capitalist legitimating stuff that we have seen being pimped both at the mall and in the consumer-friendly church. And all the charismatic enthusiasm in the world, rolling the aisles with holy joy, amounts to little more than puffed-up humanism if it is devoid of a radical transformation of entire human lives. So much religious renewal seems so attractive, so comfortable, so safe. But it is fundamentally secular. Its cultural imagination remains in captivity to an idolatrous worldview, and it has lost contact with the real source of life. It cannot sustain deep and radical growth that is subversive of the regimes of truth because it is not nourished from the source of all things—it does not grow with a growth that comes from God.

If with Christ you died in your baptism to the principles of autonomous consumerism that still hold the world captive, then why do you live in a way that suggests that you are still in the iron grip of its ideological vision? Why do you submit yourself to its regulations to consume as if there were no tomorrow, to live as if community were an impediment to personal fulfillment, to live as if everything were disposable, including relationships, the unborn and the environment? Why do you allow this deceitful vision to still have a hold on you? Don't you know that copulating with the idols of this culture is like climbing into bed with a corpse that is already decomposing?

Let's be clear about this: the postmodern vision of a laid-back pluralism where people hold only to their local narratives and abandon any attempt to make truth claims beyond their personal opinions or traditional communities may look like a way to end the violence, to respect otherness and stop marginalization and genocide, but it is in fact totally and irrevocably impotent to accomplish any of this. It has a mere appearance of wisdom; it has no depth of vision to discern between paths of wisdom and paths of folly. It looks like humility, and it will lay on the guilt pretty thick for the years of violence legitimated by various metanarratives (including the Christian one!), but it is not humble enough. It fails to see that the real issue of violence, exclusion and marginalization goes much deeper—it lies in the violence, rebellion and deceitfulness of the human heart. Self-imposed postmodern guilt trips can do nothing to heal the heart and can do nothing to stop the violence. Only the exhaustion of that violence on the cross can begin a real restoration.

You see, my friends, the postmodern incredulity of all metanarratives is well founded. The modernist metanarrative, of civilizational progress manifest in an aggressive conquering of colonized peoples, so-called scientific objectivism, a technological will to power and a market capitalism that would commodify all of life, deplete creational resources and create an ecological nightmare, was a tall tale—a lying, self-justifying ideological narrative. Yet humans are inherently storytelling creatures. And any local narrative will necessarily and invariably function as a metanarrative in the lives of those who hold it as their story.

So the issue isn't whether to live out of a metanarrative or not, but which metanarrative, and whose grand story. Without a grounding and directing story, no praxis is possible. That is why the crisis of storyless postmodern people, animated by little more than media- and market-produced images, is a crisis of moral and cultural paralysis.

But that's not the way it is with you, is it? You know which metanarrative brings life, don't you? You know whose grand story has set you free, don't you? Remember, in Christ you have died and were buried and have been raised to new life. His story is your story! Your identity and destiny are inextricably tied to the story of Jesus. And there is more to this story. The risen one is the ascended one, sitting at the right hand of God! If you have been raised with Christ, then, you must also make your own the rest of his story. Allow your imagination, your vision, your hope to be set on and directed by this image of kingly and restorative rule.

And this narrative of death, burial, resurrection and ascension still isn't the whole story. You see, Christ will return; his hidden rule in heaven will be revealed on earth—and just as his full glory will be revealed, so also will this be a revelation of *your* full glory as restored, renewed and fruitful image-bearers of God. When that happens, this whole business of exchanging your true glory as God's image-bearers for the kind of idolatry that continues to tempt and oppress you will come to a final and liberating end!

Do you feel incomplete, not yet fully who you are called to be? Good! Because you *are* incomplete, and any presumptuous sentiments otherwise would land you right back into idolatry. But we do live in hope. The struggle between the restorative rule of God in Christ and false, empty, deceitful pretenders to sovereignty—this struggle we experience deep within our bodies, our communities, our culture—will reach a final resolution in the return of Christ. Yes, we are waiting, but what we are waiting for is already stored up for us in Christ's heavenly rule and will be revealed in his coming. So live now, animated by that radically subversive hope.

What's the Deal with Idolatry?

You call that "humble and tentative"?

We knew you'd have another question.

Actually, I kind of appreciated your taking the time to anticipate some of my questions with that hermeneutical discussion that you used to set up this targum.

It was clear when we first talked that you had some misgivings about the whole enterprise of trying to read Scripture this way, so we thought it was important to put our cards on the table as clearly as we could. But you have a concern now about humility and tentativeness?

Kind of. The last thing you said before launching into the targum was that you were up to something more humble and tentative here, but I have a hard time reading this broadside against postmodernity, the church and pretty much all of capitalist culture as either tentative or humble.

Well, the tentative humility we were talking about was describing our use of dynamic analogy over against any attempt at final, direct analogy. Our approach is tentative because we are not saying in this targum that Paul had in mind the contemporary idolatries of militarism, technicism, racism and economism when he wrote Colossians. And we try to demonstrate humility by saying that this is not the only appropriate way to read this text in our context, nor the only improvisatory move available to us. It happens to be the one that we think is necessary and appropriate at this time.

It still didn't sound too humble or tentative.

Actually, there's a reason for that. There is another implicit hermeneutical principle we are working with that we neglected to mention above. We think that any rehearing of a biblical text in a different cultural situation must attempt to maintain the audacity and offense of the original text. If this section of the epistle to the Colossians has an in-your-face feel to it in its original hearing, then a faithful rehearing must have a similar emotional and rhetorical tone. We have attempted to maintain that tone.

So if the text was offensive and upsetting originally, then you won't be satisfied until you have elicited a similar response.

You got it.

Sounds like you're asking for trouble.

No, just trying to be faithful to the spirit of Paul's text.

Well, faithfulness to Paul's text is really at the heart of a larger question I have that has more to do with where the targum is coming from than where it is going. It seems to me you have imported something into the text that, as far as I can see, just isn't there.

What's that?

Idolatry. I kept hearing a refrain that contained the word idolatrous.

That's right, we mentioned "idolatrous power structures," various contemporary idolatries, "copulating with" idols and exchanging the glory of God for idolatry.

But there is no place in the text where Paul actually identifies the problem he is dealing with as idolatry. If you are going to make a dynamic analogy from an ancient text to a contemporary context, then don't you at least have to make sure that the ancient text is actually employing the language, ideas or metaphors you're using to make your analogy?

That is a very important question. You're right, we do focus the targum on contemporary idolatry. For example, instead of talking about a "philosophy," we refer to a "vacuous vision of life" and "regime of truth" that is described as deeply idolatrous and that takes our imagination captive.

That's another question I have. Why do you use the language of imagination here?

Because we agree with Walter Brueggemann's contention that one of the greatest dangers of our time is the "monopoly of our imagination."[10] Bowing before an idol, Brueggemann argues, is fundamentally a matter of "yielding the imagination" so that the world is experienced and interpreted in terms established by the idol. Consequently, "the key pathology of our time, which seduces us all, is the reduction of our imagination so that we are too numbed, satiated, and co-opted to do serious imaginative work."[11] This targum is, if you will, an exercise in subversive imagination that attempts to address head on anything that seeks to monopolize our imaginations, disempowering us from dreaming that things might be otherwise.

While the targum takes aim at various cultural realities that we perceive to be a threat to the faithful vitality of the Christian community—nationalism, advertising, certain kinds of charismatic experiences and manly pietism—the primary focus of the reading is on the various "isms" that continue to function as idolatrous forces, or "pretenders to autonomy," in our culture. A discernment of our times in terms of this particular constellation of idolatry is at the heart of the targum. Everything else revolves around this interpretation of the rulers, authorities, principalities and powers of our time. If this discernment of such idolatry is off the mark, then the whole targum fails.

Wouldn't the whole targum also fail if, in fact, the text that you are expanding or providing a gloss on does not actually talk about idolatry at all? The text under question (2:8— 3:4) never mentions idolatry. And the only reference to idolatry in the whole epistle doesn't come until 3:5. Isn't this a real exegetical complication that threatens to undermine the credibility of the targum, regardless of how good your spiritual discernment of contemporary idolatry may be?

That's true, idolatry is never mentioned in the text. But things like rulers and authorities (*archai* and *exousia* in 2:10, 15) and elemental spirits (*stoichea* in 2:8, 20) are mentioned.

That is correct.

So here's the question. How did the rulers and authorities (together with the thrones and dominions) that are created good, in, through and for Christ, in Colossians 1:16 become fallen, hostile and in need of reconciliation four verses later (1:20) and even need to be disarmed by the time we get to 2:15?

I don't know.

Well let's look at a theory from Tom Wright and see if it works:

What went wrong, then? Why are the powers so threatening? What went wrong was that human beings gave up their responsibility for God's world and handed their power over

---

[10]Walter Brueggemann, *Interpretation and Obedience* (Minneapolis: Fortress, 1991), p. 185.
[11]Ibid., p. 199.

to the powers. When humans refuse to use God's gift of sexuality responsibly, they are handing over their power to Aphrodite, and she will take control. When humans refuse to use God's gift of money responsibly, they are handing over their power to Mammon, and he will take control. And so on. And when the powers take over, human beings get crushed. (Conversely, when you see human beings getting crushed, it's usually because there are powers at work that humans are powerless to stop.)[12]

Well, it's a nice theory. And it even makes sense of the overall problem of how the principalities and powers came to be so destructively powerful. But Paul doesn't spell out the problem so explicitly in terms of idolatry.

Actually, we think that he does spell it out, but in a way that is indirect unless you have ears to hear. Consider this. What if we were to describe to you a text and tell you that it was a biblical text, and that this text is attacking something it characterizes as a force that takes people captive and controls them? The text insists that while this force has that kind of control over people's lives, it is, paradoxically, nothing in itself. Indeed it is an empty deceit, worthless and without any substance. Further, this force is described as a mere human construct, a humanly imposed way of thinking that is characterized by a puffed-up, arrogant spirituality, though in fact it is impotent, does not profit and has no real value. The text goes on to say that this force is fundamentally alienated from and antithetical to God and that it will be, and already has been, dethroned and vanquished as the impostor it is by the one true God. Now what kind of biblical text might we be describing, and what on earth might it be talking about?

It sounds like the Colossians text we're discussing.

That's true, but it also has all the telltale characteristics of Hebrew prophetic literature, though it could be a psalm. Now check this out. Consider Colossians 2:8-23. The typical biblical rhetoric against idolatry is paralleled, item by item, in Paul's rhetoric against the so-called Colossian philosophy.

- Hosea 5:4 insists that idolatrous spirituality makes repentance and the knowledge of God impossible; Colossians 2:8 describes a captivating philosophy, closing down options for a full-orbed discipleship.

- Paul's depiction of this philosophy as empty deceit (Col 2:8), a shadow without substance (2:17) that has a mere appearance of wisdom (2:23), clearly echoes earlier biblical judgment on idolatry as worthless, vanity and nothingness (Ps 97:7; 115:4-7; 135:15-18; Is 44:9; Jer 2:4).

- The prophets love to remind idolaters that their idols are constructed by humans (Ps 115:4; Is 2:8, 41:6-7; 44:11; Jer 10:1-9; Hos 8:4, 6; 13:2; Hab 2:18); the apostle repeatedly claims that the philosophy threatening the Colossians is a human tradition (Col 2:8), a human way of thinking (2:18) that imposes human

---

[12]N. T. Wright, *Following Jesus: Biblical Reflections on Discipleship* (Grand Rapids: Eerdmans, 1994), p. 18.

commands and teachings (2:20).

- Such a human tradition, says Paul, is puffed up without cause (Col 2:18) and deceives people by employing apparently plausible arguments (2:4, 8). Isaiah (44:18-20) and Hosea (4:6) say that idolatry results in a deluded mind and a fundamental lack of knowledge, and Habbakuk tells us that an idol is a "teacher of lies" (2:18).

- While Paul is clear that this philosophy with its imposed rules and regulations is of no value in checking the flesh (Col 2:23), the biblical witness insists that idolatry is impotent, without value, and does not profit (Ps 115:4-7; 135:15-18; Is 46:1-2; Jer 2:11; Hos 7:16; Hab 2:19).

- Idolatry is a matter of exchanging glory for shame (Ps 106:20; Jer 2:11; Hos 4:7; 7:16; 13:1-3; Rom 1:23); Paul says that the philosophy disqualifies, insists on self-abasement (Col 2:18) and promotes severe treatment of the body (2:23).

- Finally, Paul's proclamation that Christ disarms and triumphs over the rulers and authorities on the cross (Col 2:15) is clearly rooted in the prophetic confession that Yahweh is Lord and shares glory with no idols (Is 42:8; 48:11).

That's interesting. Those are pretty extensive parallels.

Essentially, we conclude from this analysis that the content of Paul's rhetoric against the Colossian philosophy not only legitimates but requires a reading of Colossians 2 in terms of idolatry. Whatever else we may say about the "philosophy" Paul opposes, we must say that it is idolatrous in character. Therefore any appropriation of this text in our time must similarly discern contemporary idolatry.

But that's not all. There are at least two other important parallels between Old Testament criticism of idolatry and our text. The first is that belief in and submission to idols is often criticized because Yahweh, not these false gods, is the Creator of heaven and earth (Ps 115:16; 135:5-7; Is 40:12-26; 44:9-28; Jer 10:11-16; 51:15-19).[13] In this light, it is no accident that the foundation of Paul's critique of both the empire and the Colossian philosophy is laid in the Christ hymn of 1:15-20, wherein all things—including thrones, rulers, dominions and powers—are created and redeemed in, through and for Christ.

A second dimension of the overall biblical understanding of idolatry that we find paralleled in our text is that idolatry is invariably connected to covenantal forgetfulness. The Decalogue is prefaced by a reminder that Yahweh is the God who led Israel out of Egyptian bondage, precisely because forgetting this foundational story always results in breaking the commandments prohibiting idolatry (and by extension, the rest of the Decalogue). Deuteronomy insists that the central temptation of a life of security and abundance in the land will be that Israel will forget its story of

---

[13]Interestingly, the same argument is found in Paul's sermon in Athens (Acts 17:24, 29) and in Romans 1:19-22; compare Deuteronomy 10:12-18.

liberation, will forget its liberating God and his healing word, and will embrace idols (Deut 4:23-28; 6:10-15; 8:11-19).

Paul's attack on the "philosophy" is animated by a similar concern to remember and not forget the story. His most potent weapon against the idolatrous worldview that threatens to take this community's imagination captive is precisely the retelling and remembering of the community's founding story. Having laid the foundation with reference to the local story of the reception of the gospel in Colossae (Col 1:3-8, 21), rooted that story in the new exodus effected through Christ (1:12-13), and then related that new exodus and the community's own story to the cosmic tale of the redemption of all things through the cross (1:15-20), Paul then delights to tell the story of Jesus' death, burial, resurrection, ascension and promised return (2:12-15, 20; 3:1-4). He retells this story in the heart of his attack on the philosophy because this philosophy, like all idolatrous worldviews, would take the community captive through a process of amnesia. Captivated by a system of regulations, visions and false spirituality, the community would forget its story and thus forget who they are as "saints and faithful brothers and sisters in Christ at Colossae" (1:2).

So let me see if I've got this right. Your targum is exegetically on good ground in focusing on idolatry because, first, the rhetoric of the chapter parallels Jewish diatribes against idolatry; second, the foundation of the critique is in a creation theology; and third, Paul counters the forgetfulness that leads to idolatry by rehearsing the Jesus story right in the midst of his attack on the philosophy. Is that it?

That's the argument in a nutshell.

And if Paul found it necessary to use an anti-idolatry rhetoric in this passage, then you believe any faithful contemporary reading must address the idolatries of our present culture.

That is precisely the point. Remember, idolatry is always a matter of images and imagination. In this targum we have attempted to read Colossians 2 in such a way as to engender an alternative imagination that subverts the rule of idolatry and sets us free to bear the fruit of the gospel in every dimension of our lives (1:6, 10). We have also attempted to indicate how postmodernity has a dehydrated imagination that is not up to the cultural crises and challenges that it has so clearly identified.

I guess the question is, can Christian faith do better? I mean, beyond Paul's rhetoric against the "philosophy" of his day, and your targum subverting contemporary idolatry and its postmodern cultural expression, does this "liberated imagination" actually bear fruit in everyday life?

Paul anticipates that question. That is why he deepens his reshaping of the Colossians' imagination in the next chapter by envisioning what this kind of renewed community looks like in its day-to-day praxis.

PART THREE

PRAXIS REMIXED

SUBVERSIVE ETHICS

AN ETHIC OF SECESSION

Halfway through dinner, our conversation partner announced, "I find that I am fundamentally incapable of making final or lasting decisions about ethical issues of any weight."

At this point it became clear that our "short" dinner break was going to be extended. We were in the middle of a day-long consultation on the way religion is covered in the print and electronic media, and our dinner partner was a young journalist. Twenty-nine years old and already the producer of a weekly three-hour radio news show that was broadcast nationally in Canada, Elanna was clearly on the fast track to a promising career. But our conversation about how religion fared in the media soon moved into a discussion of our own religious beliefs and ethical perspectives. That's when she made her rather remarkable ethical confession.

Confession is probably the right word. Not that she was looking for absolution (that would have required precisely the kind of ethical decision that she said she was incapable of), but it was a confession in the sense that this was a moral state of affairs that bothered her. She explained her predicament with some eloquence.

"As a woman, basically rooted in Gen X sensibilities, who works as a journalist at the end of the twentieth century, I find that whenever I'm about to come down on any issue—whether it be big issues of political, environmental or economic ethics or more personal issues of lifestyle, relationships and morality—I am paralyzed by the realization that there is always another angle on things. I'm paralyzed because it becomes clear that there are always other voices, other compelling arguments and alternative perspectives, that I need to take account of. And as I start really listening to these other voices, I end up losing my own. I have no voice in the midst of all of this. I am a listener, and when it comes time to speak, I am too confused by the plurality of options before me to be able to finally make a decision."

Notice that Elanna identifies four things that she thinks are relevant to her self-understanding. She refers first to her gender, then her generation, then her profession and finally her historical situatedness at the end of the twentieth century. While she may well acknowledge that her ethical predicament is not unique to her, she thinks it is relevant to note that she is a female, Gen X journalist living at this time in history. Perhaps the issues are heightened for her as a journalist, who professionally is always looking for new perspectives and conflicting ways of telling a story. That's just good journalism. But she also situates herself historically and generationally. When pressed, she explained that being Gen X essentially meant that she shared the postmodern aversion to final answers that rule out and marginalize all other voices. She would likely share literary critic Terry Eagleton's cultural analysis:

> We are now in the process of wakening from the nightmare of modernity, with its manipulative reason and its fetish of the totality, into the laid-back pluralism of the postmodern, that heterogeneous range of life-styles and language games which has renounced the nostalgic urge to totalize and legitimate itself.[1]

"Yes," Elanna would likely say, "modernity *was* a nightmare, and we need to adopt a more pluralistic approach to our lives. Yes, heterogeneity sure is better than the closedness of an imposed homogeneity." But her confession suggests that postmodern pluralism isn't as "laid back" as Eagleton suggests. Even if she wants to resist the "nostalgic urge to totalize," an inability to make ethical decisions of any import is disquieting for her.

She makes reference to her gender as relevant to how she understands her "inability" to make final or absolute ethical decisions. While she is probably not suggesting that all women, simply by virtue of their gender, are in the same ethical quandary, she is at least implicitly saying that in her experience at least, women are more concerned about hearing all sides than men. Perhaps she has in mind Carol Gilligan's groundbreaking work *In a Different Voice,* in which Gilligan argues that girls' moral development is much more communally and other oriented than the competitive, individualistic and autonomous orientation typical of boys.[2] If this is true, then Elanna's gender is indeed relevant to the problem she identifies. Not only does her profession, her generational sensibilities and her historical situatedness give her an aversion to absolutistic moral pronouncements, but her very gender gives her a proclivity to withhold judgment until all parties have had their say. Add it all up and she is, by her own confession, "incapable of making final or lasting decisions about ethical issues of any weight."

Elanna also thinks that this is a problem. And she is especially clear that it is a

---

[1]Terry Eagleton, "Awakening from Modernity," *Times Literary Supplement,* February 20, 1987. Quoted by David Harvey in *The Condition of Postmodernity: An Enquiry into the Origins of Cultural Change* (Oxford: Blackwell, 1989), p. 9.

[2]Carol Gilligan, *In a Different Voice: Psychological Theory and Women's Development* (Cambridge, Mass.: Harvard University Press, 1982).

problem when she finds herself faced with large ethical issues on either a societal/ cultural level or personally. Whether the issue is the ethical implications and foundations of market capitalism and its drive to globalization, or the question of military intervention, or whether she would sleep with a guy on their second date or have an abortion, Elanna really would like to be able to make some life decisions, even if this does require a "nostalgic urge" to totalize and legitimate herself.

Our conversation only explored the complexity of the problem for a while. But we left her with two thoughts. First, if we are faced with a whole generation of people who share this incapacity to make weighty ethical decisions of at least some finality, then that generation will experience disturbing levels of personal and societal paralysis. But that's not all. Second, if someone is unable to make these kinds of decisions, then someone else will come along and make those decisions on their behalf. This kind of ethical and societal paralysis establishes ripe conditions for a new authoritarianism—even a new totalitarianism—to emerge.

Anxious paralysis, however, is not the only ethical stance available in a postmodern world. Nihilism is another option.

A Vacant Space

The lecture on religion and postmodernity had just concluded, and the third-year semiotics class at the University of Toronto was dispersing. Eric came to the front of the classroom. We had already noticed Eric. He was the young man who obviously knew well the postmodern terrain we were traversing in our lecture; he also, well, kind of *looked* postmodern. At least he looked as if he'd be comfortable in the more anarchist side of the postmodern shift, given his torn blue jeans, black boots, body piercings, unkempt hair and beard. Our kind of guy! He had been thoroughly engaged during the lecture and discussion, and he wanted to continue the conversation. So he asked whether we had heard the French postmodern author Julia Kristeva when she had lectured on campus earlier in the semester. No, we replied, unfortunately we missed her lecture.

"Oh, that's too bad, because she also emphasized the importance of the 'other' in her lecture."

Trying to push the issue a little further, we asked, "Did she make any reference in her talk to Emmanuel Levinas?"

"No, why would she?"

"Well, Levinas is rather well known for his position on the ethical importance of the 'face' of the other, and it would have been interesting if Kristeva was at all indebted to Levinas' rather Jewish postmodernism. But if this isn't the case, then we are curious to know about how Kristeva spoke of the other and what she based her ethical position on."

"She based it on the only thing any ethical position can be based on—her personal experience as an immigrant, as an 'other.'"

"That seems a rather thin basis for a social ethic."

"But it's the only basis possible. Any appeal to something beyond personal experience would amount to a metanarrative, and we all know where that leads." (At this point we began to wonder who was trying to draw out whom in this discussion.)

"Well, yea, that's right," we replied, "and it seems to us that everyone does live their life in terms of one metanarrative or another, even if they are unaware of it, and even if they espouse a postmodern incredulity toward all metanarratives."

"I share that incredulity very deeply," Eric replied, "and if there's one thing that is clear from your lecture it's that you not only have a metanarrative but are also pretty sure that it's the true metanarrative and that everyone should adopt it." (Things were starting to get a little hostile.)

"You're right in discerning that we live our lives out of a particular metanarrative, and you have also discerned correctly that we hold to this story as the truth about the world. But we don't think that there is anything unique about us or about other religious people in this regard. Everyone, we contend, lives out of a metanarrative, everyone roots their life in a grounding worldview that directs their praxis and serves to legitimate that praxis."

"Not everyone! That is a totalizing move designed to reproduce everyone else in your own image. I don't have any worldview or ultimate beliefs that serve to legitimate anything. That's the point. To be postmodern is to acknowledge that the space in human life where these kind of ultimate beliefs reside remains permanently empty. It is a vacant space in which nothing will ever reside."

A vacant space of ultimacy. Nothing beyond himself that will direct his praxis in the world, and certainly nothing to legitimate his actions. In fact, for Eric, anything that would serve to give his life legitimacy would require surrendering personal responsibility. He must be his own legitimacy, with no appeal to outside standards.

Elanna and Eric are both postmodern, but they respond to the postmodern shift differently. They both live in a plural universe in which choice reigns supreme and life is devoid of any final legitimations. For Elanna, the multiplicity of choice and cacophony of voices result in an anxious paralysis. She experiences what sociologist David Lyon calls the "vertigo of relativity" and the "abyss of uncertainty."[3] Lyon puts it this way: "The postmodern context, with its emphasis on individual choice and consumer preferences, when mixed with epistemological doubt and pluralism, creates a heady cocktail that seems quickly to befuddle and paralyze."[4] Elanna is befuddled and paralyzed, and she doesn't like it. Everything in her postmodern world, indeed everything in her postmodern soul, tells her to "keep her options open," but she is finding this a confusing and lonely existence. Maybe she is looking for something

---

[3]David Lyon, *Postmodernity* (Minneapolis: University of Minnesota Press, 1994), p. 61.
[4]Ibid., pp. 64-65.

or someone to believe in. Maybe she is contemplating closing down some of her options by entering into a commitment.

Eric, however, would see this as a loss of nerve. Worse than that, closing down the options, making a commitment to one vision of life, is nothing less than a "yearning for the absolute."[5] He would find himself in David Harvey's depiction of the postmodern condition: "Postmodernity swims, even wallows, in the fragmentary and chaotic currents of change as if that's all there is."[6] Lyon describes this as embracing chaos: "Babel is valued; disorientation becomes a virtue. . . . No more nostalgia for the fixed, stable and permanent."[7] This is Eric's world. Disorientation is virtuous, because any vision of life that would provide a legitimating orientation will invariably oppress. If morality is a lie and truth is a fiction, then "the Dionysian option of accepting nihilism, of living with no illusions or pretense, but doing so enthusiastically, joyfully, is all that remains."[8]

There is something very attractive about both Elanna and Eric. Elanna's candid confession of paralysis and her longing for something that would animate her life and give it direction—without violently excluding other voices—gives expression to a deep desire for commitment and faith. And while Eric's aggressiveness can be a little off-putting, there is also something refreshing about a young man who really does attempt to live his life without illusion or pretense.

Befuddled paralysis or joyful and unpretentious nihilism? Yearning for the absolute or embracing chaos? These are two of the options facing a postmodern generation that has been shaped by the concomitant collapse of modernist epistemological self-confidence and the rise of a media-saturated, choice-driven global consumerism.

Does the epistle to the Colossians have anything to say to this kind of a world? Let us take a look at the third chapter of Paul's epistle.

Ethical Direction for a Postmodern Culture?

So if you have been raised with Christ, seek the things that are above, where Christ is, seated at the right hand of God. Set your minds on things that are above, not on things that are on earth, for you have died, and your life is hidden with Christ in God. When Christ who is your life is revealed, then you will also be revealed with him in glory.

Put to death, therefore, whatever in you is earthly: fornication, impurity, passion, evil desire, and greed (which is idolatry). On account of these the wrath of God is coming on those who are disobedient. These are the ways you also once followed, when you were living that life. But now you must get rid of all such things—anger, wrath, malice,

---

[5]Robert Jay Lifton, "The Protean Style," in *The Truth About the Truth: De-confusing and Re-constructing the Postmodern World*, ed. Walter Truett Anderson (New York: G. P. Putnam's Sons, 1995), p. 132; excerpted from Lifton's *Boundaries: Psychological Man in Revolution* (New York: Vintage, 1970).
[6]Harvey, *Condition of Postmodernity*, p. 44.
[7]Lyon, *Postmodernity*, p. 76.
[8]Ibid., p. 8.

slander, and abusive language from your mouth. Do not lie to one another, seeing that
you have stripped off the old self with its practices and have clothed yourselves with the
new self, which is being renewed in knowledge according to the image of its creator. In
that renewal there is no longer Greek and Jew, circumcised and uncircumcised, barbarian, Scythian, slave and free; but Christ is all and in all!

As God's chosen ones, holy and beloved, clothe yourselves with compassion, kindness, humility, meekness, and patience. Bear with one another and, if anyone has a complaint against another, forgive each other; just as the Lord has forgiven you, so you also
must forgive. Above all, clothe yourselves with love, which binds everything together in
perfect harmony. And let the peace of Christ rule in your hearts, to which indeed you
were called in the one body. And be thankful. Let the word of Christ dwell in you richly;
teach and admonish one another in all wisdom; and with gratitude in your hearts sing
psalms, hymns, and spiritual songs to God. And whatever you do, in word or deed, do
everything in the name of the Lord Jesus, giving thanks to God the Father through him.
(Col 3:1-17)

You know what's happening right now, don't you? William is ducking because he
just saw an absolute racing toward his face, Elanna's befuddlement just got worse
(though she *wants* to hear this ancient voice), and Eric is asking, "What fascist wrote
this bit of oppressive moral instruction?"

This text presents a postmodern reader with a whole host of problems. To begin
with, the issue at hand—for Elanna and Eric *and* William—is lived life in *this* world,
but the text seems to counsel an otherworldliness that is decidedly alien to the consciousness of any self-respecting postmodernist. Not only is the otherworldliness
alien, so also is the language in which it is couched. What does it mean to "set your
minds on things that are above"? What's this business of "hidden" and "revealed"?
And what on earth is this talk of "glory" all about?

As the text proceeds, postmodern suspicions about the meaning of this otherworldliness get confirmed. We need to think about that which is "above" because the
author seems to be driven by a vision that loathes the human body. "Put to death
whatever is earthly." What did Paul have in mind? Sex, of course! And when he moves
from sex to language and emotions, it would appear that anything that involves passion, deep feelings and anger must be replaced by—what? Bourgeois passivity and
politeness? If Paul is counseling a self-loathing passivity, then is he just legitimating
such an ethic with his heavy-handed language about disobedience and "wrath" from
above? From a postmodern perspective, this looks like a repressive totality system out
to keep people in line. How could such a perspective ever be construed as an answer
to the postmodern ethical quandary?

Even when the text moves to more positive instruction, it certainly looks like this
is an ethic rooted in an absolutistic worldview. It's not as if any of these injunctions
are negotiable. Rather, it would seem that the whole point of this ethical instruction,
the ultimate direction the discourse is taking, is toward a totalitarian subservience—

"*whatever* you do, in word or deed, do *everything* in the name of the Lord Jesus, giving thanks to God the Father through him." Never mind the patriarchal character of the language; just take a look at how all-encompassing, uncompromising and totally controlling all of this is.

Here's the question. Can a text like Colossians 3 still be heard as good news in a postmodern culture that has justifiably grown suspicious of absolutistic totality thinking? The rest of this chapter attempts to answer this question affirmatively.

What Kind of Ethic Is This?

Let's begin with the question of whether this is a life-denying, otherworldly ethic. Doesn't the text counsel us to abandon life in this world, with all of its historical situatedness, conflicting voices and intransigent ethical crises, for the sake of contemplation of higher, "heavenly" things? Isn't this what Paul is getting at when he says we need to set our minds on things that are "above," not on earthly things? And doesn't this give us an ethic that is so heavenly minded that it is no earthly good?

If this is what Paul were arguing, he would be demonstrating a profound inconsistency. Hasn't he just expended considerable rhetorical energy attempting to discredit precisely such a dualistic spirituality that is exclusionary and absolutistic? To a Christian community that might find something attractive in such a worldview, Paul insists that they are dead to this kind of otherworldly, totalitarian spirituality because they have been made alive in Christ, who sets us free from all of its rigidly imposed laws. Buying into such a spirituality, Paul argues, is to lose touch with Christ, who is the head, "from whom the whole body, nourished and held together by its ligaments and sinews, grows with a growth that is from God" (Col 2:19).

Notice again the metaphor of the "body" that is used here for the church. We have already noted that this is a term plundered from the empire. In 1:18 Paul says that the cosmic Christ is "the head of the body, the church." Bringing together these three words—head (*kephalē*), body (*sōma*) and church (*ekklēsia*)—was politically explosive, we suggested, because Paul is replacing Caesar with Christ and replacing the empire, with all its symbolic and historical power, with the church. The church is a body politic, he is saying, subject to an alternative sovereign. And he roots all of this in an understanding of the cosmos as created in, through and for Christ.

This creationally rooted political theology is at the very foundation of Paul's attack on the otherworldly spirituality in Colossians 2. Add to this the statement that the "fullness of deity dwells bodily" not only in Christ but in the Colossian believers (2:9-10), and you have a vision of life that is anything but dualistic.

Since Paul is an author of considerable insight and coherence, we should at least begin by giving him the benefit of the doubt and assuming that he does not contradict himself. If his whole argument is based upon such a radical affirmation of creation and a subversively this-worldly understanding of the gospel reconciling "all things, whether on earth or in heaven" (1:20), then how could he now change his tune and counsel an otherworldly spirituality and praxis in chapter 3? Wouldn't such a move undermine everything he has argued thus far in the letter?

Close attention to the text demonstrates that Paul is proposing no dualistic ethic. In fact the very language that he uses continues the theme of creational affirmation. "So if you have been raised with Christ" (3:1): this is a resurrection ethic, and resurrection is decidedly bodily. To affirm Christ's resurrection and to identify the Christian community with it is to affirm the goodness of embodied existence in this world. Remember how Paul put it in his poem. Christ is "the firstborn from the dead." He is the second Adam, leading the new humanity embodied in the church. This may sound exclusivistic to postmodern ears, but it is hardly otherworldly. Resurrection is this-worldly language. In this chapter Paul is offering the community the contours of a resurrection ethic for life in this world.

But this raises the question of Paul's use of heaven language. Why does an ethic purportedly for life in this world counsel meditation on that which is above? This is a very important question, and how we understand this passage hangs on it. Look closely at the text. Paul tells the readers/hearers to look above, and he tells them why: "If you have been raised with Christ, seek the things that are above *where Christ is, seated at the right hand of God*" (3:1). Why should we "seek things that are above"? Because Christ is seated there at the right hand of God.

Elanna can't make ethical decisions or embark on a path of praxis with any security because there are too many voices, too many claims on her life, and for her imagination there is nothing that matters above all else. Praxis has everything to do with *sovereignty*. What or who is sovereign in life? What is it that matters the most? What provides both a bedrock for our life—a sense of ultimacy—and an orientation? Paul's language here is all about sovereignty. The Risen One is "seated at the right hand of God," says Paul. In terms of the story he is telling, the Risen One ascends to be with the Father, and from there he begins to exercise his legitimate rule over all of creation. In this story, ascension language is sovereignty language.

The clear allusion to Psalm 110:1 ("The LORD says to my lord, 'Sit at my right hand until I make your enemies your footstool'") speaks of "a king exalted to dominion but whose rule is not yet fully achieved."[9] There is a hiddenness to Christ's rule, Paul is saying. The enemies, the principalities and powers, have not yet been brought into total submission to this Christ.

So what's going on here? In Colossians 2:15 Paul says that Christ "disarmed the rulers and authorities and made a public example of them" on the cross, thereby exercising his sovereignty, his rule over the empire. This rule was established on the

---

[9]Luke Timothy Johnson, *The Writings of the New Testament: An Interpretation,* rev. ed. (Minneapolis: Augsburg, 1999), p. 147.

cross and confirmed in the resurrection. Rome could not keep Jesus in a grave sealed by the empire. But Paul, Lydia, Nympha, Onesimus and everyone else involved in the church at Colossae knows that Rome still rules the empire through military might, socioeconomic structures and the captured imaginations of its subjects. What then do we say about the rule of Christ? We say something about the ascension. This rule is hidden in heaven. It is hidden because the earthly powers have not yet fully submitted to Christ.

Here is a classic paradox in Paul's thought. Christ has *already* defeated the powers, but his reconciling rule has *not yet* been fully established in history. The purpose of this section of the letter to the Colossians is to help them navigate life in the dynamics of that "already and not yet." Indeed, this already/not-yet that characterizes the unfinished story of Jesus also characterizes the unfinished story of his followers. They have *already* been raised with Christ, they have *already* died to the empire, but their life is hidden with Christ and has *not yet* been revealed.

So what does it mean to "seek the things that are above, where Christ is seated at the right hand of God"? Perhaps it means something like "Set your hearts on and allow your imagination to be liberated to comprehend Christ's legitimate rule." Maybe it also means something like "Allow your vision of life, your worldview, your most basic life orientation, to be directed by Christ's heavenly rule at the right hand of God." To use language from the Gospels, perhaps it means "Strive first for the kingdom of God" (Mt 6:33). Thus the passage sets us off on a direction that can lead us only to its conclusion. What begins with seeking things that are above ends with "And whatever you do, in word or deed, do everything in the name of the Lord Jesus, giving thanks to God the Father through him" (Col 3:17). Seeking that which is above is a matter not of becoming heavenly minded but of allowing the liberating rule of Christ to transform every dimension of your life. The rest of the chapter attempts to give some direction along the way.

But perhaps there is more going on with Paul's language of our life's being "hidden with Christ in God" than just the already/not-yet dynamics of the story he is telling. You see, if there is one thing any empire wants you to believe, it is that "what you see is what you get." Empires project a sense of all-embracing normality. Not only do empires want us to think that reality is totally composed of the structures, symbols and systems that have been imperially constructed, they also want us to believe that the future holds no more than a heightened realization of imperial hopes and dreams. Whether it is the eternal rule of the Pax Romana or the complete marketization of all of life and every corner of the globe, the result is the same. In fact, sameness is what it's all about. Empires "are caught in an ideology of continuity and well-being in which human reality is covered over by slogans."[10]

---

[10]Walter Brueggemann, *Hopeful Imagination: Prophetic Voices in Exile* (Philadelphia: Fortress, 1986), p. 43.

It doesn't matter whether the slogan is "Pax Romana," "There is no lord but Caesar," "Just do it," "Free trade," "Travel the information highway," "Ride the long boom of economic prosperity," or President George W. Bush's post-9/11 declaration "You are either with us or you are with the terrorists." All these slogans create a discourse that is constructed by and for the empire. The empire insists on a continuity between its present and any imaginable future. Things must remain the same or at least develop along the same ideological path. But Paul here shouts out, "You are dead to all of these lies of the empire! You are not bound by the ideology of sameness! You are no longer held captive by the powers that want to maintain the present brokenness, oppression and idolatry! What you see is *not* what you get—there is much more!"

Again the issue at hand is the imagination of the Colossian Christians, and by extension our imagination. If we can think only in terms of what the empire will allow us to see, then the empire has taken our imagination captive. What Paul is struggling for is the ability to see "just beyond the range of normal sight."[11] Praxis requires vision and orientation. But if all the maps are provided by the empire, if all the reality we can see is what the empire has constructed as reality for us, then our praxis will never be creative, and it will never be subversive to that empire.

Paul insists that not only is the redemptive rule of Christ hidden, so is the true meaning of our lives if we follow this Christ. We don't allow the empire to captivate our imagination and set the final terms of our praxis in the world, because we can see a kingdom that is alternative to the empire. And we don't allow the empire to close down the possibilities of the future for us, because we can see a future in which what is hidden is revealed—both Christ's rule and our own completion and fullness. Such a vision provides a hope that not only is subversive to the empire but also provides a radical direction for Christian praxis.

So what kind of an ethic is this? It is a *resurrection* ethic that refuses to bow the knee to the empire and its idols. It is an *ascension* ethic that refuses to be subject to the principles of normality. It is a *liberated* ethic that dares to imagine a world that is alternative to the present brokenness. It is an *eschatological* ethic of hope that engenders a this-worldly praxis in anticipation of a coming kingdom.

But Eric wants to know whether this is also a hegemonic ethic imposed by an author with totalitarian designs. And William still suspects that this ethic comes flying at him with another long series of oppressive absolutes. These questions must be addressed. So we add two more adjectives to describe this ethic. In contrast to William's absolutes, this is a *relational* ethic. And as a partial answer to Eric (though he won't be convinced by it), this is a *narrative* ethic.

---

[11]An image borrowed from Bruce Cockburn's song "Hills of Morning," from the album *Dancing in the Dragon's Jaws,* ©Golden Mountain Music, 1978.

A Relational Ethic

Absolutes, William insists, are unrelated, timeless truths that come at us as nonnegotiable moral laws. Is this what Paul is up to in the third chapter of Colossians? Partially yes, mostly no. Yes, there is something nonnegotiable about what he has to say. Paul is not proposing that we have an open conversation about whether a Christian ethic really needs to avoid idolatry or practice forgiveness. But this does not mean he is simply serving up a series of absolutes that demand our obedience. Rather than laying absolutistic moral laws on us, Paul offers us an intimately relational ethic.

Consider again the kind of language that Paul has been using. In the critique of the philosophy in chapter 2, he crafts his words carefully to bring out the relationship the Colossian Christians have with Christ. From 2:9 to 2:15 Paul uses the phrase "in him" (or its parallel "with him") seven times. "In him" the fullness of deity dwells bodily (2:9). And you have come to fullness "in him" (2:10). "In him" you were circumcised with a spiritual circumcision (2:11). When you were buried "with him" in baptism, you were also raised "with him" (2:12). And God made you alive together "with him" (2:13) because God triumphed over the rulers and authorities "in him" (2:15). This profound relationality is foundational to Paul's ethic. Since you have been raised "with Christ" (3:1), your life is hidden "with Christ in God" (3:3), and when Christ "who is your life" is revealed, then you also will be revealed "with him" in glory (3:4). Because you are so deeply identified "with Christ" and so profoundly shaped in who you are by being "in Christ," your way of life will reflect that relationship. It is not so much a matter of Christians behaving in a certain way just because God said so or because it is good for you. Rather, Paul is saying that Christians live a certain way because of the matrix of relationships that characterize new life in Christ, and especially because of a living relationship with the risen Christ, whose story of death and resurrection we share.

A Narrative Ethic

The targum offered in the last chapter suggested this gloss on Colossians 3:1-4:

> So the issue isn't whether to live out of a metanarrative or not, but which metanarrative, whose grand story. Without a grounding and directing story, no praxis is possible. That is why the crisis of storyless postmodern people, animated by little more than media- and market-produced images, is a crisis of moral and cultural paralysis.

Alasdair MacIntyre has written, "I can only answer the question 'What am I to do?' if I can answer the prior question 'Of what story or stories do I find myself a part?'"[12]

Praxis—that is, human culture-forming, ethical behavior in daily life—is narratively grounded because we act out of who we are. And who we are—our character—

---

[12]Alasdair MacIntyre, *After Virtue: A Study in Moral Theory,* 2nd ed. (Notre Dame, Ind.: University of Notre Dame Press, 1984), p. 216.

is formed by the story of our life and how that story is interpreted in the context of larger stories or grand narratives. There are two important points here: praxis depends on character, and character is narratively formed.[13] Even in a postmodern world, "the human mind continues to think in terms of stories" and "naturally seeks to order experience, looks for explanations of sequences of events, is attracted to dramas."[14] There is, if you will, a "narrative quality" to human experience.[15] In "allowing ourselves to adopt and be adopted by a particular story, we are in fact assuming a set of practices which will shape the ways we relate to our world and destiny."[16]

Adopting and being adopted by a particular story is what Paul's letter to the Colossians is all about. Paul struggles with all the strength that is in him (Col 1:29) to help this young community become secure and deeply grounded in the story of Jesus that these converts have already adopted as their own. And he does so by telling them that this story has also adopted them. They can dwell in the story and allow it to reshape their imagination because it is not a story that simply happened to someone else but is now *their* story. They are now *in* this story, and on this basis Paul calls them to adopt a set of practices that are consistent with it.

By identifying the life of these converts with every significant event in the story of Jesus, Paul reinforces the idea that the community has been adopted by the story. In the last chapter we noted how Paul counters the preferred amnesia of idolatry by retelling the story of Jesus in the midst of his attack on the philosophy in Colossians 2:8—3:4. In typically Jewish style, Paul doesn't just retell the story but ties the identity of the present generation of believers to their participation in that story. *You* have "died" with Christ (3:3), *you* were "buried" with him (2:12), *you* are "raised" with him (2:12; 3:1), *you* set your minds on Christ, "seated at the right hand of God" (3:1), and *you* "will be revealed with him" (3:4) in his coming. Death, burial, resurrection, ascension and second coming—five decisive markers in the story of Jesus. Paul tells us that Christian identity and praxis are rooted in our identification with and participation in these events. The story of Jesus is our story. This is the story that shapes our character and sets the direction of our praxis.

In the letter to the Colossians Paul is trying to shape this community in such a way that the story of Jesus, rooted in the metanarrative of Israel, becomes the medium in which they live. The third chapter of the epistle attends to that set of skills, the virtues and practices that are formed by living in this story. "Biblical narrative logic simply

---

[13]Stanley Hauerwas, *Vision and Virtue: Essays on Christian Ethical Reflection* (Notre Dame, Ind.: Fides, 1974).

[14]Walter Truett Anderson, *Reality Isn't What It Used to Be* (San Francisco: Harper & Row, 1990), p. 183.

[15]Stephen Crites, "The Narrative Quality of Experience," in *Why Narrative? Readings in Narrative Theology,* ed. Stanley Hauerwas and L. Gregory Jones (Grand Rapids: Eerdmans, 1989), pp. 65-88.

[16]Stanley Hauerwas and David Burrell, "From System to Story: An Alternative Pattern for Rationality in Ethics," in *Why Narrative? Readings in Narrative Theology,* ed. Stanley Hauerwas and L. Gregory Jones (Grand Rapids: Eerdmans, 1989), p. 186.

demands a specific, visible people, a society or societal remnant, a *polis.*"[17] And this people, this polis, must live in certain ways and not in other ways if it is to be true to its own narrative, its own story. The rest of this chapter attempts to unpack something of what this looks like.

An Ethic of Secession

This is the opening stanza of Wendell Berry's poem "The Mad Farmer, Flying the Flag of Rough Branch, Secedes from the Union."[18]

> From the union of power and money,
> from the union of power and secrecy,
> from the union of government and science,
> from the union of government and art,
> from the union of science and money,
> from the union of ambition and ignorance,
> from the union of genius and war,
> from the union of outer space and inner vacuity,
> the Mad Farmer walks quietly away.

Berry—Kentucky farmer, Christian poet, novelist, essayist—counsels an ethic of secession. Where power and science are united with money, ambition is driven by ignorance, and human genius is employed in the service of war, there is only one option, says Berry: walk quietly away. From such unions we must secede. But secede to what or whom?

> From the union of self-gratification and self-annihilation,
> secede into care for one another
> and for the good gifts of Heaven and Earth.

Secession is always from something in order to join with something else. Berry calls us to secede from a culture of concomitant self-gratification and self-annihilation (they are, in the end, the same thing) into a life of care—for one another and for the good gifts of creation. This is an ethic of gift in the face of a culture of commodity. It is such an ethic of secession that Paul proposes in Colossians 3:5-17.

We can already see the look of incredulity on the faces of Elanna, Eric and William. You call this a secessionist ethic? Take a look again at that first verse: "Put to death, therefore, whatever in you is earthly: fornication, impurity, passion, evil desire, and greed (which is idolatry)." That may be secessionist if what you want to secede from is bodily, sexual life! But why would we ever be tempted to buy into a self-loathing rejection of our sexuality?

---

[17]Rodney Clapp, *A Peculiar People: The Church as Culture in a Post-Christian Society* (Downers Grove, Ill.: InterVarsity Press, 1996), p. 90.
[18]*The Selected Poems of Wendell Berry* (Washington, D.C.: Counterpoint, 1998), pp. 162-63.

Such a question, though, is fundamentally wrong-headed. You see, if Paul is rejecting anything here, it is precisely the self-loathing sexuality that has characterized the so-called sexual revolution. Paul offers an ethic of sexual life in the face of sexual death. He calls the Colossian Christians to "put to death" a certain pattern of human relationships because those patterns are themselves deadly.

To begin with, notice that Paul is clearly rooting this ethic in the narrative that has preceded it. Since Christ "is your life" and since that life will be revealed with him in his return (3:4), "put to death, therefore, whatever is earthly" (3:5). There is, says Paul, a life-and-death struggle going on here. Clearly rooted in the covenantal traditions of Israel, in which Moses placed before the Israelites two options—life and prosperity or death and adversity—Paul here sets up a stark contrast between a lifestyle that leads to death and one that is life-giving. Like Moses, he passionately calls this community to "choose life" (Deut 30:15-20). And just as the life Moses called Israel to choose is "in the land," so also is Paul's ethic an ethic for this-worldly community building. All the sins or vices he attacks in this section of the letter are things that tear community apart, and all the virtues he recommends enhance its growth and flourishing.

So when Paul says "put to death . . . whatever in you is earthly," he is not counseling otherworldliness. Rather he is saying, "Abandon the false allegiances, the pretentious sovereignties, that have held you captive. Secede from the unholy unions of power and money, genius and war, outer space and inner vacuity, that distort your lives." Put to death what is earthly *means* put to death the remaining vestiges of an imperial imagination and praxis that still have a grip on your lives. Put all of this to death before it kills you.

Seceding from Imperial Sexuality

This is a very interesting list that Paul composes. While he is concerned primarily with promiscuous, self-gratifying expressions of sexuality outside of trothful commitment (fornication), the distortion of personal character that such practice entails (impurity), uncontrollable and insatiable sexual appetite (passion), and a desire directed only to self-gratification (evil desire), he most evocatively concludes this whole list with "greed" or covetousness, which he is quick to identify with idolatry. Sexual sin, greed and idolatry—what is the relation among these? Why end a list of sexual sins with an economic sin? Because sexual sin is fundamentally a matter of covetousness, an insatiable, self-gratifying greed that has the control and consumption of the other person as its ultimate desire. Sexual sin is sin not because it is sexual but because it is invariably covetous. It replaces the pleasure and sexual enjoyment of two people in a loving relationship with a self-centered gratification of sexual longings that can never be fulfilled apart from commitment. Such sin breaks the back of trust that is at the heart of community, and it is *a community* that Paul is striving to build here.

For imaginative resources to understand the dynamics of sex and greed we turn again to Berry, but this time to his essays rather than his poetry. Berry believes that sexual love is at the heart of community life. "Sexual love is the force that in our bodily life connects us most intimately to the Creation. . . . It brings us into the dance that holds community together and joins it to its place."[19] Both marriage and community require "trust, patience, respect, mutual help, forgiveness—in other words, the *practice* of love, as opposed to the mere *feeling* of love."[20] This practice is rooted in respect of the other, mutuality, self-sacrifice and responsibility for the consequences of sexual love.

In stark contrast to this vision of sexuality, Berry describes something he calls "industrial sexuality." "Like any other industrial enterprise, industrial sexuality seeks to conquer nature by exploiting it and ignoring the consequences."[21] This is the sexuality of the marketplace, in which "everything could be sold on the promise of instant, innocent sexual gratification, 'no strings attached.'"[22] While the ideal of the commercial economy is "the completely seducible consumer, unable either to judge or to resist," committed, trothful love exists in an economy of a "momentous giving" in which there is nothing to sell. Berry prophetically concludes, "If the community cannot protect this giving, it can protect nothing—and our time is proving this is so."[23]

When Paul says, "Put to death . . . fornication, impurity, passion, evil desire, and greed" he is desperately trying to protect this kind of momentous giving. In a world that finds it difficult to protect anything, this text calls us to an ethic that not only secedes from the commodification of all of life but also embodies a sexual praxis that is subversive to industrial sexuality. Think for a moment about how none of Paul's injunctions make any sense to a world in which all of life is reduced to marketable commodities. In a world in which sexuality is a matter of erotic encounters "with no strings attached," Christian marriage is all about "tying the knot." In an anxious world of covetousness and competition, we choose a path together rooted in trust, intimate self-giving and a shared life. In place of utility we see affection, corporate control is replaced by personal risk, and disposable consumption gives way to enduring enjoyment.

An ethic of sexuality rooted in community and fidelity subverts the fragmented world of cold economic efficiency by embracing the ridiculously inefficient life of committed love. Lovers held together in public vows of covenantal commitment have no interest in accumulating a multiplicity of intimate relationships, because they believe that their relationship, their love, is *enough*. And there is no word more offensive to a culture driven by unlimited economic growth than the word *enough*.

Late modernity and its so-called sexual liberation has given us little more than a sexual atmosphere of predation and recrimination—the most devastating opposite of

---

[19]Wendell Berry, *Sex, Economy, Freedom and Community* (New York: Pantheon, 1993), p. 133.
[20]Ibid.
[21]Wendell Berry, "Feminism, the Body and the Machine," in *What Are People For?* (New York: North Point, 1990), p. 191.
[22]Berry, *Sex, Economy,* p. 134.
[23]Ibid., pp. 134, 138.

the trust in which sexual and communal life can flourish. We live in a sexual waste-land that bears only the bitter fruit of violence, loneliness, betrayal and broken hearts. The ethic Paul is offering us here promises the good fruit of love, mutuality, fidelity and healing. John Francis Kavanaugh notes that "in a culture which portrays life-commitment as impossible and undesirable, men and women who enter into per-sonal covenant by mature and free consent are taking a radical stance."[24] It is to such a radical stance, we believe, that this text directs us.

We need to be clear that sexual practices are always of a piece with broader socio-economic and cultural practices. It is precisely an ideology of unlimited economic growth that engenders an insatiable sexual practice of unlimited partners. This is why Paul connects sexual sin with covetousness. In our culture, the unrestrained eco-nomic greed of global market capitalism pimps sexual promiscuity along with its en-tertainment products, communications systems, automobiles and running shoes.

You see, if the empire is all about economic growth driven by a lifestyle of con-sumption, then *all* of life becomes a matter of consumption—including our sexual life. Multiple sexual partners is just good capitalism.

Let's be clear about this. The neoconservative economic policies that took hold of Western societies at the end of the twentieth century, together with their free-trade global agenda, function as the ideological ground and legitimation of a cultural ethos of sexual promiscuity—regardless of how personally pious the perpetrators of this kind of economics might be.

By identifying sexual sin with covetousness, this text gives us the resources to cut through this kind of duplicity. There is no point in getting all morally absolute about sexual promiscuity if Christians are screwing around with the same consumerist way of life as everyone else. This text gives us the language to identify what is going on here for what it is: idolatry.

Seceding from Imperial Idolatry

We have already argued that Paul has been addressing questions of idolatry through-out his critique of the philosophy in chapter 2 of the epistle. The only explicit refer-ence to idolatry, however, is found here in Colossians 3:5, and it comes as no surprise that this idolatry is connected to covetousness and sexual sin. In the prophetic tradi-tion idolatry invariably resulted in sexual sin wedded to economic injustice.[25] Paul's

---

[24]John Francis Kavanaugh, *Following Christ in a Consumer Society: The Spirituality of Cultural Resistance* (Maryknoll, N.Y.: Orbis, 1981), p. 132.

[25]For example, consider Hosea. This prophet condemns Israel for an idolatry (2:5, 11-13; 4:12-19; 8:4-6; 10:1-6; 11:2; 13:2; 14:8) that results in a lifestyle of sexual sin (4:18; 7:4) and economic injustice and violence (4:2; 6:8-9; 7:7; 10:4, 13-14; 12:1, 7-8). Moreover, the dominant metaphor in this prophet for Israel's sin is adultery or whoredom (1:2-9; 2:1-13; 4:10, 12; 5:3-4; 6:10; 9:1), which results, Hosea in-sists, in fruitlessness and barrenness (4:10; 8:7; 9:11-14, 16; 10:1, 8; 13:14-15).

ethic of secession from all idolatry is deeply rooted in Israel's faith. In biblical perspective, human beings are constitutively, structurally image-bearers. That is to say, human beings are created in such a way that they invariably root their lives in an ultimacy that is authoritative, grounding and directive of all that they do. We are, if you will, *Homo religiosus*. Created in the image of God, we can do nothing other than seek a God (or god) to serve and image in the totality of our life, especially in our stewardship of the rest of creation.[26] If we turn away from our covenanting Creator, this does not mean we are no longer image-bearers. Rather, such turning away will necessarily result in idolatry: we will find something in the creation to serve as our god, something to which we give ultimate allegiance. We will take some thing, or more usually some dimension of creatureliness that is in itself a good gift from the Creator, and make it into our god, thereby distorting it (whether it be fertility, national or ethnic identity, security, scientific analysis, technological power or economic growth) in such a way that what was good comes to have demonically evil power over our life.

There is, however, a certain dynamic to idolatry. Graven images not only usurp our proper place as God's image-bearers, they also serve to transform our lives in their own image. After describing the impotent sterility of idols, the psalmist offers this observation and curse: "Those who make [idols] are like them; so are all who trust in them" (Ps 115:8). Idols may well be human products, but they act back on their producers with demonic power. Once humans relinquish their calling to image the Creator in covenantal faithfulness and give their hearts to false images, alien gods, it is inevitable that their lives will be deformed in the image of the idol. Kavanaugh puts it this way: "Remade in the image and likeness of our own handiwork, we are revealed as commodities. Idolatry exacts its full price from us. We are robbed of our very humanity."[27]

So why must we put to death a life of sexual immorality rooted in a culture of insatiable consumption? Because such a life is ultimately idolatrous and it will kill us. The path of idolatry is a path of death because it (a) cuts us off from Jesus Christ, who is our life, (b) cuts us off from who we are as God's proper image-bearers and stewards of all of life (including sexuality and economic activity), and (c) cuts us off from what we really desire. The goodness, meaning and enduring pleasure of our sexuality is lost and killed in a promiscuous, self-gratifying lifestyle. The life-giving, fruit-bearing joy of creation is lost and killed by a consumptive, greedy and idolatrous worldview that leaves our lives fundamentally barren.

It is not surprising that God is incredibly angry about all of this. It is not surprising that Paul then says, "The wrath of God is coming on those who are disobedient" (3:6). This God, after all, is the Creator God of life who comes to redeem all of creation and to

---

[26]For a powerful analysis of the biblical notion of humankind created in the image of God, see J. Richard Middleton, *The Liberating Image* (Grand Rapids, Mich.: Brazos, 2005).

[27]Kavanaugh, *Following Christ*, p. 26.

restore his image in humanity. Is it any wonder that he is angry when the object of his love is constantly distorted and abused through idolatry? If this God did not respond to such a travesty, such a mockery of his good creation, with wrath, we would wonder how deep his love really went. Wrath is the right response to screwing around with idols. Wrath is the appropriate emotion in the face of adulterous infidelity. God's loving wrath can be seen both in the very brokenness, dehumanization and barrenness that such idolatry produces in sociocommunal life and in eschatological judgment. This is necessary if we are to live in a moral universe. Those who have been sexually brutalized, economically oppressed, ecologically raped and reduced to commodities in a world system of global consumerism need to have a court of appeal before which they can bring their legitimate complaint. That court, Paul assures them, is the judgment seat of God.

Paul concludes this discussion of sexual/economic sin by saying, "These are the ways you also once followed, when you were living that life" (Col 3:7). That is the life of the empire—not just the Roman empire or the empire of global consumerism but the empire of darkness. In Christ we have come to say to the darkness, "We beg to differ."[28] We have seceded from the empire of darkness and been granted citizenship in the kingdom of the beloved Son. So why would the death-dealing lifestyle of the empire have any more appeal for us?

While some readers of Foucault might see in this text an attempt to create docile bodies that are acted upon but do not themselves act, the opposite is the case. In the face of an imperial consumerism that commodifies sexuality and renders us disempowered and docile, this text calls us to live sexual lives that are set free by trothful commitment and that are therefore subversive to the empire.

The Discourse of Violence

We could summarize what we have just said about Colossians 3:5-7 thus: Economic brutality always results in sexual brutality, and that idolatry is the brutality of all brutalities—doing violence to our very identity as creatures called to image our God. An ethic of secession calls us out from such a culture of violence.

The next list of vices Paul offers brings our attention to this kind of violence as it is manifest in our feelings and our language. After reminding the Colossians that they no longer live according to the empire, Paul says, "But now you must get rid of all such things—anger, wrath, malice, slander, and abusive language from your mouth. Do not lie to one another, seeing that you have stripped off the old self with its practices" (3:8-9). Is this a call to bourgeois passivity and middle-class politeness? Is this a repression of any and all strong emotions and deep feelings that might be uncomfortable? Given the fact that Paul's whole discourse in this letter, especially in chapter 2, is full of strong language and emotions and that just two verses ago he has spoken of God's wrath, it

---

[28]Mary Jo Leddy, *Say to the Darkness, We Beg to Differ* (Toronto: Lester and Orpen Dennys, 1990).

would seem that middle-class politeness and the repression of emotions is not what he is talking about here. Rather, he is talking about the discourse of violence that serves to justify the sexual and economic violence he calls us to abandon.

Just as Paul opposes sexual sin and economic injustice that reduce other people to objects of sexual greed and economic exploitation, so he is here concerned with the emotional dynamics of such objectification. The anger, wrath and malice he warns us against all entail the reduction of another person to an object of contempt with whom we have no connection, no compassion, no community. Such seething anger results in a rage that justifies any and all malicious intent in relation to other people. These are violent construals of other people that necessarily result in their marginalization and exclusion at best and violent extermination at worse. In a world of jihad, ethnic cleansing and tribal holocausts, together with the objectification of the poor, drug addicts, homosexuals, immigrants and visible minorities, Christians do well to secede from a culture of such violence.

Violent emotions give rise to violent language. The objectifying and demonizing of the other in anger, wrath and malice comes to expression in slander and abusive language. Interestingly, slander is the translation of the Greek word *blasphemia*. To bear false witness against someone, or to cast a whole community in a negative light that would justify violence against them, is blasphemy, says Paul, because it slanders people who are also created in the image of God. Such slander necessarily gives way to abusive language that dehumanizes its object.

Now we need to ask ourselves, is Paul really concerned about suburban politeness here? Is he concerned about cleaning up the language of the local youth so that they stop using *fuck* as a punctuation mark in their discourse? Well, yes, that is an abusive form of language—and it is uncreative. But is that the only kind of abusive language we face? Or might there be another kind of violent discourse that is integrally tied to the kind of market sexuality we were addressing above?

Isn't there something deeply abusive and dehumanizing about the way advertising uses sex to sell everything from condos to cars? Isn't the ubiquitous presence of advertising in our lives and the total domination of space by commercial life—on the Net, on the street, on television, in the elevator, at the urinal—an abusive invasion of consumerism into the very warp and woof of our daily lives? And from a Christian perspective aren't slogans like "Just do it," "Coke is the real thing," "The American Way of Life" and "Homeland security" all discourses of violence? After all, the American way of life and national security serve to legitimate the escalation of global warming through withdrawing from the Kyoto Accord, and isn't this an act of anticreational and unneighborly violence? Doesn't Nike's slogan come part and parcel with sweatshops in the Third World?[29] Aren't all of these slogans em-

---

[29]Naomi Klein, *No Logo: Taking Aim at the Brand Bullies* (Toronto: Vintage Canada, 2000), pp. 198-201.

bedded in an imperial agenda of global domination?

In his 1994 annual report, the president of Campbell's Soup Company wrote, "As I look forward to the future, I shiver with business excitement. That's because Campbell's Soup Company is engaged in a global consumer crusade."[30] This is a crusade to capture both consumer taste and culinary practice. There is nothing that Campbell's would like better than to have more markets of people who will forget how to make soup for themselves and will become dependent on a can. Or consider this moment of enlightened business ethics from David Glass, CEO and president of Wal-Mart: "Our priorities are that we want to dominate North America first, then South America, and then Asia and then Europe."[31] Business development is couched in the language of domination. This, we contend, is the abusive language of our time. When "free trade" means corporate sovereignty, "fiscal responsibility" means that the poorest in our society have to put up with even less, "quality of life" means quantity of consumption and the "liberation" of Iraq means the expansion of the Pax Americana, then our language has been debased and deformed into a discourse of deceit that justifies violence.

Or consider an advertising campaign from McDonald's which tells us, "There's a little M in everyone." The global arches have so branded our consciousness that we all bear their image. For Christians who confess that humans bear the image of God, this language is both abusive and blasphemous.[32]

If we want to find abusive language and identify the discourse of violence of our time, we are terribly short-sighted if we don't look beyond the obscenities of the street or the schoolyard. It is in the double-speak of corporate executives, the spin of politicians, the come-on of the advertisers, the cultural lies of the pharmaceutical companies and the biotech firms, and the false humanistic optimism of the cybernetic revolution that we meet abusive language in this culture. Paul is saying that this was the discourse of our past life in the empire, the discourse of lies that we were liberated from when the "word of the truth" came to us (1:5). And sometimes we need to employ strong language in the face of such lies.

Vancouver street poet and activist Bud Osborn opens up new vistas for us when it comes to the nature of abusive language. In his poem "Amazingly Alive" Osborn tells the remarkable story of his experience of resurrection in "a culture teachin ten thousand ways/ways to die/before we're dead."[33]

---

[30]Quoted in *Adbusters: Journal of the Mental Environment* 31 (August/September 2000): 2.

[31]Ibid.

[32]The sad fact is that this campaign, though abusive, is telling the truth. Eric Schlosser notes that 96 percent of American schoolchildren can identify Ronald McDonald and that "the Golden Arches are now more widely recognized than the Christian cross" (*Fast Food Nation: The Dark Side of the All-American Meal* [New York: HarperCollins, 2001], p. 4).

[33]Bud Osborn, "Amazingly Alive," in *Hundred Block Rock* (Vancouver, B.C.: Arsenal Pulp, 1999), pp. 7-11.

so here I am
here we are
amazingly alive
against long odds
left for dead
north america tellin lies
in our head
make you feel like shit
better off dead

so most days now
I say shout
shout for joy
shout for love
shout for you
shout for us
shout down this system
puts our souls in prison

say shout for life
shout with our last breath
shout fuck this north american culture of death

shout here we are
amazingly alive
against long odds
left for dead
shoutin this death culture
dancin this death culture
out of our heads

In an ancient culture of death, the apostle Paul mounted a rhetorical attack on those forces that would separate us from Christ who is our life. He used the biblical language of idolatry to make his point. In a late modern culture of death Bud Osborn uses graphic language to depict the violence this culture inflicts on the souls of the most vulnerable, and he does so in the context of a joyful testimony of resurrection. We think that Paul would approve. The real abusive language isn't found in Osborn's critique of a culture of death in the light of resurrection life. Rather, the real abusive language is in the often sanitized ways of talking and thinking that serve to make this culture of death appear normal and acceptable. Indeed, when the church's language, in all of its piety, serves to give an air of normality to an idolatrously constructed culture, thereby functioning as a polite cover-up for a comfortable life in the empire, then that language is also abusive.

Perhaps the air of normality that characterizes life in the empire is the crux of the issue for this ethic of secession. The ethical crisis of Christianity at the turn of the millennium is that Christians by and large accept the empire as normal. Here is Wendell Berry's prophetic appraisal of the church:

> Despite protests to the contrary, modern Christianity has become willy-nilly the religion of the state and the economic status quo. Because it has been so exclusively dedicated to incanting anemic souls into Heaven, it has been made the tool of much earthly villainy. It has, for the most part, stood silently by while a predatory economy has ravaged the world, destroyed its natural beauty and health, divided and plundered its human communities and households. It has flown the flag and chanted the slogans of empire. It has assumed with the economists that "economic forces" automatically work for good and has assumed with the industrialists and militarists that technology determines history. It has assumed with almost everybody that "progress" is good. . . . It has admired Caesar and comforted him in his depredations and faults. But in its de facto alliance with Caesar, Christianity connives directly in the murder of Creation.[34]

A predatory economy has ravaged the world. Christianity has flown the flag, chanted the slogans of empire and made an alliance with Caesar. Christian faith has made itself comfortable in the empire and taken up the role of comforter of the empire in its murder of creation.

We will never embrace an ethic of secession until we cease to be comfortable in the empire. Christians should feel "disjointed and out of place in a civilization which divinizes the thing."[35] Kavanaugh says that since Christian faith "at rock bottom conflicts with American culture, even subverts it . . . the practicing Christian should look like a Martian. He or she will never feel at home in the commodity kingdom. If the Christian does feel at home, something is drastically wrong."[36]

If Christians are not at home in a consumerist culture, then where do they feel at home? If they attempt to put to death the vices and character traits that are taken to be normal in our society, what kinds of virtues do they put in their place, and what kind of alternative community do such virtues engender? If sexual sin, economic greed and the discourse of violence characterize life in the empire, what is the alternative character of the kingdom?

---

[34]Wendell Berry, "Christianity and the Survival of Creation," in *Sex, Economy,* pp. 114-15.
[35]Kavanaugh, *Following Christ,* p. 99.
[36]Ibid., p. 112.

— 10 —

AN ETHIC OF COMMUNITY

Let's come back to Elanna, Eric and William for a minute. In befuddled paralysis, in unpretentious nihilism or on the defense against aggressive absolutes, our three friends know there is something wrong with the moral culture of late or post modernity, but they aren't at all sure about how to respond. Elanna's ethical pluralism is paralyzing because it suffers from an "over-exposure to otherness."[1] With so many voices to attend to, how does she discern her own voice? How does she make decisions about ethical issues of any weight? However, Eric's nihilism is more disastrous. We mean that term quite literally and not as a value judgment on Eric's situation. *Disastrum* means to be without a star, a light in the darkness, a point of orientation.[2] If in the past metanarratives provided such orientation and functioned as stars in our ethical cosmologies, then to be postmodern, says Eric, is to learn how to do without such narrative legitimations, to learn how to live in the darkness.

In the midst of this, William has no nostalgia for the absolutes of any grand systems, whether of modernity or of traditional Christianity. But he is also not happy to remain in the befuddled paralysis of ethical pluralism—he has seen too much in the world that he just knows (somehow) is wrong—nor to embrace Eric's nihilistic disaster. Perhaps Bruce Cockburn sums up William's stance evocatively: "at home in the darkness but hungry for dawn."[3] William can find his way in the darkness of a postmodern culture with neither befuddlement nor abandonment. But he longs for a dawn that would shed light on his path.

The question is, where can such light be found, and can it shine with enough

---

[1]Walter Truett Anderson, introduction to *The Truth About the Truth: De-confusing and Re-constructing the Postmodern World,* ed. Walter Truett Anderson (New York: G. P. Putnam's Sons, 1995), p. 6.

[2]John D. Caputo, *Against Ethics: Contributions to a Poetics of Obligation with Constant Reference to Deconstruction* (Bloomington: Indiana University Press, 1993), p. 6.

[3]Bruce Cockburn, "Birmingham Shadows," on the CD *The Charity of Night,* ©Golden Mountain Music, 1996. Brian Walsh has discussed the dynamics of homecoming in the lyrics of Bruce Cockburn in "One Day I Shall Be Home," *Christianity and the Arts* 7, no. 1 (Winter 2000): 28-32.

power to illumine clear paths through the present darkness? Here we meet one of the most devastating contradictions of the postmodern imagination. You see, paths require choice. Choosing one path invariably requires rejecting other paths, and it is impossible to walk on more than one path at once if you are actually trying to get somewhere.

Choices in the Postmodern Mall

A postmodern cultural ethos wants to keep all the options open. It is here that postmodern pluralism and global consumerism come together. As long as "the moral world, like the material world, is supremely represented as a shopping mall,"[4] and as long as human beings are fundamentally consumers, the forces of global consumerism have little to fear from postmodern pluralism. After all, if you are paralyzed in the befuddlement of postmodern pluralism, where will you find the moral resources to actually oppose the oppressiveness of global capitalism? And while your intuitions might lead you to be suspicious of the structures of international markets and dismissive of the manipulations of advertising agencies, what basis will you have for either a sustained critique or a subversive lifestyle if you are unable to appeal to an alternative narrative as better than the lies of the market? Without embracing a narrative that you believe is more ethical, how could you ever engage in the kind of secession that we counseled in the last chapter?

If we want to insist that narrow notions of economic efficiency, manipulative approaches to shaping consumer desire, repressive labor policies and ecologically unsustainable environmental practices are all to be opposed, then we need to know why this is taken to be an unacceptable moral culture and what the alternative would look like. In other words, we need to offer a different set of ethical principles as a critique of and an alternative to the moral culture we are rejecting. As long as we lack the courage to take a stand and remain unrooted in a narrative that would be subversive to the principalities and powers, the empire can remain secure. The inner anguish of Elanna, Eric and William ends up being impotent in the face of the empire.

There is, however, an even deeper problem with all of this talk about ethical decisions in a postmodern culture. The whole discourse assumes that somehow there are still some decisions to be made. But it is precisely the perverse genius of empire that all the decisions have already been made. Empires, we have seen, engage in a massive campaign of indoctrination in which we are all taught that resistance is futile. Kalle Lasn puts it this way:

American culture is no longer created by the people. . . . A free, authentic life is no longer pos-

---

[4]Nicholas Boyle, *Who Are We Now? Christian Humanism and the Global Market from Hegel to Heaney* (Edinburgh: T & T Clark, 1998), p. 80. See also John Pahl, *Shopping Malls and Other Sacred Places: Putting God in Place* (Grand Rapids, Mich.: Brazos, 2003).

sible in America™ today. We are being manipulated in the most insidious way. Our emotions, personalities and core values are under siege from media and cultural forces too complex to decode. A continuous product message has woven itself into the very fabric of our existence. Most North Americans now live designer lives— sleep, eat, sit in car, work, shop, watch TV, sleep again. I doubt there's more than a handful of free, spontaneous minutes anywhere in that cycle. *We ourselves have been branded.*[5]

Lasn likens life in what he calls America™ to life in a cult in which "we have been recruited into roles and behavior patterns *we did not consciously choose.*"[6] Does the child who sits in front of a television set for three to four hours a day, shops at the mall with her parents, goes to school and recites the Pledge of Allegiance, plays computer games, listens to her president encouraging everyone to go out shopping in order to defeat terrorism, wears clothes from the Gap, and plays with the toys created out of the imagination of Disney and Hollywood, ever actually *choose* the American way of life? Did she go through a ritual of initiation beyond getting her first Barbie? Was there a moment of conversion in her life when the American dream became her dream? No. She imbibed this monoculture consumerist dream in the fast food she ate, the polluted air she breathed and the visual culture she inhabited. And so she was converted, made into a cult member, before she ever knew what was happening. Lasn points out that "dreams, by definition, are supposed to be unique and imaginative. Yet the bulk of the population is dreaming the same dream. It's a dream of wealth, power, fame, plenty of sex and exciting recreational opportunities."[7] When a whole population dreams the same dream, empire is triumphant.

An alternative to the empire requires different dreams, animated by a different narrative. While we understand Elanna's befuddlement, Eric's nihilism and William's ethical allergies, it seems to us that we can no longer afford the luxury of keeping our options open. We can no longer afford an ethical paralysis. The decisions have already been made. And if there is something deep inside of us that knows that this consumerist dream is a sociocultural nightmare, then we must ground our lives in a narrative that will break through our paralysis. In the face of the ensnaring sovereignty of the empire, we must submit to a subversively liberating sovereignty. Our lives must be animated by an alternative narrative, sovereignty and hope.

Sounds like Colossians 3, doesn't it? So we turn again to Paul's letter to a struggling band of Jesus-followers in the midst of the Roman empire, and we move from an ethic of secession to an ethic of community.

---

[5]Kalle Lasn, *Culture Jam: The Uncooling of America™* (New York: Eagle Brook, 1999), p. xiii. Italics in original.

[6]Ibid., p. 53. Italics in original.

[7]Ibid., p. 57.

An Alternative Community

Paul follows his secessionist ethic of "putting to death" the vestiges of empire and "stripping off" the old self that was deformed by that empire, with a call to the resurrection life of the new self that is clothed in a different set of virtues. If the story of the empire no longer has a hold on you, then allow the narrative of Jesus—crucified, buried, risen, ascended and coming again—to shape your character as a community that is alternative to the empire.

In this section of the letter Paul must make good on a number of earlier claims. If the risen Jesus replaces the emperor as the head not of the body politic of the empire but of the church—the body of Christ (Col 1:18)—then what does that alternative body actually look like? If the reality of love and encouragement within the church renders all competing claims to ultimacy implausible (2:1-4), then how is such a community shaped? And if the ensnaring philosophies of this world are subject to pretentious rulers and authorities that are usurpers of sovereignty and are therefore impotent in bringing real blessing to human life (2:16-23), then what kind of a community is formed subject to the sovereignty of the Crucified One? How does a relationship with this Messiah shape the life of the discipleship community?

Paul's response is to offer his readers a kingdom in contrast with an empire. If the problem with the empire was idolatry (3:5), then the alternative of the kingdom is the renewal of the image of God (3:10). If the problem with the empire was that it was embedded in the lies of a violent and estranged way of thinking (1:21; 3:9), then the alternative of the kingdom is a renewal of knowledge (3:10). If the problem with the empire was that it imposed religious, ethnic, cultural and economic divisiveness and marginalization, then the alternative of the kingdom is a community in which Christ is all and in all (3:11). So Paul writes in 3:9-11:

> You have stripped off the old self with its practices and have clothed yourselves with the new self, which is being renewed in knowledge according to the image of its creator. In that renewal there is no longer Greek and Jew, circumcised and uncircumcised, barbarian, Scythian, slave and free; but Christ is all and in all!

As Paul understands things, the conflict of history, indeed the conflict for the salvation of the world, cuts through the very heart of the cosmos. "All things," we recall, are created in, through and for Christ. He is preeminent and has "first place in everything," and "all things" are reconciled through his death on a Roman cross (1:15-20). Such a comprehensive salvation must permeate all of life. This means that the ethic Paul will propose in this letter could never be limited to personal life. All of creation is at stake in this narrative of salvation, and Paul is describing the church as a community alternative to the empire. But the church isn't just a body politic, narrowly conceived. Rather, the church is the beginning of the new humanity for the new creation. The new self that has replaced the old self with its imperial allegiances and idolatrous commitments is the restoration of the image of God in history. In Christ we are restored to our full humanity as God's stewards of creation and shapers of culture. And since a misplaced grasp for autonomous knowledge was the origin of our estrangement in the story of the Garden of Eden, our restoration in the image of God must entail a renewal of knowledge.

As we have seen, Paul has been concerned with themes of knowledge throughout the letter. Here all of those themes come to their culmination. The falsehood of the empire and the lies of the philosophy find their correction in this most radical and foundational of all epistemological revolutions. We are renewed in knowledge—of who we are, of who God is, of what the story of Israel has been all about, of the gospel, of Jesus—and this renewal enables us to have a transformed imagination that engenders an alternative praxis. The whole letter has been driving to this end, from its opening prayer that the community "be filled with the knowledge of God's will in all spiritual wisdom and understanding" (1:9) to this remarkable passage. Just as that prayer at the beginning of the letter was directed to praxis—"so that you may lead lives worthy of the Lord, fully pleasing to him, as you bear fruit in every good work" (1:10)—so also is this renewal of knowledge immediately manifest in a transformed social order.

To make sure we catch the fact that this renewal has social, economic and political implications, Paul tells us that the old imperial divisions that provided the grounds for marginalization and exclusion no longer have any validity in a community renewed in the image of God. The ethnic division between Greek and Jew; the religious division of circumcised and uncircumcised; the civilizational and cultural disdain for barbarians of any kind, but especially those barbarians of all barbarians, the Scythians; the political and economic divide between slave and free that served as the very foundation of the Roman empire—all of this is deconstructed in Christ. These "barriers and habits are . . . neither natural nor normal. They are, ultimately, a denial of the creation of humankind in the image of God."[8] In postmodern terms, Paul is denaturalizing these reified societal structures and unveiling them as the cultural lies they are.

All of this is done away with, says Paul, because "Christ is all and in all." Again, just as "all things" are created in, through and for Christ, he is before "all things," in him "all things cohere," and "all things" are reconciled in him (1:15-20), so also the community that bears his image is called to embody that reconciliation in its hospitable inclusiveness. "If Christ is all in all in relation to the cosmos, then nothing less can be the case within the community of the new humanity."[9]

---

[8]N. T. Wright, *Colossians and Philemon,* Tyndale New Testament Commentary (Leicester, U.K./Grand Rapids, Mich.: Eerdmans, 1986), p. 140.

[9]Andrew T. Lincoln, "The Letter to the Colossians," in *The New Interpreter's Bible,* ed. Leander Keck (Nashville: Abingdon, 2000), 11:644.

What is the character of a community that is shaped by the narrative of Jesus' death, burial, resurrection, ascension and return? Once we have seceded from the empire, what does the kingdom look like? What do people shaped by this kingdom vision actually do? How are they different in thought, word and deed? Recall again the text (3:12-17):

> As God's chosen ones, holy and beloved, clothe yourselves with compassion, kindness, humility, meekness, and patience. Bear with one another and, if anyone has a complaint against another, forgive each other; just as the Lord has forgiven you, so also you must forgive. Above all, clothe yourselves with love, which binds everything together in perfect harmony. And let the peace of Christ rule in your hearts, to which indeed you were called in the one body. And be thankful. Let the word of Christ dwell in you richly; teach and admonish one another in all wisdom; and with gratitude in your hearts sing psalms, hymns and spiritual songs to God. And whatever you do, in word or deed, do everything in the name of the Lord Jesus, giving thanks to God the Father through him.

What does a community renewed in knowledge according to the image of the Creator look like? It looks like the Creator. It *images* this God. How? By embodying in its communal life the virtues that are formed by this God's story.

Paul calls the community members to "clothe themselves" with certain virtues. They are called, if you will, to drape themselves, surround themselves, present themselves with and embody the character traits of compassion, kindness, humility, meekness, patience, forgiveness and love. They are called to be a people rooted in and dedicated to peace, living lives characterized by gratitude, wisdom and worship. While there is merit in attending to each of these virtues in turn, it is important that we first get a sense of the whole. In this passage Paul conjures up a sense of the style and ethos of a particular kind of community, shaped by a particular story—a biblical story of hope for the reconciliation of all things.

In Paul's vision this community not only abandons the discourse of violence and exclusion that characterizes the empire; it manifests an ethos that embraces the pain of the world, a *compassion*, a shared passion, that pays attention to the deepest brokenness of its human and nonhuman neighbors. This is an ethic of compassion, because the God of Israel revealed in Jesus is a God of compassion who hears his people's cry and knows their suffering (Ex 3:7). Jesus calls his followers to be compassionate just as their Father is compassionate (see Lk 6:36).[10]

In contrast to the coldhearted bottom line of profit margins and market shares, Paul envisions a community that places something as inefficient and unprofitable as *kindness* at its heart. In stark antithesis to the self-assured bravado of the modernist

---

[10]Sylvia Keesmaat, "In Defense of Hermeneutics and Compassion: A Response to Allen Verhey," in *The Ethos of Compassion and the Integrity of Creation,* ed. Brian J. Walsh, Robert Vandervennen and Hendrik Hart (Lanham, Md.: University Press of America, 1995), pp. 158-65.

or postmodernist self-constructed ego, this community values *meekness*—replacing the clenched fist of self-protection with an open hand of welcome and service. It abandons the arrogance of cybernetic mastery and global economic dominance for the *humility* of people who recognize that the fruit of creation is received as a gift from the hand of the Creator. Only in such humility is there the possibility of a *wisdom* that can never be achieved through mere accumulation of information. The immediate gratification of insatiable desire has no hold on a community that is suffused with *patience*. We are here for the long haul, we measure time in terms of eternity, and our hope is for the restoration of all of creation. And since we know who finally accomplishes such a restoration, we can afford to be patient—waiting in hope.

This is not a naive or romantic view of community. Community can be sustained only in an ethos of *forgiveness*. Paul uses the word *forgive* three times in one sentence because he knows that community is possible only where there is forgiveness. Forgiveness must characterize this community restored in the image of its Creator precisely because its very existence is founded on the forgiveness that has set it free from the empire (Col 1:13). When people manifest the vices Paul has just called the Colossians to put off rather than the virtues he enjoins them to clothe themselves in, the path of healing, reconciliation and renewal will not be through condemnation but through forgiveness. A community is a place where people "bear with one another" in repeated forgiveness.

Such forbearance is possible, however, only where there are deep resources of *love*. Paul portrays love as the garment that wraps it all together because he knows that love holds the very creation together. Wendell Berry puts it this way:

> I believe that the world was created and approved by love, that it subsists, coheres and endures by love, and that, insofar as it is redeemable, it can be redeemed only by love. I believe that divine love, incarnate and indwelling in the world, summons the world always toward wholeness, which ultimately is reconciliation and atonement with God.[11]

It is such love, in the face of all of the violence, selfishness, narcissism and self-enclosure of our times, that establishes community and sustains it.

Love, says Paul, binds life together in perfect harmony. The harmony of the community has been a concern throughout the letter. Paul commends the Colossians for their love for each other in the opening greetings (1:4), reminds them that such enacted love is foundational to their secure understanding of the new worldview they have adopted in Christ (2:2-4), and attacks the forces of division and exclusion that have disrupted the harmony of the community (2:16-23).

Now Paul says that in this community the *peace* of Christ rules. In radical contrast to the violent, imperial rule of the Pax Romana, or the economically motivated vio-

---

[11]Wendell Berry, "Health's Membership," in *Another Turn of the Crank* (Washington, D.C.: Counterpoint, 1995), p. 89.

lence of the Pax Americana (in which people will be "liberated" by military force if the economic well-being of America is threatened), Paul subverts what the empire calls peace by appealing to a peace achieved through a victim of the empire: allow that all-pervasive, cross-shaped peace to rule your life as a communal body.

"And be *thankful*" (3:15). In a culture caught in an insatiable craving for more, a culture of perpetual dissatisfaction because there is never enough, the community renewed in the image of the Creator is characterized by "radical gratitude." "We are held captive by dissatisfaction," writes Mary Jo Leddy.[12] As a consequence, "ingratitude is ingrained within every social class within the culture of money. It is how sin takes shape within us, conditions us, and holds us captive."[13] Therefore "the longer we live ungratefully, the more we strengthen the claims of a culture that takes everything and everyone for granted."[14] Deep experiences and expressions of thankfulness—for creation, for the gifts of our lives, for the redemption and peace of Christ—break through this culture of ingratitude and loosen its claim on our lives. It is no wonder that Paul makes the call to gratitude three times in three verses!

We have argued throughout this book that the primary way any imperial culture claims our lives is through the captivity of our imaginations. Take an average of twenty-six hours of television a week, thousands of brand-name logos a day, an education system structured to produce law-abiding consumers who always crave more, and dress it all up with a mythology of divine right to world rule, and it is not surprising that the dominant worldview is so deeply internalized in the population—including the church—that it is simply taken to be the only viable, normal and commonsensical way of life. In the face of such a deeply ingrained worldview, Paul says, "let the word of Christ dwell in you richly" (3:16). Let this word of Christ—this word who *is* Christ—take up its residence in you, be so at home in you, so close to you, that this word—not the false and empty words of our culture—is like the very air you breathe (Deut 6:6-9). Let this word become your first vocabulary; let it be the lens through which you engage the world. Let this word—this word of truth which is the gospel of Jesus, this narrative of redemption—provide you with the metaphors with which you make sense of life.

The community is called on to allow the word of Christ to dwell in them richly because the impoverished word of the empire is pervasive. The teaching ministry of this community, then, is a matter of life and death. Dwell in this word of Christ, so that the words of death don't destroy you!

The word of Christ dwells in this community richly when the community indwells the liberating narrative as it engages in the mutual ministry of teaching and admonishing one another "in all *wisdom*." In an information culture that esteems quick ac-

---

[12]Mary Jo Leddy, *Radical Gratitude* (Maryknoll, N.Y.: Orbis, 2002), p. 23.
[13]Ibid., p. 61.
[14]Ibid.

cess and is preoccupied with the cybernetic production of knowledge, this community seeks wisdom. In a culture that turns knowledge into power—and often the power to do violence to the other—the church is a community that roots wisdom in the indwelling presence of the One who was powerless on the cross.

All of this is impossible apart from *worship*. The community cannot be formed with these kind of virtues, cannot take on the character of the renewed image of God, without singing "psalms, hymns, and spiritual songs to God" (Col 3:16). Worship is a world-making endeavor. By singing songs of praise to God, we proclaim the source of ultimate sovereignty in the world. By singing the poem of Colossians 1:15-20, the early church subversively announced that Christ, not Caesar, is Lord. By singing that song today, we proclaim that Christ—not the global market, not the president of the United States, not Microsoft, not military might—is Lord of our lives. In the face of empire, "what is needed is imaginative, liturgic world-making that enacts a world more credible than the world of the empire."[15] By reciting these stories to each other in worship, we shape our imaginations in a way that engenders an alternative praxis, a character shaped in the image of God.

For this community, it all begins and it all ends with Christ. "Christ is all and in all." When the community so indwells his story that its very imagination is transformed by this narrative and its daily life in the empire embodies these counter-imperial character traits, "whatever" this community does, "in word or deed," will be done "in the name of the Lord Jesus, giving thanks to God the Father through him" (3:17). Again, the comprehensive nature of Paul's vision must not be missed. *Whatever* we do—voting or shopping, writing a poem or a check, shaping educational curricula or a sculpture, establishing a household or a business enterprise, having babies or caring for the elderly, paying taxes or lobbying the government, singing praise or singing the blues, making a film or making a pie, building housing for the homeless or protecting an endangered species—will be done in the name of the Lord Jesus and will thereby be giving thanks to the Creator in whose image we have been renewed.

The Poetics of Community

There is something wildly audacious about all of this. This is a vision of life and an ethic that are hardly imaginable to most of us. And so again we must turn to poetry to help us find the images that might make this radical ethic real in our lives. Wendell Berry and Bud Osborn again prove to be wise guides through the terrain of an alternative ethic in the face of our captivity.

In "Manifesto: The Mad Farmer Liberation Front," Berry offers us resources of a transformed imagination by contrasting the anonymous world of "the quick profit,

---

[15]Walter Brueggemann, *Israel's Praise: Doxology Against Idolatry and Ideology* (Philadelphia: Fortress, 1988), p. 46.

the annual raise," in which we receive "everything ready-made" and in which "when they want you to buy something they will call you," with a subversive alternative rooted in love.[16]

> So, friends, every day do something
> that won't compute. Love the Lord.
> Love the world. Work for nothing.
> Take all that you have and be poor.
> Love someone who does not deserve it.
> Because this is a vision of life that embraces humility and patience,

> Give your approval to all that you cannot
> understand. Praise ignorance, for what man
> has not encountered he has not destroyed.
> Ask the questions that have no answers.
> Invest in the millennium. Plant sequoias.
> Say that your main crop is the forest
> that you did not plant,
> that you will not live to harvest.
> Say that the leaves are to be harvested
> when they have rotted into the mold.
> Call that profit. Prophesy such returns.

As we have seen, in the face of the empire Paul proclaims a gospel that calls forth a community of fruitfulness. If this is true, then Berry's advice about how to discern ethically life-giving paths of wisdom in the day-to-day rhythms and decisions of life is worth heeding.

> Ask yourself: Will this satisfy
> a woman satisfied to bear a child?
> Will this disturb the sleep
> of a woman near to giving birth?

Is this cultural action, this communal decision, this political policy or ecological practice, this artistic product or technological development life-giving or not? Is it the kind of thing that bears good fruit in our lives? Would it make sense to a woman about to bring vulnerable new life into the world? Is it something that would be worth disturbing the sleep of a woman between the contractions of birthing? If not, then abandon it for the path of death it is. This "Manifesto," this community, is committed to life, and life more abundant. "Practice resurrection."[17]

Resurrection can be practiced only in the face of death. And death is often

---

[16]Wendell Berry, "Manifesto: The Mad Farmer Liberation Front," in *The Selected Poems of Wendell Berry* (Washington, D.C.: Counterpoint, 1998), pp. 87-88.
[17]This is the last line of the poem.

where the Christian community finds itself. Bud Osborn's poem "The Truth of Community" tells the story of the Franciscan Maximillian Kolbe, who took the place of another man in the starvation cell at Auschwitz and while in a death cell comforted his fellow prisoners and sang canticles of love.[18] The poem ends with this testimony:

kolbe
who created community even in auschwitz
kolbe
who lived community while naked and starving to death
kolbe
who sang community into a situation without hope
kolbe
who demonstrated that community cannot be destroyed
though buildings are demolished
though people are scattered and lives are shattered
kolbe
who taught that community cannot be extinguished
as long as a single human being
steps forward
out of line
and speaks out
for the sake of another's life
kolbe

We might add: Kolbe, who follows a Savior who stepped out of line and gave up his life for the sake of us all. Christian community, as demonstrated by Maximillian Kolbe and countless others, is founded in the love of God and reflects that love.

Like the love of God for his creation, the love of the Christian community "longs for incarnation."[19] Love cannot remain an abstract idea; it must take on flesh in the embodied life of the Christian community in particular places and at particular times. Rodney Clapp offers this historical observation: "The original Christians, in short, were about creating and sustaining a unique culture—a way of life that would shape character in the image of their God. And they were determined to be a culture, a quite public and political culture, even if it killed them and their children."[20]

What shape might this alternative public and political culture take in our time?

---

[18]Bud Osborn, "The Truth of Community," in *Hundred Block Rock* (Vancouver, B.C.: Arsenal Pulp, 1999), pp. 45-48.

[19]Wendell Berry, "Word and Flesh," in *What Are People For?* (New York: North Point, 1990), p. 200.

[20]Rodney Clapp, *A Peculiar People: The Church as Culture in a Post-Christian Society* (Downers Grove, Ill.: InterVarsity Press, 1996), p. 82.

A Christian Political Vision

If the church is a body politic, what kind of political vision might be engendered by the virtues of community that we meet in Colossians 3:12-14? What would a political vision shaped by compassion, kindness, humility, meekness, patience, forgiveness, love and peace look like? How could we envision a politics of *compassion* that insists on standing with the most vulnerable members of our society? Would this be a politics of greed that is preoccupied with tax cuts for the richest members of society and international trade policies that aim for economic growth for its own sake? Or is the community renewed in the image of God committed to a politics for "the least of these" (Mt 25:40)—for aboriginal peoples, drug addicts, gays, the homeless and the poorest of the poor?

Further, what would a political vision suffused with *kindness* look like? Would it be a politics of care that seeks to attend to questions of ecological stewardship and sustainability *before* we confront environmental crises? Would it engender an economics of care that places questions of quality of life, ecological principles, social well-being and health at the forefront of all policy discussions, legislation and personal/communal decision-making?[21]

Or consider *humility* as a political virtue. While a Christian political vision is all-encompassing because it serves Christ, who is all and in all, this is not a politics of grandiosity or arrogance. Recognizing that Christ—not we—restores the creation, we need have no pretense or anxiety about what we are doing. We are called to a politics of humility because we know who saves the world. Further, this is a servant politics that is characterized by humility because it seeks to serve the humble, not the haughty. Rather than enacting policy that makes our nation "great" or our town a "world-class city," this politics serves "the least of these." Perhaps this will mean shifting the agenda away from amassing economic power to addressing the scandal of child poverty, or away from focusing on national security to forming refugee and immigration policies suffused with hospitality.

How might we envision a politics of *meekness?* "Blessed are the meek," Jesus says, "for they shall inherit the earth" (Mt 5:5). They inherit the earth because they never grasped the earth and claimed proprietary rights over it. A politics characterized by meekness is a politics of gift. It doesn't grasp but receives this creation, this city, this wonderful land in all of its richness and beauty as a gift from the Lord. Over against the reduction of land to a salable commodity and the eclipse of the family farm by monoculture agribusiness, a politics of meekness may see the farm crisis as foundational because the very giftedness of creation is at stake.[22] In a scientific culture of dangerous arrogance about what we can accomplish both medically and agricultur-

---

[21]Bob Goudzwaard and Harry de Lange, *Beyond Poverty and Affluence: Toward an Economy of Care,* trans. and ed. Mark Vander Vennen (Toronto: University of Toronto Press, 1995).

[22]Wendell Berry, *The Unsettling of America: Culture and Agriculture* (New York: Avon, 1977).

ally through genetic modification, a politics of humility and meekness cuts through such arrogance and counsels a much more careful approach to biotechnology.[23]

In a political culture in which politicians and party strategists seldom look beyond the next election because they are preoccupied with either gaining or maintaining political power, consider the shape of a politics of *patience*. In a politics that is addicted to the quick fix, it would seem that patience is not a political virtue. But it is a Christian one. Christians can be patient about righting the world's wrongs (though still passionate about justice!) because we know that the establishment of the just society— what the book of Revelation calls the New Jerusalem—and the healing of the earth are finally not in our hands but in God's. We long to see Christ revealed, and we live our political lives anticipating his kingdom, but we do so with patience. Ours is a political vision for the long haul, not preoccupied with power or the quick fix.

But what would a politics embedded in an ethic of *forgiveness* look like? Surely a community that actively promotes forgiveness would not want to limit this virtue to its internal life with no public implications. Imagine the radical impact forgiveness would have if applied to international conflict, penal reform, race relations and the crippling indebtedness of the poorest nations.

Shuttle diplomacy without somehow calling nations to reconciliation through real forgiveness is doomed to failure in regions like the Middle East, Africa, Latin America and the Balkan states.[24] More repressive prisons and sanctioned state murder will not produce a safer and more law-abiding society. Race relations will not improve simply through our trying harder "to get along." But what if penal reform and race relations were negotiated in an ethos of mutual forbearance and forgiveness, not retribution and vengeance? That such an ethos can take an institutional shape in a society has been proven by the remarkable success of the Truth and Reconciliation Commission in postapartheid South Africa.[25] And that a biblical understanding of forgiveness can capture the imaginations of people from all over the world and all the world religions has been proven through the success of the Jubilee 2000 campaign to provide debt relief to the most indebted nations of the world.[26]

---

[23]Brewster Kneen, *Farmageddon: Food and the Culture of Biotechnology* (Gabriola Island, B.C.: New Society, 1999). See also Bill McKibben, *Enough: Staying Human in an Engineered Age* (New York: Henry Holt/Owl, 2004).

[24]Miroslav Volf, *Exclusion and Embrace: A Theological Exploration of Identity, Otherness and Reconciliation* (Nashville: Abingdon, 1996).

[25]James Cochrane, John de Gruchy and Stephen Martin, eds., *Facing the Truth: South African Faith Communities and the Truth and Reconciliation Commission* (Capetown: David Philip/Athens: Ohio University Press, 1999); and Desmond Tutu, *There Is No Future Without Forgiveness* (New York: Doubleday, 2000).

[26]Hans Ucko, ed., *The Jubilee Challenge: Utopia or Possibility? Jewish and Christian Insights* (Geneva: WCC Publications, 1997). See also the three volumes of essays from the Canadian Ecumenical Jubilee Initiative, *Making a New Beginning: Biblical Reflections on Jubilee* (Toronto: CEJI, 1998); *Jubilee, Wealth and the Market* (Toronto: CEJI, 1999); and *Sacred Earth, Sacred Community: Jubilee, Ecology and Aboriginal Peoples* (Toronto: CEJI, 2000).

What all of this is about is *love*. A politics rooted in love is not the sentimentality of warm feelings in the political arena. Rather, love takes on political shape in justice. Justice as the political face of love is never impartial but is always biased. In the kind of biblical faith that occasions Paul's understanding of love, justice is always suspicious of the powerful and biased toward the powerless. Justice is first and foremost directed toward the orphan, widow and stranger precisely because these people lack the economic and political power to defend themselves. Love shapes the very content of justice. God's love takes sides with the most vulnerable, the most oppressed. Therefore a Christian political praxis of love seeks justice for those who are the most marginalized, the most oppressed and downtrodden. While an idolatrous culture of greed is always willing to allow the powerless to be oppressed by the powerful and will always tolerate homelessness, disease and violence amongst the disfranchised, and an ever-growing income gap between the rich and the poor, a Christian community of love will strive to bring justice to those at the bottom of society. Love, Paul says, "binds everything together in perfect harmony" (3:14). Love unifies and love heals. In a society that has gaping wounds in its social fabric, the Christian community, through its example and its societal and political witness, is called to be an agent of reconciliation and justice.

Reconciliation is at the heart of peacemaking. *Peace* is not simply the absence of war; it is the presence of well-being and justice in social and international relations. A community whose hearts are ruled by "the peace of Christ" is a community of peacemakers. Empires are built on violence and maintain their power through violence. The United States spends more on its armed forces than the rest of the world put together. The military is the largest single employer in the United States, and the United States is the largest arms exporter in the world.[27] While the U.S. administration was willing to go to war against Iraq under the false pretenses of "weapons of mass destruction," supposed connections to Al Qaeda and 9/11, and the "liberation" of Iraq, Christians are called to let the peace of Christ that rules in their hearts to rule in their political lives as well. Pious language about God blessing America notwithstanding, the geopolitical agenda of the Pax Americana is not the agenda of the kingdom of God. And if the control of oil stocks is fundamentally a matter of fueling the machinery of economic growth for the sake of a consumerist society, then Christians should declare themselves noncombatants in this kind of war.

A war-mongering empire should find no support from a community that worships the Prince of Peace. Stanley Hauerwas reminds us that "a nation at war has no time for the poor, no space to worry about the extraordinary inequities that constitute this society or about those parts of the world ravaged by hunger and genocide. Everything—civil liberties, due process, the protection of the law—must be subordinated

---

[27]See "The Other America: The Facts," *New Internationalist* 351 (November 2002): 19.

to the one great moral enterprise of winning the unending war against terrorism."[28] Not if the peace of Christ rules in your hearts! Then everything—whatever we do in word or deed—is directed to a politics of peacemaking. *Everything!* Whether it be protesting the war, refusing to serve, withholding taxes, going to the enemy country to stand as a witness for peace, engaging in civil disobedience, supporting the victims or boycotting the corporate players in the military-industrial complex, everything a Christian community does in a time of imperial war should be directed to peace.

This peacemaking, this persistent though patient politics of care, compassion, kindness, humility, meekness, reconciliation, love and justice, is generated by an alternative and liberating "word" and sustained in an ethos of gratitude. As an alternative to the foolish belief that peace, prosperity and social well-being are secured through the growth of the economy and the military expansion of imperial control, the Christian community seeks political wisdom by being rooted in *the word of Christ.* While a politics of economic growth "flounders in a time of economic scarcity, when the economic pie begins to shrink," because it has created a sullen culture of entitlement and unending growth, a politics of *gratitude* can live with limits and can say "Enough."[29] Mary Jo Leddy argues that "the choice to affirm that *there is enough for all* is the beginning of social community, peace, and justice" and "frees the imagination to think of new political and economic possibilities."[30] Such a politics of enough, rooted in the fullness found in Christ, is the calling of a Christian community that would take Colossians as a charter for its social, political and economic life.

Again, it all comes down to *worship.* You see, while Paul rightly calls the community to sing, pray and teach, the proof of our worship is demonstrated in "whatever we do, in word or deed." This is, if you will, a worshipful politics. The Christian community is not unique in bringing together worship and politics. After all, what was the Roman empire up to when it provided legitimation of its regime by means of the imperial cult? And what other role do civic events such as Independence Day, the State of the Union Address and Remembrance Day, together with reciting the Pledge of Allegiance, singing "The Battle Hymn of the Republic" and "God Bless America" (these are *hymns,* remember!), have but to provide a moment of ritual that gives religious legitimation to the American empire? But these are not the worship events of the Christian community! In our worship we tell and retell another story than that of the republic, hear another word proclaimed, eat an alternative meal of remembrance, pledge allegiance to another sovereign, and sing hymns, psalms and spiritual songs that set our imaginations free for another way of life, another politics.

---

[28]Stanley Hauerwas, "Nonviolence and the War Without End," *The Other Side* 38, no. 6 (November/ December 2002): 30-31.

[29] Leddy, *Radical Gratitude,* p. 123.

[30]Ibid., p. 57.

Touching Down in Daily Life

I think we need to talk.

Yes, we probably do.

Are you saying that I can't be a patriotic citizen of my home country and also a citizen of the kingdom of God?

In a context in which patriotism has become an idolatry of nation, yes, we are saying that Christians are not called to patriotism. The Bible never calls us to be patriotic to the empire.

In Romans 13 Paul tells us to be subject to the governing authorities, to not resist those authorities, to pay our taxes and give respect and honor to the authorities. You seem to be calling us to disrespect and dishonor our political leaders. How can you justify all of this?

Let us answer that with a few questions of our own. In Acts 16, Paul and Silas are imprisoned in Philippi after being beaten and severely flogged. That night an earthquake shakes open the prison doors, but Paul and Silas don't escape, and the jailer and his family are converted to following Jesus. In the morning, the magistrates send the local constable over to say that Paul and Silas are free to go.

So far, so good. Paul will subject himself to authority even to the point of not escaping when he has a chance. But listen to his response to the message from the magistrates: "But Paul replied, 'They have beaten us in public, uncondemned, men who are Roman citizens, and have thrown us into prison; and now are they going to discharge us in secret? Certainly not! Let them come and take us out themselves.' The police reported these words to the magistrates, and they were afraid when they heard that they were Roman citizens; so they came and apologized to them. And they took them out and asked them to leave the city" (Acts 16:36-39). Now let us ask you, did Paul respect and honor these magistrates?

I don't know.

Think about it. The authorities decide that these two guys whom they have imprisoned for a night and given a good beating to should be set free. So they send a lesser official—a cop—to tell them they can leave. And Paul will have nothing of it. "You tell those officials to get themselves down to this jailhouse and tell me to my face that I am free to go," Paul says. He is saying that after such a public display of injustice, such a disregard for due process, these magistrates can't get off so easily.[31] They must now publicly right the wrong they have done. So we ask again, did Paul honor these magistrates?

Well, when you put it that way, I guess not.

---

[31]The U.S. Patriot Act, passed in the wake of the September 11, 2001, terrorist attacks, gives the state the authority to detain noncitizens indefinitely without recourse to legal counsel and without even a charge being brought against them. Empires attend to "due process" only when it suits the imperial agenda. For a profoundly Christian response to these political developments, see Wendell Berry, *Citizenship Papers* (Washington, D.C.: Shoemaker and Hoard, 2003), esp. chaps. 1-2.

Actually, when we put it that way, we think Paul *did* honor those magistrates. You see, Paul is insisting that they exercise the authority invested in them—an authority that he will say in both Romans 13 and the Colossian poem is from God!—in a manner appropriate to their public office. Public officials who misuse their authority must face up to that misuse in public. Paul honors these magistrates precisely by calling them to task. And because he believes that their authority is not ultimately rooted in the authority of the emperor but instituted by God, Paul demands that they exercise their authority in a way that demonstrates that they really are servants of God.

Now we suggest that this sheds some light on the matter of subjection to political and legal authorities. Rather than read this text as providing carte blanche legitimation for any regime, regardless of how idolatrous and oppressive it might be, we suggest that Paul is actually limiting the authority of the state. The state is a servant of God for our good. It has no legitimacy or authority in and of itself, apart from subjection to the rule of God. And when the state clearly abrogates its responsibility to do good, when it acts against the will of God, then the Christian community has a responsibility to call it back to its rightful duty and even to engage in civil disobedience (see Acts 12:6-23). The state has no authority to do evil.

If Paul is suggesting here that the authority of Rome is relativized, then why does he tell the Roman Christians to be subject to those authorities and to pay taxes?

This book is on Colossians, but you are right to raise these questions about Romans 13. So let's take a closer look at that text. In the first place, we need to take seriously the context in which Romans 13:1-7 occurs. This teaching can't be isolated from what Paul is saying in the surrounding passage. It is preceded by a radical call against conformity to this age (12:1-2), within a context of persecution at the hands of the empire in 12:9-21.[32] It is followed by a call to "owe no one anything, except to love one another" (13:8). In the midst of this clear context of nonconformity, persecution and the call to love not only the community but also one's enemies, Paul's comments about the state have ambiguous overtones. It was, after all, the state that had persecuted the Roman believers and caused their suffering.

In the second place, the violent nature of the state is underlined by references to "fear" and to the state's bearing of the sword. Paul emphasizes that the state should be obeyed because of the fear of wrath (13:5), a fear that is underlined in 13:7: "Pay to all what is due them—taxes to whom taxes are due, revenue to whom revenue is due, fear to whom fear is due, honor to whom honor is due" (our translation). Note that we have translated the Greek word *phobos* as "fear" to show that this is the same word that is used in verses 3-4. The use of the language of fear in relation to the state, along

---

[32]"Be patient in suffering" (Rom 12:12); "bless those who persecute you" (12:14); "if your enemies are hungry, feed them; if they are thirsty, give them something to drink" (12:20); "do not be overcome by evil" (12:21). On the broader context of suffering in the Roman Christian community see also 8:17-39.

with the mention of the sword, heightens the ambiguity of the passage.[33] On the one hand Paul is echoing Jewish sources such as Philo who use the language of fear in describing both the brutality of rulers and the need to be obedient out of expediency;[34] on the other he is using language that is "quite out of pace with the contemporary propaganda of the empire" that touted Nero as a ruler who engaged in no bloodshed and no wielding of the sword.[35]

As Neil Elliot puts it, "'Honor' may be due the authorities—at least some of them—but so, given the reality of the Roman sword, is fear. . . . Given the reality of Roman rule, one may 'do good' and hope for the best (13.2); but under the circumstances, open resistance cannot be contemplated, so long as the authorities wield the sword (13.4)."[36] What sounds to our ears like a completely straightforward call to obey governing authorities, especially when read out of the context in which this instruction was given, has overtones of persecution, fear and bloodshed for the community reading this letter. Romans 13:1-7 is not a call to blind obedience to the state but to prudent action; its very vocabulary hints that this particular authority is not living up to its God-given calling. In a nutshell, Paul is saying, "Be careful."

If Paul's language is so ambiguous here, how do you translate what he is saying into the kind of "politics" you just read out of Colossians 3?

When the state functions as an empire, when it bears an uncanny resemblance to Babylon, then "seeking the welfare" of the state requires shaping an alternative community that practices an alternative politics (Jer 29:7). Our discussion of Colossians 3 was an attempt to broadly sketch out what that kind of politics might look like in our present context. If the empire is war-mongering, then the Christian community is called to be a witness for peace. If there is racial oppression in the empire, then a community that believes there is neither Jew nor Arab, black or white, Hispanic or Asian, because Christ is all and in all, will lay down its life for the sake of racial justice. If women and racial minorities receive unfair treatment in the marketplace and the public square, then the church calls for, and demonstrates, equal opportunity. If homelessness and hunger are on the rise in our society, then a community suffused with kindness builds housing, feeds the hungry and then gets busy addressing the root causes of that homelessness and hunger. If the empire enacts social policy that leaves the poor destitute, establishes trade policy that legitimates unfair trade practices, and passes environmental law that allows global warming to go unchecked, species to go extinct at alarming rates, and our waterways to become chemical sewage

---

[33]Neil Elliot, "Romans 13.1-7 in the Context of Imperial Propaganda," in *Paul and Empire: Religion and Power in Roman Imperial Society,* ed. Richard A. Horsley (Harrisburg, Penn.: Trinity Press International, 1997), pp. 196-203.

[34]Ibid., pp. 200-201 and references cited there.

[35]Ibid., pp. 201-3 and references cited there.

[36]Ibid., p. 201.

dumps, then a Christian politics of compassion, kindness and meekness both lobbies for alternative policies and attempts to live in a way that is consistent with these foundational Christian virtues.[37]

Are you saying that the state should be Christian?

Actually, in the present context of North American politics, the state is saying itself that it is Christian, and we are denying that claim. No, we are not calling for a "Christian state." All such attempts in the past have been failures. And such a move would make Christian faith into precisely the kind of violent and absolutistic regime that we have spent this book trying to avoid. Our agenda, and we think Paul's agenda, is both less and more ambitious. It is less ambitious because we do not believe the kingdom of God is established until Christ returns to establish a new heavens and a new earth. Our task is to live in that coming kingdom now.

Remember how Paul began and ended this section of the epistle: Since you have been raised with Christ, set your minds on where Christ is, the enthroned one, seated at the right hand of God. And if that messianic rule is what animates your life and shapes your imagination, then whatever you do, in word or deed—including your political life as well as your professional, familial, recreational, artistic, economic, social and ecological life—will be done in the name of Jesus. So our modest agenda is to live our lives fully subject to Christ's rule in the midst of an empire that recognizes no rule but its own. We do not plan to overthrow that empire but simply to be faithful witnesses to the kingdom in the face of the empire. We don't expect to see America, or any other empire, ever being Christian. Our agenda is not that ambitious.

On the other hand our hope is in some respects even more ambitious. We long for, and hope to anticipate in our daily life, nothing less than the kingdom of God renewing all of creation. This means that we dare to hope for peace on earth, for the beating of swords into plowshares and spears into pruning hooks (Is 2:4; Mic 4:3), for the healing of the nations (Rev 22:2), for justice to roll down like a river (Amos 5:24). This means that we are willing to live—or at least attempt to live—as if a politics of compassion, kindness, humility, meekness, patience, forgiveness, love and peace makes sense.

What does this look like, then, in daily life? What kinds of ordinary decisions do you make that reflect this character?

That's *the* question that we are asked over and over again, by our students, by our friends, by our church community, even by our academic colleagues. That is why in our narrative about Nympha we suggested that this was the kind of question the Colossian community had to struggle with. How do we live in the shadow of empire? What cultural, economic and social practices ought to characterize the community that finds its identity and direction in the story of Jesus?

---

[37]Michael Schut, ed., *Simpler Living: Compassionate Life* (Denver: Living the Good News, 1999).

We need to admit at the outset that this is a lifelong challenge. We always find ourselves in a struggle to discern the shape of a Christ-directed life and to live it. And this struggle is full of compromises and tensions all along the way.[38]

But let's put the question this way: if the empire in which we live bows the knee before the golden calf of economism and believes that economic growth is the purpose of life, the engine of progress and the meaning of history, then how does a community that refuses to pay homage to that false god actually live? Well, let's begin with what we do with our money. Condemning the idolatry of economism does not mean that Christians withdraw from economic life. Economism is the absolutization of a *good* dimension of human interaction in this creation: economic exchange. We must not respond to the idolatry by abandoning what is good in economic life. Rather, if we understand economics as a matter of the just and fruitful stewardship of creational resources, including money, we must reclaim this dimension of our lives for the sake of the kingdom.

How?

Well, to begin with, we should be careful to not allow the empire to use our resources for its idolatrous purposes. For example, consider banking and retirement funds. When we place our money in the bank or a retirement fund, managers at those institutions invest that money wherever they think it will get the best return. The problem is that in the context of the global economy, the best return is often found in industries that oppress the poor in sweatshops, destroy the environment, and produce products that a Christian understanding of stewardship would find useless, frivolous or offensive. Should Christians have money in industries that are based on cash crops in Third World nations, produce plastic toys in sweatshops for children of the wealthy or bolster the military-industrial complex? We don't think so. Nor do we think that money should be invested in money. The whole business of currency speculation seems to us to be economic idolatry at its worse. When money is invested in money in the global market of currency speculation, people make a profit without ever producing a product or a service that might be of some use or benefit to anyone else. This is an incredible travesty of stewardship.

So we need to think long and hard about our investments. Perhaps a credit union or a local bank with a social conscience will provide a viable alternative to large charter banks.[39] Perhaps ethical funds that uphold standards regarding the ecological, social and political impact of our investments are a better place for our retirement sav-

---

[38]Deedee Williams offers honest counsel on these struggles in "Living into the Hard Choices," *The Other Side* 38, no. 6 (November/December 2002): 10-15. We have been helped over the years by Loren and Mary Ruth Wilkinson's book *Caring For Creation in Your Own Backyard* (Ann Arbor, Mich.: Servant, 1992).

[39]An example of such a bank is Dwelling House Saving and Loan, 501 Herron Avenue, Pittsburgh, PA 15219-4696.

ings. And perhaps we just need to be giving more away. The level of giving in churches at the beginning of the twenty-first century is certainly well below anything like a 10 percent tithe! One guidepost we work with is that if we ever find in a given year that we have invested more in our own future by way of retirement savings than we have given away for someone else's present need, there is something terribly wrong. We tend to think the ratio should be at least two to one: for every dollar we invest in retirement savings, two dollars should be given away to an agency that will serve the poor.

Well, investments and retirement savings are pretty far from my reality right now. I don't generally have enough money to think about those things yet.

Do you eat?

Yes, I eat.

Where do you buy your groceries?

At the supermarket, like everyone else.

Maybe we need to reconsider the local supermarket as the source of our food. Food production in the global market is as tied to the bottom line of profits as is any other commodity. The result is that Mexican peasants produce strawberries for our tables while their own children go hungry. Colombian farmers cut down their citrus groves to increase their coffee crop and find that they have only one source of income, so if there is a crop failure or the price of coffee goes down, they are left destitute.[40] Our point is that food is deeply political, and we need to pay attention to where our food comes from and what is in it.[41] Attractiveness and longevity on the shelf require that various chemicals be added to much of our produce and processed foods. And increasingly we will find that our foods are genetically modified, though the producers will fight to keep that information away from us.

Now the question is, how does a community committed to justice and love for our Mexican and Colombian neighbors, and committed to an economics of humility and kindness in relation to the stewardship of natural resources, develop an alternative lifestyle when it comes to food? In the first place, we need to be aware of where our food is coming from and what its real social, ecological and economic costs are. What is the social implication of cash crops in the Third World? What does switching to cash crops for export do to those communities? What are the ecological costs of the chemically intensive and single-crop practices of the agribusiness sector? To whom are we really paying the 69 cents a pound for our bananas? How much is the farmer getting? How much goes to the wholesaler and the retailer?

Shopping at the large chain supermarkets will never allow you to get enough con-

---

[40]Gregory Dicum and Nina Luttinger, *The Coffee Book: Anatomy of an Industry from Crop to the Last Drop* (New York: The New Press, 1999).

[41]Stephen H. Webb, *Good Eating* (Grand Rapids, Mich.: Brazos, 2001); and Michael Schut, ed., *Food and Faith* (Denver: Living the Good News, 2001).

trol over your food consumption to be able to be free of the empire. So we suggest that people set up food co-ops. A food co-op is a nonprofit enterprise that serves its members with quality food produced as locally as possible, in environmentally responsible ways, and that seeks to do justice to the producer of the food.

Aren't food co-ops expensive?

That depends. Since food co-ops provide many basic food items in bulk and do not add exorbitant markups, their products are often less expensive than a supermarket's. But because many food co-ops carry organic and health foods, the meats and vegetables may be more expensive than the agribusiness-produced food at the larger chain stores. But the quality is better, and the price more accurately represents what the food really costs to produce. And the producers are getting a fairer return on their investment of time and labor in producing that food.

There is also another side to "expense." In our culture people are increasingly paying for someone else to produce and process their food for them. We think one of the most radical things we can do in the face of an imperial food economy is to start growing our own food again. Indeed, in the face of the empire, backyard gardens are potentially subversive. In growing our own food we are saying no to the corporations, no to genetically modified foods, no to supermarket control of the vegetables and fruits we eat, no to the use of chemicals to produce perfect-looking but toxic food.[42] Neighborhood and communal gardens take this a step further, saying yes to healthy food for the poor and for those with no access to land.

Of course these are not the only ways to produce and eat food in an alternative way. There are also community-supported agriculture programs, in which urban folk make a contract to buy the produce of a particular farmer, who then delivers the produce throughout the season as crops come ripe. In such programs the community that buys the food shares both the risks and the benefits of food production with the farmer. A set price is paid for the crop when it is planted. If there is a crop failure, the whole community bears the cost of that failure, but if there is a bumper crop, the whole community benefits. It doesn't all hang on the shoulders of the farmer.[43]

Then there is the question of how food is processed. One of the most expensive things we do in our time-starved society is buy processed foods. We pick up food at the takeout counter or go to that massive wall of freezers in the supermarket with all the meals ready for the microwave. From a purely dollars-and-cents perspective, this is vastly more expensive than buying organic foods and cooking them yourself. From an ecological perspective, the ways these processed food products were produced— the heavy use of pesticides and herbicides, the high-energy processing in the factory, the preservatives that must be used, the high cost of freezing and transporting these

---

[42]Sylvia Keesmaat, "Gardening in the Empire," *The Banner* 137, no. 3 (February 25, 2002): 28-30.
[43]Bill McKibben, *Hope, Human and Wild* (St. Paul, Minn.: Hungry Mind, 1995), pp. 197-98.

products—make this a very expensive way to produce food.

But there is another way in which this is an expensive way to eat. This fast-food convenience not only is unsustainable from an economic and environmental perspective, it also engenders an unsustainable personal and familial life. There is a world of difference between sitting down at a table with food produced in a factory and now piping hot out of the microwave and sitting down with a meal that has been lovingly prepared from the basic raw materials of foods cooked in the adjoining kitchen throughout the afternoon. Not only do so-called convenience foods often feed into a lifestyle in which there is no time for a family meal, they also render us so dependent on the imperial structures of food supply that we don't even know how to cook anymore. What could serve the interests of the empire better than that? When we become dependent on unsustainable and oppressive structures for our daily bread, not only do we make a mockery of the Lord's Prayer, but we have become docile subjects of the empire rather than free citizens of the kingdom.

So you think Paul is advocating organic gardening and home-cooking in Colossians 3?

No, *we* are advocating organic gardening and home cooking as one faithful expression of the community ethic that Paul is offering, once we begin to reflect on the nature of food production and consumption in the context of our own imperial realities.

What other things do you think are important for our daily lives?

We've talked about the basic need for food; why not consider transportation next? We live in a automobile-addicted society, and that addiction is quite literally killing us and killing others. Not only do we never get the exercise we need because of the car, we are also destroying the environment through this addiction. Perhaps global warming has already gotten to a point of no return, but the evidence that makes the connection between fossil-fuel consumption and global warming is conclusive.[44] It's time for the bicycle again! While complicated science may be needed to understand global warming, it doesn't take rocket science to see that reducing our burning of fossil fuels is necessary if we want to be ecologically responsible. So Christians should reduce their use of automobiles and increase old-fashioned modes of transportation: riding a bike or walking. If these are not feasible, then Christians should be at the forefront of promoting public transit.

The automobile is the preferred mode of transportation for autonomous human beings. But the new self renewed in the image of God in Jesus Christ knows that autonomy is quite literally a dead end. If we are not autonomous individuals but persons-in-relation made for community, then we should seek modes of transportation that enhance community. The car is decidedly not such a technology.

It sounds as if your understanding of community goes beyond the church, beyond the

---

[44]See Steven Bouma-Prediger, *For the Beauty of the Earth: A Christian Vision for Creation Care* (Grand Rapids, Mich.: Baker, 2001), pp. 61-64. Also important is Bill McKibbin's powerful though disturbing book *The End of Nature* (New York: Doubleday, 1989).

community of those who follow Jesus. Are you saying that we have a responsibility to the community as a whole?

That's right. As we live as a community shaped by the story of Jesus, we are to be a witness to and in service of the community beyond the church. To secede from the empire does not mean withdrawal from the local community. Let's stay with the example of transportation for a minute. When a city plan called for a new expressway to be built through the heart of a residential neighborhood and down an existing ravine, we joined others in protest. And we actually managed to stop that expressway. The ravine with its rich biodiversity has been saved as a green zone in the city. Neighborhoods have remained intact, and a new subway system has been constructed underneath the proposed expressway route. Participating in the protest and helping to seek a better solution, we felt, was an integral expression of our Christian faith, in solidarity with our neighbors.

Or consider another example. When McDonald's announced plans to rebuild its local restaurant to include a drive-through window, we actively supported the local neighborhood group and the local city politician in opposing this development. Why? Just because we think McDonald's is one of the most egregious examples of imperial food? Not really. The pressing issue was the health of the neighborhood. Is a drive-through that would increase traffic and create a hazard for parents, children and the elderly on the sidewalk conducive to good community? We didn't think so, and neither did our neighbors. So the megacorporation had to deal with a group of angry residents who would take the issue as far as it needed to go in order to stop this incursion into the community.

Of course, all of this brings us back to politics. It's no use talking about a Christian political vision if you are not prepared to take political action. For our family, municipal elections have become one of our favorite events as we take the kids to our local councilor's office and get busy going door to door to get him reelected. That this man is a Christian is a bonus for us, but we would support him even if he weren't. You see, his politics demonstrate the character of Christ. His first political questions about any policy or conflict have to do with justice, kindness and service to the most vulnerable. Such a politician is rare and needs our support.

You have talked about politics, community action, transportation, food and money. And I imagine we could go on to discuss things like education, media, healthcare and the arts. But one thing I've noticed is that environmental concerns seem to underlie an awful lot of what you've been saying a Christian communal ethic should look like. Now I had always read Colossians 3 in rather personalistic ways, and your interpretation has opened up this text as a communal ethic, even a political ethic. Would you say it contains an environmental ethic as well?

If we start talking about the environment, we're not sure you'll be able to get a word in edgewise for the rest of the chapter.

That's a risk I'm willing to take.

Well then, yes, we think that Colossians 3 has significant environmental implications.[45]

An Ecological Ethic

Again, let's be clear about what we are and what we are not saying. Paul didn't have food co-ops in mind when he described the character of the Christian community, and he didn't have an ecological worldview in mind either. But it is fair for us to ask whether this ethic has ecological consequences for our lives as a Christian community in the twenty-first century. The text itself gives a profound legitimacy to our question. After all, this is a community for whom Christ "is all and in all," says Paul. And what is that "all"? Remember the cosmic scope of the poem about Christ in chapter 1. "All things have been created through him and for him," "in him all things hold together," and "through him God was pleased to reconcile to himself all things, whether on earth or in heaven" (Col 1:15-17, 20). This gospel has been preached to *all creatures* (1:23). This is a cosmic redemption that extends to the very stuff of creation, and therefore this view of Christ and creation must have ecological consequences.

Remember also that Paul says the new community "is being renewed in knowledge according to the image of its creator" (3:10). The clear allusion to the opening chapters of Genesis raises the question for us of how this renewed image-bearing community tills and cares for the rest of creation. If we are renewed in the image of the Creator, then we must ask how the virtues of such a renewal transform and reshape our stewardship of the earth.[46]

So take a look again at Paul's list. This is a community of *compassion* that shares in the pathos and pain of creation. Is compassion an appropriate response to the suffering of nonhuman creatures? Ought we to be driven to compassion by something as immediate as the plight of animals in our own bioregion and something as abstract as the thinning of the ozone layer? Yes, compassion is precisely the appropriate response. When fellow creatures, whether they be particular animals or complex ecological systems, are in distress, when they cry out in anguish, a compassionate community responds, because it has the ears to hear those cries.

Recognizing with Paul and the whole biblical witness that creation in all of its rich, complex diversity is good, a delight to its Creator, means that those who are renewed in knowledge according to the image of this Creator will act "so as to preserve diverse kinds of life."[47] The renewal of the image of God in our lives will engender an *ecolog-*

---

[45]Many of the insights in this section were suggested by our students in the Creation Care Studies Program in Belize in November 2002.

[46]Among Steven Bouma-Prediger's most significant contributions to Christian environmental ethics are his proposals for a character ethic that discerns ecological virtues: *For the Beauty of the Earth,* chap. 6.

[47]Ibid., p. 142.

ical kindness: we will receive the creation as a gift and refuse to engage in aggressive mastery and subjugation of the earth. Creation care rooted in kindness wants to ask whether a given activity—choosing a mode of transportation, deciding how to deal with our waste or establishing the family menu for the week—will serve to honor the integrity, stability and beauty of a biotic community or harm that community. Kindness will always privilege care over harm, protection over destruction.

Kindness, however, is impossible where the relationship is unequal and based in an arrogant power "over" the other. Therefore an ecological ethic of *humility* rooted in Colossians 3 calls us to replace the arrogance of modern ecological control and destruction with a more respectful and careful mode of ecological engagement. It was a lack of humility in relation to our knowledge and technological abilities that led to a nuclear power industry that has littered the world with radioactive waste. Industry developers arrogantly insisted that while they didn't know how to safely dispose of such waste when it was first being produced, they were sure that future science and technology would be able to solve the problem. The future is now, and there is still no solution.

In a similar way, humility would want to slow down the march toward genetic modification of our food sources. In humility we should raise questions about the long-term ecological and economic consequences of genetically modified seed stocks. What happens, we ask, when crosspollination modifies more and more of the ecosystem, eventually wiping out the natural genetic development of species that has taken millennia within God's good time? Not only does this continue the ecological foolishness of large-scale monoculture farming (one blight or disease and the whole crop is gone), it also entrenches an agribusiness system of total control over farmers. Using genetically modified patented seeds means that farmers must pay the seed companies every year for their seed. Even farmers whose crops have been tainted by genetically modified seed from their neighbor's fields are being forced to pay the companies. A rice farmer in the Philippines puts the matter clearly: "If seeds are patented, it's like cutting off a farmer's arm since you are removing the farmer's freedom to choose seeds and preserve them."[48] Of course, the perpetrators of this revolution in genetic modification view the raising of such issues as little more than the paranoid fear-mongering of opponents of progress. But these questions arise not out of fear of progress but out of a fear of arrogance. These are the questions of humility.

Again, in the mode of arrogant control, there is only one voice that gets heard—the so-called voice of progress and profits. The one voice that is always drowned out in our cultural cacophony—until it screams at us through ecological disasters—is the voice of creation. It takes a certain *meekness* and receptivity to hear that voice. A community renewed in knowledge according to the image of the Creator embraces meek-

---

[48]Quoted by Devlin Kuyek in "Rice Is Life," *New Internationalist* 349 (September 2002): 17.

ness as integral to its way of engaging the world, because it follows a Lord who said, "Blessed are the meek," and who was recognized as the Messiah by the very stones on the side of the road (Mt 5:5; Lk 19:40).

The meek do not assume to control the earth, nor do they live beyond their means. They realize that people cannot continue to abuse the earth with impunity, because they are receptive enough to discern the forces of creation that are beyond our control. If it is true that the meek will inherit the earth, then a community that embraces meekness as a virtue will want to make sure there is an earth worth inheriting. Reducing the production of waste, reusing materials as often as possible and recycling waste once it cannot be reused any further should be second nature for such a community.

Integral to an ecologically sustainable way of life is rest. Not only must human beings receive rest and experience sabbath, but so also must all of creation. In our culture, however, no one gets real rest. An economically driven culture is always on the go, seven days a week, twenty-four hours a day. We have to keep moving because we might be left behind and we might not get what we want *now*. Ours is a culture of impatience. We can't rest because we wouldn't know what to do with ourselves if we weren't producing and consuming. For leisure we need the numbing presence of television, otherwise we would go crazy with impatience, waiting for the next thing to do. A culture of impatience has no time to slow down, plant and tend flowers, observe the changing of the seasons, or notice migrating bird species flying over our backyard or the park. A culture of impatience has no conception whatsoever of what it might mean to allow the creation to rest for its rejuvenation. For such an ethos of rest we need a community suffused with *patience.* An ecological mode of being in the world requires slow, attentive dwelling with creation, and only patience can provide us with the character to hang in there for the long haul of ecological healing.

From a biblical perspective, ecological brokenness is rooted in human sin. Creation groans in travail (Rom 8:22) because of the disobedience of the human steward of creation. In the graphic language of Leviticus, the land will vomit out the inhabitants because of their idolatry (Lev 18:28). So Paul calls the Colossian community to abandon all idolatry, all graven images, and be renewed in the image of the Creator. Such renewal, however, requires *forgiveness,* and this has been a repeated theme in Paul's epistle (Col 1:14; 2:13; 3:13). But what can be the ecological meaning of forgiveness?

Forgiveness is necessary if there is to be a renewed relationship. When covenant is broken, it can be repaired only when that break is healed through forgiveness. Our renewal as image-bearing caretakers of the earth must be rooted in a renewed relationship with the Creator through receiving forgiveness for our covenant-breaking idolatry, and perhaps there is a sense in which we must also seek forgiveness from creation itself. When we do injustice to another, deny their rights and inflict violence on them, reconciliation requires confession and forgiveness. If this is the case in human relations, why not in our relationship with the nonhuman creation? Wendell Berry has said, "Our destruction of nature is not just bad stewardship, or stupid economics, or a betrayal of family responsibility; it is the most horrid blasphemy. It is flinging God's gifts into His face, as if they were of no worth beyond that assigned to them by our destruction of them."[49] It is blasphemy because it holds both the Creator and the creation in contempt. Now, if all of creation is included in the covenant God makes through Noah (see Gen 9:8-17), and if Jesus comes to redeem all things, then ecological renewal and restoration require a spirituality of repentance for our blasphemous destruction of this good earth. That repentance means taking a stance of contrition before both God and the creation that we have wantonly destroyed. We will find that, like the Creator, creation can be a very generous and gracious covenant partner.

As we sat on a dock with a group of students late one night, the conversation turned to the question of why God made the world. We listened as the students went around and around on this one. Did God *need* the world? Was God lonely? Was there some preexisting force that God had to tame and direct toward a creation? None of these answers were satisfying, until at last one student suggested that God made the world because God is *love*.

A reverent silence came over the group, and for a few minutes we all lay out on the dock looking at the stars, hearing loons calling from across the lake and feeling the air chill as we entered deeper into the night. Then someone quoted from Psalm 33: "For the word of the LORD is upright, and all his work is done in faithfulness. He loves righteousness and justice; the earth is full of the steadfast love of the LORD" (vv. 4-5). The earth is full of the steadfast love of God! Even in the face of our ecological hate, our contemptuous rape of this creation of delight, the creation in its very being radiates the love of God.

Knowing the world in love is the only viable alternative to a knowing aimed at objective mastery. But such knowing is never divorced from doing. To know in love, to receive the world as full of the love of God, calls forth an ecology of love. As a mode of knowledge, ecology is the study of things in their complex and dynamic webs of relationships. Paul's ethic of *love* translates into an ecological practice (and theory) that wants to see those relationships directed by love. Whether the lion that eats the gazelle is engaging in a relationship of love is not for us to say. But we do know this, that *our* relationship to lions, gazelles, wetlands, ozone layers and backyard gardens —that is, *our* mode of ecological relationality—is to image the love of God that fills the earth.

Relating to nonhuman creation in love, however, is not an easy thing to contemplate

---

[49]Wendell Berry, "Christianity and the Survival of Creation," in *Sex, Economy, Freedom and Community* (New York: Pantheon, 1993), p. 98.

in our cultural context. Responding to the world in love is possible only when our imagination is set free from the worldview of commodification and objectification. When we can confess that the world is full of the steadfast love of God, and when our lives are brought together in a love that binds all things together in perfect harmony—that is, a love that makes things ecologically whole again—we will know deep within our being, with every breath we take, that love is stronger than any darkness, even the cultural darkness of our times, and stronger than death, even the ecocidal death that surrounds us.

So we are called to "let the *peace* of Christ rule" in our hearts. Just as peace in our hearts must lead us to be peacemakers in a world at war, so also must that peace in our hearts lead us to be peacemakers in a world that is at war against the very biotic, genetic, chemical and physical structures of creation. In this war Christians are called to be conscientious objectors. Christians will seek to be ecological peacemakers through their political activism, their patterns of consumption, the way they heat their homes and churches, the materials they use in constructing homes and churches, the way they deal with their waste, the cleaning products they use, and the kinds of technology they employ.

Let's put it this way. If Christians are committed to a covenant of peace with all of creation, they will seek to reduce the amount of waste thrown into landfill sites. How might this influence Christian parents' decision about how to deal with the waste that comes from their baby's bum? That's what it comes down to: what do we do about diapers? If the peace of Christ rules in our hearts, and if it is a peace for all creation, then does it matter whether we use disposable or cloth diapers? Is this a matter of Christian integrity?[50] Yes, it is. Christians committed to ecological restoration and peace will want to put cloth diapers on their baby's bottom, because this is healthier for the child and puts considerably less strain on our ecosystem.[51]

Ecological care is fundamentally a matter of homemaking. Just as the word *economics* refers to the laws or rules of the household (*oikos* = house, *nomos* = rules), *ecology* is a study of how the household of life is structured, how the world works (*oikos* = house, *logos* = study). When the structures of life have been broken, when the rules for the household are transgressed, the world is increasingly rendered uninhabitable. Without ecological care, without a life that reflects something of the virtues that Paul commends in Colossians 3, our creational home is broken, and we find that we can no longer dwell in it as our home. So what happens if in this condition of ecological homelessness we allow the word of Christ to *dwell in us richly*? Does the word of Christ

---

[50]If we are going to talk about disposable diapers, why not also think about disposable menstrual products? Why are we dumping blood-stained tampons and pads into landfill sites when there is the ecologically more appropriate option of washable organic cotton pads?

[51]See Laura Schmitt, "Crazy for Cloth: The Benefits of Cloth Diapers," *Mothering* 116 (January/February 2003): 36-39. In a profound article in this same issue, the staff of the magazine offer a comprehensive history of the disposable diaper: "The Politics of Diapers: A Timeline of Recovered History," pp. 40-46.

taking up residence in the very heart of our lives affect the way we take up residence in the world that was created, coheres and is being redeemed in, through and for this very Christ? Does this word of Christ shape the way we dwell in this world? Does this word shape our way of inhabiting the world?

Inhabitation requires attention to, intimacy with and even love of a particular place. Only then are we at home in that place, and only then do we respect its integrity.[52] If we are to be a community in which dwells the very word that called all of creation into being and calls all of creation to reconciliation, then we must nurture the skills of *inhabitance.*

Paul connects this indwelling of the word of Christ in our lives to three things: "teaching in all wisdom," gratitude and worship. For this word to indwell our lives, transform our imagination and shape our ecological engagement with the world, we must teach each other in all *wisdom,* says Paul. In what could be seen to be the quintessential environmentalist's psalm, the psalmist proclaims,

> O LORD, how manifold are your works!
>   In wisdom you have made them all;
>   the earth is full of your creatures. (Ps 104:24)

The author of Proverbs writes, "The LORD by wisdom founded the earth; by understanding he established the heavens" (3:19). Biblical wisdom is the tracing of the divine wisdom of creation.[53] Such wisdom—such an understanding of things in their interrelatedness—is in short supply in the fragmented culture of postmodern pluralism and global commodification. Wisdom understands that in a world of ecological interconnectedness there is no such thing as "away." We don't throw things "away," we simply put them someplace where they defile the land, foul the water, pollute the air or change the earth's atmosphere.

Knowing the world in wisdom, however, engenders a response of *gratitude.* A culture of entitlement, exploitation, greed and dissatisfaction can never know anything of gratitude. When the earth is reduced to raw materials for our economic acquisitiveness and all its "goods" are no more than commodities to be purchased on the global market, gratitude is impossible. Gratitude insists on receiving this world as gift. Creational life is a gift of a covenantal partner who, for no apparent reason apart from wanting to love us, called us into being. Rejoicing in the gift of creation precludes proprietary control of the gift and engenders a care born of gratitude. Steven Bouma-Prediger says, "Gratitude is the grammar of a grace that fosters respectful care for God's creatures." He adds, "Grace begets gratitude, and gratitude care."[54]

---

[52]David Orr, *Ecological Literacy* (Albany: State University of New York Press, 1992); Wes Jackson, *Becoming Native to This Place* (Washington, D.C.: Counterpoint, 1994).
[53]Roland Murphy, "Wisdom and Creation," *Journal of Biblical Literature* 104, no. 1 (1984): 3-11.
[54]Bouma-Prediger, *For the Beauty of the Earth,* p. 178.

Finally, this is an ecology rooted in *worship*. The word of Christ indwells us, says Paul, when we teach each other in all wisdom and when "with gratitude in [our] hearts" we "sing psalms, hymns and spiritual songs to God."

Now we know what William is saying right now: "You think that the romanticized, individualistic and ethereal spirituality of either traditional hymnody or contemporary 'praise and worship' songs will engender a decent environmental ethic and ecologically sensitive lifestyle? Take another look at the SUVs in the church parking lot!" And of course William would be right. We can probably tell as much about the real spirituality and the real worldview of a people by looking at the cars they drive, the food they consume, the gadgets that fill their homes and the garbage they throw out as we can by listening to the songs they sing and the prayers they pray. That is precisely our point. An otherworldly spirituality that is preoccupied with "me and Jesus," and escaping from this world into heavenly bliss, will never engender the kind of ecological ethos we are here suggesting. Moreover, an individualistic spirituality will inevitably legitimate an ecologically disastrous lifestyle.

Paul would not recognize such worship as having anything to do with the gospel that he proclaimed. Indeed, in light of our discussions of Paul's rhetorical attack on the "ensnaring philosophy" of Colossians 2, we could easily imagine him addressing contemporary evangelical spirituality in the same tone. If your worship serves to give you an ecstatic experience of personal relationship with Jesus without challenging you to see more deeply the way Jesus comes to reconcile all things in creation—including your ecological practices—then Paul would have a hard time recognizing it as a response to the gospel that he proclaimed "to *every* creature under heaven" (Col 1:23).

We have argued that Paul's understanding of the word of Christ that is to dwell richly in the Christian community is deeply rooted in Hebrew understandings of creation and wisdom. In those traditions, human worship is always to be in accord with the worship offered by all of creation. It is not just humans who sing praise to the Creator; so do rocks and trees, hills and mountains, snow and sleet, oceans and rivers. All of creation sings praise to God.[55] Unless there is something that inhibits that praise. Unless creation is choking in the pollution of human idolatry and can hardly raise more than a whimper of longing to the divine throne. Unless the rich symphony of creation is impoverished through the loss of many unique and wonderful voices because of unnecessary extinction.

Why does the Christ-following community strive for an ecologically responsible way of life? Because it is a worshiping community that joins its song with all of creation. When it is renewed in knowledge according to the image of the Creator, this community knows that its worship must both be in harmony with the rest of creation

---

[55]Terence E. Fretheim, "Nature's Praise of God in the Psalms," *Ex Auditu* 3 (1987): 16-30. See Psalms 19; 93; 96; 97; 98; 104; 148.

and must facilitate and make possible the free praise of our creaturely kin.

As we have said above, this is an ethic that begins and ends with Christ. Because "Christ is all and in all," whatever we do—whether recycling our garbage or deciding to reduce the amount of plastic we use, lobbying for better environmental policy or cleaning up the local river valley, conducting an energy and environmental audit on our home and church or choosing to eat only foods that are grown in sustainable ways, leading a summer camp in ecological literacy for kids or deciding to ride the bike rather than take the car—will be done in the name of Jesus and in gratitude to the Creator God. It all begins and ends with Christ.

Paul's ethic in the third chapter of Colossians is rooted in the narrative of Christ—died, buried, risen, ascended and coming again. This is not a narrative that imposes a series of absolutes to oppress us; it is a story of liberation from an empire that would take captive our imagination while it rapes and plunders the earth. This is not a violent metanarrative of exploitation of the earth. This is a story of restored relationships, a love story that calls forth an alternative community characterized by compassion, kindness, humility, meekness, patience, forgiveness, love, peace, gratitude and wisdom. This is a story of creational restoration, a renewal to full humanness, in the image of the Creator. This is a community in which the word of Christ dwells richly. This is a community that is shaped as a countercultural force through the subversive worship of a subversive Lord.

AN ETHIC OF LIBERATION

We were nearing the end of a course in which we had explored the book of Colossians in some depth with our students. In this session we were addressing one of the most difficult and controversial passages in the book: Paul's instructions in Colossians 3:18—4:1 to wives and husbands, children and fathers, slaves and masters.

As we finished reading the passage, Anthony, one of our students, began the discussion. It was clear that as far as he was concerned, this passage called into question everything we had done so far in the course. His argument was this: We can argue until we are blue in the face that Colossians is good news for an oppressed and marginalized community at the heart of the Roman empire, but unless this good news is for those truly at the margins—slaves, children and women—it is nothing but a noisy gong and a clanging cymbal. And this household code not only reinscribes the traditional oppressive ordering of a household in the empire, it is also "the integral consequence of Christ's universal lordship."[1]

Anthony continued: The letter doesn't just root the household codes in the transcendent language about Christ's lordship over all. These instructions also contradict those places where Paul does appear to be proclaiming a liberating gospel. Thus this code makes it possible for subsequent Christian interpreters to ignore the message of liberation that flashes out occasionally in the letter. This tension, according to Anthony, is handled in the letter by an overspiritualizing of the Colossians' baptismal identity with otherworldly overtones and by a personalizing of their calling.[2] He supported this interpretation by reading the beginning of chapter 3 as an attempt to transcend the Colossians' earthly situation and by reading the ethical injunctions of chapter 3 in terms of personal conduct.

---

[1]The phrase is from Mary Rose D'Angelo, "Colossians," in *Searching the Scriptures,* vol. 2, *A Feminist Commentary* (New York: Crossroad, 1994), p. 322. Quoted by Anthony J. Ricciuti in "An Open Letter to Onesimus of Colossae: An Examination of Colossians 3.18—4.1 in Context," unpublished paper submitted at the Institute for Christian Studies, Toronto, 1999, p. 3.
[2]Ibid., p. 11.

We have already suggested an interpretation of chapter 3 which challenges such a dualistic, personalistic reading, but Anthony's questions still remain. Does Paul's teaching about the structure of a Christian household stand in fundamental tension with the rest of Colossians? Are the injunctions to wives, children and slaves legitimated by a language of transcendence that is oppressively hierarchical? And if so, then does our whole reading of Colossians as a text subversive of empire—both ancient and contemporary—come crashing down under the weight of a repressive household ethic? If Paul is reinforcing an imperial view of the household—and especially slavery—then how can this really be an ethic of secession? And if this is an ethic of community, just how liberating is it for those who were at the bottom of the social structures of the day?

When Anthony framed these questions for us in print, he did so by writing an open letter to Onesimus, asking for his voice to be heard in the reading of Colossians. Because the questions Anthony raised provide a profound challenge to our reading of Colossians as a whole, we have answered his letter with one of our own. Our letter, however, explores these verses from the perspective of Onesimus, a carrier of Paul's epistle to the Colossian community (Col 4:9).

The Epistle of Onesimus the Slave to Paul the Apostle

Onesimus, a servant of Christ Jesus by the will of God, to Paul, my father in the faith. Grace to you and peace from God our Father and the Lord Jesus Christ.

I thank God for you when I remember you in my prayers, because of your encouragement in the Lord and the love you have shown me. Such encouragement provides steady hope in the controversy that has erupted with our coming to Colossae. Indeed, *controversy* is a mild word to describe the chaos your letter created in the community. Not that I myself am in any danger. Tychicus has made it clear that I am under his protection, and not only his but also yours, and so no harm has come to me. In fact I was so able to efface myself that the discussion your letter generated took place in my presence, though my input was not solicited, in spite of your commendation that I could tell them about everything.[3]

The community here is very much as Epaphras had reported it to us, and indeed much as I had left it. Tensions notwithstanding, the brothers and sisters continue to live in faith, love and hope. But fear of further persecution is also prevalent. And that fear shaped many of the responses to the letter you sent with Tychicus and me.

As you can imagine, every member of both house churches in Colossae was present for the reading of your letter. By God's grace Nympha was also present, since she was in Colossae to meet with one of her textile merchants. No small interest was generated by my presence, since everyone knew that your letter would address my

---

[3]See Colossians 4:9.

status in the community. What would Paul suggest be done with Onesimus, runaway slave, supposed thief, betrayer of his master? As they listened to the letter I could feel that tension was building, along with bewilderment and unease.

Then when you did finally mention Tychicus and described me as a good and faithful brother, the room erupted. Tychicus had to restore calm to finish the letter. As he did there was a look of blank disbelief. That's all? No *specific* advice to Philemon? Everyone looked disappointed—more than that, enraged—except for Archippus, who flushed and then went pale. He clearly knew what was up.

Well, before Tychicus could even announce that he had another letter for Philemon—the letter, in fact, that would answer their concerns—the arguing began. And Tychicus, with a little mischievous grin, sat back and enjoyed the fun. You would have enjoyed it yourself, I think, if only as an example of how people read and misread your letters. There were three basic views on what you were saying.

The first was the predictable one, the position you actually argued against throughout the letter. (I'll call these men "the philosophers.") "See," they argued, "Paul is affirming the household structure as we've inherited it from Aristotle. Paul would never try to undermine the natural order of society. He affirms the God-given order of husband over wife, father over children and master over slave. Without such a structure our society would lose its moral and economic moorings; it would crumble." In fact, one young scholar got up and began to solemnly intone the crucial sentences from Aristotle:

> For the male is by nature better fitted to command than the female . . . and the older and fully developed person than the younger and immature. . . . All human beings that differ as widely as the soul does from the body . . . are by nature slaves for whom to be governed by this kind of authority is advantageous. . . . For the free rule the slave, the male the female, the man the child in different ways; for the slave has not got the deliberative part at all, and the female has it but without full authority, while the child has it but in an undeveloped form.[4]

He was stopped when an elderly Jewish brother broke in. "But this is precisely the kind of philosophy according to *human* tradition that Paul referred to in his letter! A philosophy that takes us captive and makes us take and keep others captive. Paul is definitely *not* affirming Aristotle here. Why, look at how widely his instructions differ from Aristotle's!" And he stopped for a breath.

One of the philosophers jumped in the breach. "Of course he is affirming Aristotle. Even your own philosophers affirm that this is the divinely ordained structure of society!"

---

[4]Aristotle *Politics* 1.125.3b, 9b, 4b; 1.126.0a, quoted in Elisabeth Schüssler Fiorenza, "The Praxis of Coequal Discipleship," in *Paul and Empire: Religion and Power in Roman Imperial Society,* ed. Richard A. Horsley (Harrisburg, Penn.: Trinity Press International, 1977), pp. 238-39.

"One of our own philosophers?" While the older man kept calm, he was white with anger. "And who might 'our own philosophers' be?"

"Philo, of course, and Josephus. They both affirm that 'the male head of the household is intended by nature to rule as husband, father and master, and that not to adhere to this proper hierarchy is detrimental not only to the household but also to the life of the state.'"[5]

"You would do well to remember," the older man replied, "that a Hellenistic Jew such as Philo"—he almost spat the words out—"and a Roman sympathizer such as Josephus"—then he did spit—"hardly reflect the views of faithful Jews."

But he knew the philosophers had touched the point that was crucial for the community. Not to adhere to this hierarchy could be interpreted by outsiders as treasonous to the empire, as an undermining of the social order. And we know that over the last number of decades the emperors have made legislative changes directed at ensuring that the social order be strengthened and maintained.

Various people in the group spoke to this concern. What the argument boiled down to was this. It is fine for you, Paul, to say that Jesus has triumphed over the principalities and powers, but the daily experience of this community is that the evil spirits of this age are very present and working against them, and the rule of Rome and its military authority still hold all the power that matters. It's very well for you to say that those who are clothed in Christ no longer need the sabbath and food regulations, asceticism or the beneficial intercession of angels. But this community needs such practices for good order, to deflect outsiders' suspicion that Christian households are undermining the social order. Moreover, as a number of the leaders pointed out, to tamper with such an obviously natural order would be economically disastrous. Best to have a severe, though restrained, ethic, and best to uphold the economic status quo of the empire when it comes to the paterfamilias.

Even if such a status quo can be brutal at times (*as it was for Onesimus,* I could see some of them thinking), the way to deal with such suffering is to patiently wait for our escape from this world of death. In a higher spiritual realm such earthly situations are irrelevant. This is the true wisdom.

They didn't look at me as they spoke, but I could tell what the result of such a philosophy would be for me. No matter how unbearable my situation, I should have stayed. I should glory in my abasement and realize that I'm not really a slave before God. But in this earthly life I need to take what my master dishes out. And that would likely mean stiff punishment for running away, I could see that immediately.

Others wanted a softened version of this stance. It was true: Paul would not want to undermine a social order that is a natural outworking of the very order of creation.

---

[5]Andrew Lincoln, "The Household Code and Wisdom Mode of Colossians," *Journal for the Study of the New Testament* 74 (1999): 100. The relevant texts are Philo *De Decalogue* 165; *De Hypothetica* 7.1-14; Josephus *Contra Apion* 2.190-219.

But they wanted to take the rest of the letter a little more seriously. After all, Paul had talked at length about Jesus' reconciling all things in heaven and on earth. Surely such reconciliation should affect the structures of the household. And surely his exhortations to get rid of anger, wrath, malice, slander and abusive language, to be clothed in compassion, kindness, humility, meekness and patience, to live in forgiveness and peace and thanksgiving, should affect the way we work within creational structures.

They argued that this ethic does affect creational structures. Paul doesn't just speak to husbands, fathers and masters. He also speaks to wives, children and slaves. And it is clear that he recognizes that they have some will in this matter, that they can *choose* to be subject. What he says to the heads of the household is also unusual: husbands are to love their wives, fathers are not to provoke their children, masters are to treat slaves justly and fairly. Surely what Paul has done is transform the natural order of things so that it might undergo the reconciliation of Jesus. While he may be supporting the status quo, he is doing so in a way that makes the natural order of things palatable. Love patriarchy, that's what Paul is arguing for.[6] This is a kinder, gentler economic and social hierarchy.

The men who argued for this position did look at me as they spoke. They even smiled. You could see that they felt they were being very generous toward me. And given the way most slaves are treated, they *were* being generous. With such a love patriarchy, Philemon would be bound to take me back gently, treat me fairly and justly, and not abuse me. Not bad.

While this group was speaking, the older man who had spoken earlier was shaking his head sadly. Finally he looked pointedly at Archippus and said, "Archippus, you heard what Paul said to you: 'See that you complete the task that you have received in the Lord.' Perhaps now is the time."[7]

Archippus took a deep breath, stood up and addressed the assembly.

"Men of Colossae," he began, "holy and beloved, called to bear fruit and grow in the wisdom and knowledge of God. You know that I have now for many months been attending the synagogue in order to receive instruction in the Scriptures of Israel, the ancient texts of our Messiah, Jesus, and of many of his followers both here in the Lycus Valley and throughout the world. The story found in these texts is known to many of you, as is the story of Jesus the second Adam, in whom the image of God dwells fully, the One who came to bring salvation to Israel and bring God's new kingdom of peace to both Israel and the whole world through his death on the cross and his rising from the dead. As you know, I have been studying this story and these Scriptures for some time now in preparation for my teaching ministry in this community. Today I must begin this ministry.

---

[6]The term was coined by Gerd Theissen, *The Social Setting of Pauline Christianity* (Philadelphia: Fortress, 1982), p. 107.
[7]Colossians 4:17.

"It is indeed true that in the letter we have heard today Paul refers to the ordering of our households as found in the ancient philosophers and as taught by imperial decree. But I ask you today, do we worship the gods of the philosophers? Do we worship the gods of the empire? Or do we worship the living God, who raised Jesus from the dead *to free us* from all bondage to powers on earth and in heaven, whether thrones or dominions or rulers or powers, even the authorities we have been taught are according to nature?

"In this letter Paul appeals not primarily to the ancient philosophers, nor to the edicts of the emperor, but to the ancient stories of Israel. Those stories describe how, in the shadow of empire, Israel was called to form an alternative covenant community rooted in the Torah of a God who freed the slave, loves the refugee and cares for the widow and the orphan. As that community was called to be holy, so we are called saints, the holy ones.[8]

"The kingdom of Jesus is just such a covenant community. Paul describes the story of that kingdom as a story of forgiveness. He began his letter to us by calling the kingdom of the Son a kingdom of forgiveness. He said that through Jesus all things in heaven and on earth are reconciled to God; he also said that God made us alive in Jesus when he forgave us our debts, erasing the record that stood against us with all its legal demands. And then he called us to forgive each other; just as the Lord has forgiven us, so we should forgive.[9]

"And the story of forgiveness in Jesus is rooted in an even larger story. Remember how God decided during the exodus that the way he will deal with a stiff-necked people, who glory in a golden calf, is by forgiving them.[10] In our Scriptures, forgiveness of sin and redemption from slavery are always at the heart of God's dealing with the covenant people. In the community God called together to bear his image, such forgiveness and redemption were to be most obviously evident in the forgiving of debt and freeing from slavery.

"Every seven years the Israelites were to forgive debts and free slaves.[11] In fact, Israel's Torah reaches its climax in the jubilee year, when a complete economic leveling was to take place involving not only release of slaves but also the return of land.[12] Laws like this were rooted in Israel's memory of its God: because God releases slaves out of Egyptian bondage, so Israel is called to image that God by being a slave-releasing community.[13] This story shows that in the new covenant reality to which God calls his people, forgiveness permeates all of life, especially our households. In this epistle, Paul has told us that through Christ, God was pleased to reconcile all

---

[8]Colossians 1:2; Exodus 19:6; Leviticus 19:2; 20:26; cf. Psalm 16:3; 34:9; Daniel 7:18; 8:24.
[9]Colossians 1:14, 20; 2:13-14; 3:13.
[10]Exodus 32—34.
[11]Deuteronomy 15.
[12]Leviticus 25.
[13]Deuteronomy 15:15.

things. His whole letter has been calling us to live out of that reconciliation and to practice the reign of Christ in every area of life. And he explicitly told us that in this renewal there is no longer Greek and Jew, circumcised and uncircumcised, barbarian, Scythian—slave and free![14]

"So far no one has mentioned these breathtakingly radical words of Paul and asked how they might shed light on his advice for our household lives. Are these empty words? Or do they mean a radical change in how we followers of Jesus organize ourselves?

"You see, Paul didn't use just the language of forgiveness to describe our story; he also used the language of *inheritance*. As I recall, it went like this: we are enabled to share in the inheritance of the saints.[15] In Israel's story, forgiveness and inheritance always come together.[16]

"Now it may be that you are thinking Paul's language about inheritance is irrelevant to the problem of slavery. After all, Onesimus here is more likely to *be* part of an inheritance than receive one.[17] But Paul did say something about an inheritance when he was talking to the slaves. Tychicus, perhaps you could read that section to us again."

So Tychicus read the relevant section, that bit we had labored so hard over: "Whatever your task, put yourselves into it, as done for the Master and not for your masters, since you know that from the Master you will receive the inheritance as your reward; you serve the Master Christ."[18]

Then Archippus went on. "Paul seems to think that slaves will receive the inheritance. This is the central theme in Israel's story, a story lived always in the shadow of empire, a story of a kingdom that turns empire on its head. Don't forget that *we* are a people who were freed from slavery in the exodus. The laws appeal to this event again and again, especially when calling for Israel to free slaves (with a good portion of wine and grain and livestock) and when calling for Israel to practice not merely justice but unexpected graciousness and generosity to the orphan, the widow and the alien.[19] Is-

---

[14]Colossians 1:20; 3:11.

[15]Colossians 1:12.

[16]The biblical texts regarding inheritance are plentiful. The promise to Abraham that he will inherit the land is found in Genesis 12:1-7, 15:7-12 and 17:1-8. The promises to Israel in the exodus that they will be given the land as their inheritance are found in Exodus 3:7-8 and 23:20-33; Leviticus 20:24; Numbers 34:2; Deuteronomy 4:20-40, 12:10 and 1:20. The promise during the exile that the land will be given as an inheritance in a new exodus event is found in Ezekiel 36:8-12. And in intertestamental Judaism, the promises that the faithful will inherit the whole earth are found in *Jubilees* 22:14-15 (in a blessing on Abraham) and 32:19; *1 Enoch* 5:7. This is affirmed by Paul in Romans 4:13, where he restates the promise to Abraham as a promise that Abraham would inherit the whole earth.

[17]In Leviticus 25:46 slaves are listed as part of the inheritance that may be passed on to one's children.

[18]Colossians 3:23-24, our translation. It needs to be noted that the Greek word *kyrios* can be translated "Lord" or "Master." By using "Lord" for God and Jesus but "master" for human masters, most English translations lose some of the nuancing that is found in the repetition of the same word in the Greek.

[19]See Deuteronomy 15:15; 24:18; 24:22; cf. Deuteronomy 5:15; 16:12.

rael and we ourselves are called to be gracious and generous because we once were slaves in the land of Egypt and God saved us from our slavery.

"This movement from being slaves to being sons who receive the inheritance is central to the story of Israel. And forgiveness is central to slaves receiving the inheritance as well. This is why the sabbath laws are about rest and freedom for slaves.[20] The jubilee, which is the climax of the sabbath, is precisely about slaves receiving an inheritance. They are freed, and they inherit once again the land that was taken from them. In fact, some groups interpret this story to mean that Jews should not keep slaves at all, because the God we worship is a God who sets slaves free.[21]

"Look at what Paul does. Yes, he addresses wives, children and slaves. Yes, he transforms the relationships by asking husbands to love wives, fathers not to provoke children and masters to treat slaves justly and fairly. But he does more. You serve the Master Christ, the messianic Master! This is your *true* Master. He completely strips earthly masters of their ultimate sovereignty over their slaves. In fact he tells masters that they have a Master in heaven. The categories are completely undermined by Paul's language here. They no longer have validity.

"This is what Paul is really saying. This is our story. The letter is clear if you know the story, if you are aware of the way our God has acted in history up to now. In contrast to the economics of the empire, Paul here proclaims a countereconomics of sabbath and jubilee rooted in the forgiving love of Jesus. By telling the slaves in our midst that they have an 'inheritance,' Paul is recalling for us the traditions of jubilee; he is reminding us that Israel's story—and now, through Jesus, our story—is a slave-freeing story.

"Look closely at what Paul is doing here. First he says that there is no longer Greek and Jew, circumcised and uncircumcised, Scythian and barbarian, slave and free. Then he says that in Jesus' kingdom slaves who follow the messianic Master (the Lord Christ) will receive the inheritance. We are called to fill in the missing step."

Well, by the time Archippus had finished speaking, I felt like cheering. Well done!

Then Tychicus, with that grin of his still hovering, spoke up and told one of the parables that Luke loves about Jesus. You know, the one about the master who comes and finds his slaves waiting to open the door, and so he sits the slaves down and serves them the banquet.[22] He didn't push it, just pointed out the reversal.

And then came the question, the main one. If Paul wanted to say that slaves are to

---

[20]See Exodus 20:10; Deuteronomy 5:14; 15:12-18.

[21]Both Josephus and Philo, in their descriptions of the Essenes, assert that the Essenes have no slaves, for they consider slavery an injustice and a transgression of the law of nature (Philo *Omn. Prob. Lib.* 79; Josephus *Jewish Antiquities* 18.21). See Geza Vermes and Martin Goodman, *The Essenes According to the Classical Sources* (Sheffield, U.K.: JSOT Press, 1989), pp. 21, 55. However, see also *Damascus Document* 12.11, which indicates that some Essenes may have owned slaves. That slavery was a contentious issue in both preexilic and postexilic Israel is evident in Jeremiah 34:8-22 and Nehemiah 5:1-13.

[22]Luke 12:35-38. On Luke's presence with Paul when Colossians and Philemon were composed, see Colossians 4:14 and Philemon 23.

be freed, then why didn't he come out and say it? But even as it was asked, everyone knew the obvious answer.

Even so, Tychicus replied: "You know what happens to these letters. They're read aloud at many gatherings, copied, sent to other cities, such as Laodicea. You know the importance of slaves, wives, even children in the social and economic hierarchy of the empire. You know what would happen if Paul ever committed such advice to paper, ever made such a declaration public.[23]

"For those who do not have ears to hear, for those who do not know the story, either of Israel or of Jesus, this advice seems innocent enough. It appears to uphold the status quo while advising tolerance. But for those who know the story, the clues are there, the allusions are made, and the hidden meaning is understood. For those with ears to hear, the message is clear: this is a God who proclaims a different kingdom from the ensnaring oppression of the empire, a God who frees slaves and calls for his followers to do likewise."

Then he stopped.

So there it was, our whole rhetorical strategy laid out in simple terms. And it looked as if the debate would go on for some time, especially about the economic feasibility of such a teaching ("so many of our house churches *depend* on slaves"). Of course Philemon, who had been pretty quiet, pointed out that if he freed one runaway slave he would have chaos in his household.

As if on cue, Tychicus drew out the letter for Philemon, Apphia and Archippus. By that point everyone in the community wanted to hear what you, Paul, had to say in this more private epistle. They wondered if you would dare to put your wishes more clearly in writing to these three leaders or if you would be circumspect once more. They weren't disappointed. For even though you had chosen your words carefully to this community that had already experienced persecution, your wishes were pretty clear: that I be released by Philemon as a voluntary good deed, that Philemon welcome me, that he forgive my debts or at least transfer them to you, and that you are asking more than you even dare say in the letter.[24]

By this time it was clear that you were walking a pretty narrow tightrope between what you dare say explicitly in a public epistle and the hidden message of the ethic you are actually espousing. (I should add that such circumspection is appreciated by almost everyone here; no one wants the authorities to pay more attention to us than is absolutely necessary, especially in the current political climate).

But then the totally unexpected happened. As the room fell silent a voice was

---

[23]On the distinction between public and hidden transcripts, see James C. Scott, *Domination and the Arts of Resistance* (New Haven, Conn.: Yale University Press, 1990). While the public transcript of Colossians 3:18—4:1 might appear innocuous to an outsider, the hidden transcript—the jubilee text for those who had ears to hear—was socially, economically and politically subversive.

[24]Philemon 13-14, 17-21.

raised at the back, "What about the women?"

There was a stir as people turned around to see who had spoken. It was Nympha, the textile merchant from Laodicea. As I have mentioned, she was in Colossae on business when your letter arrived. Since she leads the Christian community that meets in her house, she had stayed to hear the reading of the letter.

As the people in the room gaped at her in surprise, especially as they had just heard your letter ask them to send her your greetings,[25] she continued, "Paul doesn't just talk about slaves here, although that is clearly his main concern; he also addresses husbands and wives. If this really is a story about liberation for slaves, is it also a story about liberation for women? Are women also to be freed from the cruelty and abuse that the heads of households often display? Are women also to be freed from the power of their husbands?"

No one said a word. For some reason none of the men wanted to break their silence. Then Apphia spoke up. "Nympha," she said, "Paul is concerned in this letter about slaves, not about women."

Nympha wasn't convinced. "But you just heard what Paul said to wives. They are to be subject as is fitting *in the Lord*. Our Lord is the Lord Messiah, not our husband, and in Jesus we are all to be subject to one another, husbands and wives alike. And Paul tells husbands to love their wives. Such love can only mean that the hierarchy is gone. You know, Apphia, how harshly authority is practiced in our homes. There is no room for that where love is."

Apphia countered. "Scripture doesn't support that. It is clear about slaves but not about women. There is no jubilee for women; there's no provision for women to be set free from their husbands."

Nympha was having none of it. "Jubilee is rooted in sabbath," she argued, "and the sabbath laws applied equally to women. It says in the law, 'On the sabbath you shall not do any work, you or your son or your daughter, your male slave or your female slave.'[26] Rest and freedom are for men and women equally, whether slave or free.

"And what about the Messiah?" she continued, "Did he not have women followers who provided for him and who proclaimed that he had risen from the dead? Were they not the first to proclaim the gospel of the resurrection?"[27]

She paused. When no one responded, she singled out one man. "Tell me, Tychicus," she said. "You brought this letter here; you work with Paul. What is Paul's practice in this matter? Are women subject to an enslaving philosophy that slaves are to be freed from?"

Tychicus answered slowly but truthfully, pointing out that throughout the communities in which you minister there are women in positions of authority—even some

---

[25]Colossians 4:15.
[26]Exodus 20:10; Deuteronomy 5:13.
[27]Matthew 28:1-10; Mark 1:10; Luke 24:1-12; John 20:11-18.

whose husbands are not. "Phoebe is a deacon in Cenchreae, Junia is a prominent apostle, Priscilla is a woman who teaches and proclaims the gospel equally with (some even think better than) her husband, Aquila, and many other women work hard to proclaim the gospel in their respective places," he said.[28]

Apphia remained skeptical, remarking that while women in leadership might go over in the larger metropolitan centers such as Rome or Corinth, it's a different story here in the Lycus Valley. But she trailed off as she realized that she was speaking to Nympha, not only a successful textile merchant but the leader of a house church in Laodicea, just ten miles from Colossae.

Tychicus added that he had heard the formulation "There is no longer Greek and Jew, circumcised and uncircumcised, barbarian, Scythian, slave and free" also include "There is no longer male and female."[29]

Nympha pursued the point. "It's clear that Paul is undermining the structure of the household in the empire, especially in relation to slaves. We need to listen clearly to his words, for when he suggests that slaves be freed, he does so in the context of the whole household system by also mentioning both women and children. My fellow believers, you know that when we became part of this Christian community, we gave up these allegiances. You know that we all became part of a new household, which does not support the hierarchical economic structures of the empire but in which all exist for the benefit and mutual service of others. You all experienced the coming of the Spirit, promised to both old and young, sons and daughters, slaves and free. You know how Paul's teachings have challenged the very basis of our society by contradicting the emperor's edicts on compulsory marriage, by urging widows to remain single, by urging us all to choose a life free of the encumbrances of marriage.[30] It is no surprise then that Paul is also challenging the basis of the *paterfamilias,* which the empire regards as fundamental and which we have replaced with a new household in Christ Jesus our Lord."

As she paused, the older Jewish brother slowly got to his feet. "Our sister is right," he said. "We should not let our fear of the emperor keep us from following the call of our brother Paul to end these worldly structures. We have suffered for this gospel before. It may be that we will suffer again. But we are subject to Jesus, not Caesar. And we are citizens of the kingdom of the beloved Son, not the empire.

"We now need to spend some time in prayer, so that we may wisely discern how

---

[28]Romans 16:1-12; Acts 18:26; Philippians 4:3; Colossians 3:15.

[29]Galatians 3:28.

[30]In the *Leges Iuliae* "widowers and divorcees of both sexes were expected to remarry after a period of one month. Widows at first were expected to remarry after a one year period, but, following protests, that period was extended to three years" (Schüssler Fiorenza, "Praxis of Coequal Discipleship," p. 233). Cf. 1 Corinthians 7; Paul Zanker, *The Power of Images in the Age of Augustus* (Ann Arbor: University of Michigan Press, 1990), p. 157.

to be a community of mutual submission. And I would like to ask our sister Nympha to lead us in such prayer, for I perceive in her the working of the Spirit." It was a benediction as well as an invitation.

As Nympha prayed, Philemon quietly left and did not return. The meeting ended.

Tychicus and I are enjoying the hospitality of Archippus, and tomorrow I await my judgment. Philemon could choose to do as little as the philosophers expect, or he could choose to do even more than you have asked of him. Either way, his choice is not easy.

I am left with one question, the tension between what is safe or prudent to commit to writing when advising these struggling communities on the one hand and the actual outworking of the gospel that is practiced by you and your followers on the other. Perhaps in a hostile world it will never be safe to bluntly state the radical demands of the gospel; from the gospel as Luke told it to us, even Jesus seemed to hold back from speaking clearly until he knew the end was in sight. But his lived ethic conveyed much more than his words. When will the followers of the gospel ever be able to commit to the insecurity of written word the radical ethic they are called to obey? Will it not be until the kingdom has dawned and the glory for which we await has been revealed?

Give my greetings to Epaphras, Aristarchus and especially Luke, who labored so carefully on my behalf. The grace of the Lord Jesus Christ be with your Spirit.

What Slaves?

I would really like to believe this reading of Colossians 3:18—4:1, but it raises even more questions for me. I am wondering what this whole discussion of slavery has to do with our world. How would you translate the question of slavery into the twenty-first century? What names would you name?

Listen to this description of working conditions in factories located in "export processing zones," where low-wage workers make products cheap:

> Regardless of where EPZ's [Economic Processing Zones] are located, the workers' stories have a certain mesmerizing sameness: the workday is long—fourteen hours in Sri Lanka, twelve hours in Indonesia, sixteen in Southern China, twelve in the Philippines. The vast majority of the workers are women, always young, always working for subcontractors from Korea, Taiwan or Hong Kong. The contractors are usually filling orders for companies based in the U.S., Britain, Japan, Germany or Canada. The management is military style, the supervisors often abusive, the wages below subsistence, the work low-skill and tedious.[31]

Sure looks like slavery to us. What names would we name? Well, just take a look at the tag in the clothing that you are wearing. If that article of clothing was produced

---

[31]Naomi Klein, *No Logo: Taking Aim at the Brand Bullies* (Toronto: Vintage Canada, 2000), p. 205.

in what was just called an Economic Processing Zone, then the odds are pretty good that you can name the brand of clothing you are wearing as a slave trader. And all of us who purchase these goods are thereby complicit in slavery.

But let us allow one of the largest clothing manufacturers in the world to explain how this works. Explaining his decision to shut down twenty-two plants in North America, John Ermantinger, president of the American division of Levi-Strauss, said, "Shifting significant portions of our manufacturing from the U.S. and Canadian markets to contractors throughout the world will give the company greater flexibility to allocate resources and capital to its brands. These steps are crucial if we are to remain competitive."[32] Translation? Move the production side of the operation to Economic Processing Zones, where there is no restrictive labor legislation or bothersome environmental protection laws, thereby producing the clothing more cheaply and releasing more resources to the more important local task of advertising the brands.

It all sounds rather sinister when you put it that way.

There is nothing innocent about economic oppression. There is no room for Christians to be "balanced" and "careful" when we are talking about an economic idolatry that will sacrifice children in its service. Slavery *is* sinister no matter how it gets packaged.

Then what are we to do? How do we proclaim Colossians' liberating word to slaves when they are halfway around the world? It's not as if we have any power over their working conditions. It's not as if they are our *slaves whom we need to release.*

But that's just the point. They *are* our slaves. Every time we step into a Wal-Mart or Niketown or Gap or Winners and exclaim over the great deal we can get on an article of clothing, or how trendy we now look, we've made sweatshop workers our slaves. Every time we buy coffee that isn't shade grown and fairly traded, we've made those coffee producers and their children into our slaves.[33] Every time we have purchased a product—any product—that says Made in China, or Indonesia, or the Philippines, or Sri Lanka, it is pretty likely that we have made someone our slave.

But we have no choice about buying products made in those places. Some things can be bought only from these companies! Buying some of these products is inevitable.

The language of inevitability is the language of empire. Whenever we hear "We have no choice," our ears should perk up. It is precisely the strategy of the empire to take our imagination captive so that we think we have no choice. When a certain lifestyle seems to be inescapable, you need to realize that you are imprisoned.

The truth is that we have many choices. The simplest action anyone can take is to stop purchasing these products. There are still local tailors and seamstresses who make clothes and sell them in shops, and there are clothes made in cooperatives all over the world that are part of an international fair-trade network. Such clothes are

---

[32]Quoted in ibid., p. 196.
[33]Emily Polk, "Children: The Other Side of the Coffee Trade," *Whole Earth,* no. 108 (Summer 2002): 16-17.

available through Oxfam's Bridgehead stores and through the Ten Thousand Villages stores sponsored by the Mennonite Central Committee. But maybe you can't afford to pay more for clothes that are locally or fairly made. Perhaps you will simply decide to have fewer clothes as a result. Or perhaps you will decide that if you are going to end up wearing sweatshop-produced clothing, then at least you will do it in a way that will serve the poor locally by making your purchases at secondhand shops. That way, a local charity benefits from your purchase.

But maybe that won't be enough for you. You might decide to lobby these corporations to end their oppressive labor practices. Or you might decide to join one of the projects or campaigns that work to end child labor and support workers' rights.[34] Maybe you will lobby your government to withdraw from trade agreements that legitimate oppression and call on your political leaders to draft new legislation that seeks to end the global market's equivalent of slavery.

Our point is that when there are options available—whether various consumer choices or lobbying—to decide not to do anything at all is itself a choice. The Gospels call it the wide and easy path. But we can choose another path. There are ways to proclaim and enact Paul's word of release to slaves, women and children.

All these choices that you list seem overwhelming to me.

That's why we spent so much time talking about an alternative community in the previous chapter. No one can attempt to nurture an alternative imagination on their own without a community gathered around a crucified and risen Lord and enlivened by the Holy Spirit. Perhaps since Paul felt it important to spend a significant amount of time instructing this community about slavery, we should take that seriously and devote some adult Christian education time in our churches to discussing the contemporary manifestations of slavery and how we as followers of Jesus live in the face of it.

That would sure put a different twist on Sunday school in my church. But I want to ask about the issue of parents and children. You discussed in your epistle what Paul's words might mean for husbands and wives, but the passage also talks about fathers and children. Did Paul's liberating message to slaves also apply to parents and children? And what would that look like in the way we structure our families today?

Well, what do *you* think? If the household structure of women, children and slaves was crucial to the economy of the empire, and if contemporary slavery is crucial to the economy of the empire today, then how is it that the structure of our families, par-

---

[34]Some projects and programs concerned with child labor issues include Coffee Kids, Plaza Esperanza, 1305 Luisa Street, Suite C, Santa Fe, NM 87505 (800-334-9099); United Nations Works Programme, Department of Public Information, Room S-955, New York, NY 10017 (ask for information on child labor). On general labor issues related to workers in Economic Development Zones, consult International Labour Organization, International Labour Office, 4 Route de Morillons, CH-1211, Geneva 22, Switzerland (41-22-799-6111); U.S. Labor Education in the Americas Project, PO Box 268-290, Chicago, IL 60626 (773-262-6502).

ticularly the way we raise our children, is still in service of the empire? Do our children have any function in this empire?

You mentioned earlier the way advertising targets children, so I guess they are seen as valuable consumers.

That's true, children are increasingly targeted as consumers. And where does such targeting happen?

Television would be the obvious place, and the Internet.

Exactly. Television is one of the most obvious places that our children are shaped to be part of an economy of consumption. So maybe one way to wrest our children from the control of the empire is removing the television.[35] Such a simple act, but so deeply subversive!

The Internet brings us to an even more insidious form of marketing to our children. Not only does regular Internet service enable companies to place "cookies" on e-mail addresses in order to send targeted marketing, but the in-school computer network Zap Me! "monitors students' paths as they surf the Net and provides this valuable market research, broken down by gender, age and zip code, to its advertisers. Then, when students log on to Zap Me! they are treated to ads that have been specially 'microtargeted' for them."[36]

This last example brings us to another place where our children are trained to be obedient to the authority of the empire: schools. Schools are the latest avenue for corporations to reach children. With the mandatory viewing of "Channel One" in schools, which reaches an estimated eight million students in North America, as well as cafeteria menu items named by Disney and Kellogg's, fast-food chain kiosks in cafeterias, exclusive sale deals with Pepsi and Coke, sports team sponsorships, and curricula provided by Nike and other corporations, students are now surrounded by advertising in every aspect of their school life.[37] This sort of education not only creates consumers but trains our children to be promoters of consumption as well.

What does this have to do with the question of parents—or, in Paul's case, fathers—having authority over their children? This seems to me to be an abdication of authority, not a misuse of it.

Precisely. Remember what Paul says, "Fathers, do not provoke your children, or they may lose heart" (Col 3:21). Handing our children over to the captivity of the empire actually allows the empire to provoke them to become dutiful subjects, obedient consumers who have lost the heart for any kind of resistance.

This is our deepest suspicion of mass, mandatory and state-controlled education.

---

[35]See Barbara Kingsolver, "The One-Eyed Monster and Why I Don't Let Him In," in *Small Wonder* (New York: HarperCollins, 2002), pp. 131-42; and Ann Vorisek White, "Breaking out of the Box: Turn Off TV, Turn on Life," *Mothering*, no. 107 (July/August 2001): 70-75.

[36]Klein, *No Logo*, p. 94.

[37]Klein, *No Logo*, chap. 4.

While it may seem to be self-evidently a good thing that we have established school systems to educate our children, and that it is clearly a matter of civilizational progress for us to attempt to ensure that all children gain literacy and numeracy skills, there is also a downside. You see, the role of schooling in producing docile consumers in the empire is consistent with the vision of mass education from the beginning. We must remember that "schooling" is not the natural and necessary way of educating the young that it purports to be.[38] Rather, schooling as we know it is a relatively recent phenomenon, dating back no further than the industrial revolution.[39] Together with the media, schooling shapes our children into obedient subjects of the empire.

How does all of this relate to my question about parental authority? Are you saying that simply by sending our kids to school we are handing over their formation into the hands of so-called experts who will socialize them to be servants of the empire?

We are at least raising the question.

So what's the alternative? Are you saying we all have to send our children to Christian schools?

Actually we believe we need to rethink the whole notion of schooling—Christian or otherwise.[40] Our question is this: if it is true that schooling is an institution of the modernist progress myth and is preoccupied with quantification, testing, standardization, passivity, docility and consumption resulting in a dazed, numbed-out, stupefied, disinterested, disempowered and unmotivated population of unthinking consumers, then why are Christians playing this educational game of schooling at all?[41] Why are we subjecting our children to an institutionalized education system that strips them of their creativity, discourages alternative thinking and literally makes them "lose heart"? And insofar as Christian schools are applauded in our society as producing fine, middle-class, hardworking and hard-consuming citizens, we are not sure that they are providing much of an alternative.

So what would an alternative educational practice look like?

Let's begin by asking the question of what education is *for*. Why do we think it is important to "get" an education?

---

[38]From a postmodern perspective, we need to "denaturalize" the idea of schooling and demonstrate that this is a cultural construct designed for social control. See Peter McLaren, *Critical Pedagogy and Predatory Culture: Oppositional Politics in a Postmodern Age* (New York: Routledge, 1995).

[39]Ivan Illich, *Deschooling Society* (New York: Harper & Row, 1971). See also Brian Walsh, "Education, Tall Tales and the End of An Era," *Christian Teachers Journal* 8, no. 2 (May 2000): 4-9.

[40]An example of such a rethinking of education is the Small School in the U.K. See Satish Kumar, "Human-Scale Education: Re-inventing Schools to Meet Real Needs," *Green Teacher* 73 (2004): 9-13. See also David Sobel, *Place-Based Education: Connecting Classrooms & Communities,* Nature Literacy 4 (Great Barrington, Mass.: Orion Books, 2004).

[41]John Taylor Gatto, *Dumbing Us Down: The Hidden Curriculum of Compulsory Schooling* (Gabriola Island, B.C.: New Society, 1992); John Taylor Gatto, ed., *The Exhausted School* (New York: Oxford Village, 1993); Paulo Freire, *Pedagogy of the Oppressed,* trans. Myra Bergman Ramos (New York: Continuum, 1986); John Holt, *How Children Learn,* rev. ed. (Reading, Mass.: Perseus, 1983).

Well, apart from all the lofty language about the benefits of gaining literacy skills and knowledge—that is, the "three R's"—I think the real issue behind education these days is that it is the prerequisite for life in our society. Without an education there are few doors open to us for employment, few paths up the career ladder.

Interesting metaphor, isn't it—"up"? The proper place for an educated person in our society is "up." Wendell Berry has some comments on this metaphor. Observing that "education is the way up" and that the popular aim of education is to put everyone "on top," Berry wryly notes, "Well, I think that I hardly need to document the consequent pushing and tramping and kicking in the face" involved in getting to the top and staying there.[42] He muses that perhaps "up" is "the wrong direction."[43] We would add that "up" is the wrong metaphor and misshapes the imagination of our young. Rather than instilling in them a desire to get to the top, to move up, we want to encourage our children to develop a sense of calling and service, including an awareness that this may require a process of *downward* mobility, a decision not to strive for the top but to care for those who are on the bottom.

Environmental ethicist David Orr points out, "Education is no guarantee of decency, prudence or wisdom." Indeed "more of the same kind of education will only compound our problems."[44] Orr questions education from an ecological perspective. Simply stated, Orr wants to know, if we are the most educated people in history, then why are we so ecologically blind, stupid and malevolent? Why does a rise in linguistic literacy seem to parallel a concomitant increase in ecological illiteracy? In biblical terms, what is lacking is wisdom. And if our children are not to lose heart in this confusing and fragmentary culture, then we need to instill wisdom in them.

How do you do that?

Primarily by example, we suspect. If they are raised in a household and a community that exercise the kind of ethic of secession and virtue we have been talking about in the last few chapters, it is certainly more likely that they will have the resources within themselves to live an alternative life. And if their imagination is shaped by the life of that community, its literature, poetry, music and art—and most foundationally, its subversive narrative of a kingdom that turns the values of the empire on their heads—then that liberated imagination will, we pray, engender a liberated child. We hope that our children will not need to secede from the empire, because they were never captive to it.

---

[42]Wendell Berry, "A Remarkable Man," in *What Are People For?* (New York: North Point, 1990), p. 25. See also Steve Bouma-Prediger and Brian Walsh, "Educating for Homelessness or Homemaking? The Christian College in a Postmodern Culture," *Christian Scholar's Review* 32, no. 3 (Spring 2003): 281-96.

[43]Ibid., p. 26.

[44]David Orr, *Earth in Mind: On Education, Environment and the Human Prospect* (Washington, D.C.: Island, 1994), p. 8.

But doesn't this mean that you'll need to isolate your children from the world? Won't they end up being social misfits?

We hope so. Yes, social misfits, that's what we long for. May it be that we raise up a generation of social misfits, because to "fit into" this culture, to find your place of comfort in it, is to be accommodated to the empire. We have argued that this is precisely what this subversive little tract called Colossians is arguing against.

But no, it's not a matter of isolationism. The issue here is not to isolate our children from the world but to expose them to the world through the liberating vision of a biblical worldview. Precisely where the powers that be don't want children to make connections, don't want them to really *see,* we want our children's eyes to be opened. We want our kids to see through the targeted advertising of McDonald's toys, games and playlands and recognize them as the manipulative come-ons they are. We want them to see through the packaging and grease in order to see that the stuff being served is not food. We want our little girls to be offended, not enamored, by Barbie's figure. We want them to know that while the news of war that they are constantly hearing on the radio and on the street makes them worry, there are other little girls in places like Palestine, Israel, Iraq, Colombia, Guatemala, Sierra Leone and Zimbabwe who have to live with the daily fear of war in their very neighborhoods. We want them to think about the little girls who work the fields producing cash crops or who slave in the sweatshops producing cute clothes for little girls in North America.

But that's not all. If all of this is rooted in our desire that our children grow up to be people of deep prophetic discernment, we also long that they be wise. Wisdom is a matter of making connections. To be wise is to know one's place in the world and to know the web of interconnections in which one lives. So it is important to be able to identify the migratory and nonmigratory species of birds in the neighborhood and to take delight in those creatures. It is important to know that there are foxes, and now coyotes, in the ravine down the street and to know what kinds of environmental factors make these species either flourish or decline. To be wise is to be able to make connections between the food you eat, the store where it was purchased, the transportation systems that brought that food, the land where it was produced and the people who produced it. It's good to know why the local organic strawberries this year were so small and how that might be related to climate change. And children should know how to grow their own food and be involved in the garden work, rejoicing in the harvest. Just as we want them to see through the lies of the empire, so also do we want them to delight in the truth that is still to be received from this gift known as creation. Our prayer is that they will have a rich imagination and an abiding curiosity about this world God has given us, so that they will learn how to be careful and loving stewards of our creational home.

We could go on and on, but the point we're making is simply this. From a Christian perspective influenced by this reading of Colossians, responsible parental authority, and responsible education of the young, is an authority that subverts the principalities and powers of the culture and educates our children for discipleship. Whether this educational responsibility is exercised in schools, churches or homes, the goal is the same: to raise up children who are subversive to the empire because they are subjects of the kingdom. Parents, do not provoke your children, do not break them, and for God's sake, do not offer them up for sacrifice before the idols of our age. Model for them an alternative way of life, a kingdom vision with a lifestyle and daily habits that engender the virtues of compassion, kindness, humility, meekness, patience, forgiveness, love, peace, gratitude, wisdom and worship. Then, whatever they do, in word or deed, will be done in the name of the Lord Jesus.[45]

---

[45]On children see also Marva Dawn, *Is It a Lost Cause? Having the Heart of God for the Church's Children* (Grand Rapids, Mich.: Eerdmans, 1997).

— 12 —

A SUFFERING ETHIC

Nympha's Trial

It has turned out to be quite the day; the summons I feared has finally come. I, Nympha, follower of Jesus, leader of a house church in Laodicea, successful businesswoman, have finally been called to meet with the city magistrates to explain the conduct of my community. I've been expecting the summons, and I'm not overawed by these magistrates. Most of them were still wet behind the ears when I became a prominent benefactor, and few of them have been able to contribute to the upbuilding of this city as much as I did in my day. To this day I walk past archways and courtyards built by my workers that contain statues of the emperor paid for by my wealth. And some of the imperial games that I sponsored are still spoken of for their opulence and lavish ceremony. I can easily hold my head up in front of these magistrates.

What surprised me is the way I was summoned. No protocol, no proper deference shown to a woman of my stature. Just a short command from a slave that I had better present myself as soon as possible. Or else.

So what could I do? I summoned my foreman and outlined which of my workshops and farms needed to be visited today. I also asked him to make arrangements for the evening meal for those of our community who were currently assisting with the fieldwork. Then, donning my plainest robes, I made haste to the place of the magistrates, beside the marketplace.

As I walked I pondered what might have prompted the summons. Ever since we Christians in Laodicea had begun meeting, we were viewed with suspicion. At first we were viewed as a potentially subversive political group just for meeting together and sharing a meal at which everyone was equal. But then some of our other actions began to get attention. It became known that we did not attend the festivals and imperial games staged by the empire. Our attitudes toward marriage were unpopular, especially since the emperor had decreed that marriage was mandatory for everyone.

Business leaders were incensed when some members of our community began to free their slaves. A number of our members have been tried and even found guilty for treason and subversion. Some have been sent to Rome; more have become fodder for the gladiatorial games here in Laodicea or in neighboring Colossae.

But today was different. Up until now the magistrates had tended to pick on those in the community who had no civic connections. Say what you will, it is easier to throw some poor peasant to the lions than a prominent member of the business community who might have family willing to fight for them. And today's summons felt different. It was a summons to me to come and speak for my *ekklēsia,* my church. What could that mean?

When I arrived at the marketplace, I saw that everyone there knew about me. Conversations abruptly ceased or became muted as I went by. And as I reached the portico of the magistrates' offices, I could sense an expectant hush behind me. Suddenly I was struck by the absurdity of the situation. Was this not the sort of summons to be expected by a follower of Jesus? I felt a lightening of my mood, and on a whim, I turned around and waved at the crowd. They were taken aback; I could hear the collective gasp. But far at the back I noticed a few hands waving back. I would not be alone.

As I entered the magistrates' atrium, the same slave who had summoned me led me through to the largest room. They were all there, all seven of the magistrates who administered the laws of the emperor to the people of Laodicea. I knew them all; some of them had been my friends when I walked in the way of darkness; some of them still were business cronies of my husband. I looked around the table: Rufus, Felix, Cassius, Aquila, Eutychus, Trolius, Lucius. Cassius indicated where I should stand.

Trolius, who was pontifex magnus, began without preamble. "A document has come to our attention, Nympha, which indicates that the followers of Christus who meet in your house are part of a larger movement of subversion against the emperor. We have only a fragment of the document, so we do not know what kind of revolutionary activities it outlines, but the portion that we have obtained indicates treason of the highest order. How do you answer this charge?"

Well, even though I was a woman, I knew something about judicial procedure. "What is this document, Trolius, and how did you obtain it? How do you know it is a fragment of a document from followers of Christus? I cannot defend myself if I don't even know the evidence on which I am being accused."

Trolius looked at the others. Some were shaking their heads, others nodded. Clearly there had been some disagreement about how the trial should proceed. And I could see why. As a woman I had no legal standing; they could easily have imprisoned me without this trial. It said something about my own—and my husband's— status in the community that they had summoned me at all. Trolius thought for a moment; then he picked up a fragment of parchment, unrolled it and began to read.

He is the image of the invisible God, the firstborn of all creation; for in him all things in

heaven and on earth were created, things visible and invisible, whether thrones or dominions or rulers or powers—all things have been created through him and for him. He
himself is before all things, and in him all things hold together. He is the head of the
body, the church; he is the beginning, the firstborn from the dead, so that he might come
to have first place in everything. For in him all the fullness of God was pleased to dwell,
and through him God was pleased to reconcile to himself all things, whether on earth
or in heaven, by making peace through the blood of his cross.

As he read, the silence in the room deepened. And no wonder, for the magistrates
had got their hands on one of the most widely circulated poems about Jesus. It had
first appeared in Paul's letter to the assembly in Colossae but had spread quickly
throughout the communities in Asia Minor as a word of hope for weary Christians.
And I couldn't imagine a more damning document to have to defend. If treason was
the charge, then this document surely supported it.

Of course I didn't say that to them. I knew that in the end the charges could be
sustained. But that air of absurd lightheartedness was still with me. First I would have
some fun. I would make them explain the whole document to me, and in so doing I
might have a chance to show them a little more about Jesus than they could ask or
imagine. Bearing witness happens in the most unlikely places; this would be mine.
But for the moment I kept silence.

"Well, Nympha." Trolius spoke sharply, "What have you to say? Is this or is this
not the Christus whom you worship?"

"Yes," I answered. "Yes, this is a description of Jesus the Christ, the One whom I
worship."

"Then would you be so kind as to explain this document to us?" Trolius asked.

"Certainly," I replied. "It would be a pleasure." I saw Rufus raise his head sharply.
He had caught the note of laughter in my voice and looked puzzled.

"You see," I began, "this is a hymn to Jesus modeled on the poetry of the ancient
Hebrew Scriptures. More specifically, it is a creation story that moves from the first
creation, when humanity was created in the image of God, to the new creation, where
humanity is reconciled to God. The language used is that of the wisdom writings,
where Sophia, Wisdom, is the firstborn of the creation and assists the Maker of the
Universe in bringing all things into being."

"Enough!" The word cut me off sharply. "Enough of this rubbish!" It was Lucius,
one of the youngest magistrates. "This may look like an ancient Hebrew poem, but it
is a direct attack on the emperor. Jesus is the image of God, indeed! If we want to see
the image of the one who represents the gods to us, we look to Caesar, no one else.
That is why his image is everywhere we look: in the marketplace, on the city gates, at
the entrance to the temple, even above our heads here in the chambers of the magistrates. In our homes, on our coins, everywhere we acknowledge that it is the image
of Caesar to whom we owe thanksgiving, honor and devotion. Do you tell us that you

deny the rule of Caesar, Nympha? You see how this poem continues; don't you dare tell me that any more of it is ancient Israelite Scripture," he sneered.

"Actually," I replied, "that's exactly what it is. This hymn asserts what every Jew has confessed throughout Israelite history: that God is the One who has created all things, that all things hold together in God. But unlike the ancient Israelite Scripture, this hymn proclaims that Jesus is the One through whom God did all these things, he is the One who created all rulers and authorities and throne and powers . . ."

"Can't someone stop this woman?" Lucius cried out. "Not only does she claim that Jesus, not Caesar, is the image we should worship, she also claims that this Jesus has ultimate authority over all other rulers and powers! She denies the lordship of Caesar, she puts another ruler over him!"

"Surely you don't believe this, Nympha." It was Aquila who spoke. He had known me for many years. "You may say that you believe this poem, but surely you don't *live* as if this Jesus is lord. You can't tell me that you no longer have images of Caesar in your household. Surely your murals, the images over your lintels, those exquisite goblets you had made in Rome, those things are still central to your life. You haven't given everything over for this Jesus, have you?" He ended on a pleading note, and I knew what he was trying to do. He was trying to give me a way out, a chance to redeem myself before the council.

But before I could answer, someone answered for me. "But of course she has," came a deep, slow voice. It was Eutychus, an old friend of my father who had come to see me about some of my recent business practices that had puzzled him. "Of course she has," he continued. "I myself have been to her house. Nothing remains to remind her of the empire and its rulers and its glorious history. No murals, no statues, no goblets with the vines of prosperity. Not so much as a hairbrush with the symbols of peace or a lamp with the symbols of victory. All is gone.

"And there is more. Her business has become tainted by this Jesus as well. She has released all of her slaves. She has given many of her farms away to the poor in surrounding villages, and the remainder she works with hired laborers who are fed and clothed. She has refused to provide the purple cloth for the dignitaries of the emperor, as you well know, and has reduced the fortune of her father dramatically. It is beginning to have an adverse affect in the villages. Now the peasants are asking other merchants why they are not returning the farms that the farmers lost in the famine, and the slaves of our households are working themselves up to revolt with dreams of freedom. This teaching is not only treasonous to the empire, it is fundamentally bad for business, and with all due respect, the latter is of as much importance to me as any sacrifice. If we lose our entitlement to the cheap labor of slaves and the amassing of property, where will the basis be for our growth?" Eutychus stopped, amid nods from the other magistrates.

"You see that you are accused of undermining the social fabric," said Trolius. "Your actions are eating away at the foundations of our society."

Before he could continue, I took a deep breath and plunged in. "Me, undermining the social fabric?" I said mildly. "Me? Look at your business practices! You think that working slaves to death for your own profit makes for healthy community and a solid society? You want to keep collecting farms, but in order to do so you need to prey on those who cannot pay their taxes to the emperor, those who are impoverished because they work only to keep food on your tables. You can't claim to be weaving a solid social fabric yourself when you drive people into poverty so that your profit margin can keep rising. You can say that business is more important to you than sacrifice to the emperor, but you know, Eutychus, that the two go hand in hand. You know that with an emperor as the head of this body politic, you will always have tax laws that favor the rich, you will always be able to seize the land of the poor, you will always be able to eat your sumptuous feasts during the festivals while your neighbors get the smallest oatcakes and a sip of wine.

"Lucius is right. This text about Jesus is fundamentally opposed to the lordship of Caesar. But I am right too: this text is just like an ancient Hebrew prophetic text which stands as a challenge to the empire."

Since they were all staring at me in stunned silence, I continued. "But the body that Jesus heads is fundamentally different. That's why we call Jesus the head of the body, not the body politic of the empire but the body of something new, the *ekklēsia,* the assembly. We know that you call your political organizations the *ekklēsia,* and we know they are places where the grossest inequality rules, where some are fed twice as much food as others and some are relegated to the fringes of every banquet even if they have paid their dues. Well, our *ekklēsia* is in direct challenge to all of this. Do you wonder why people are flocking to our meetings? It is because we offer hope for a better kingdom, where all meet together as equals, where all are fed at the table of our Lord, where the poor are cared for and none go hungry, where forgiveness and love are practiced. This is a kingdom where peace rules. And that peace is rooted so firmly in the hope of Hebrew prophecy that everyone who hears the promise of peace that Jesus offers knows that a new world has come, where the Creator God is partisan on behalf of all those the empire excludes."

"But surely, Nympha," said Trolius, "you must acknowledge that Caesar is the one who truly brought peace. Look at the empire; it encompasses the whole of the world. There has never been such a ruler."

I confess that what I said then surprised even myself. "Caesar has brought peace? Let's look at the peace brought by your Caesar. Let's take as an example Galilee, the homeland of Jesus. All the Jewish people want to do is live in peace in their own land, free to follow their ancestral laws, with a king from their own people and a high priest from the priestly line. And the Romans continually beat them down, imposing rulers who oppress them and impoverish them. When they rebel they are ruthlessly cut down, their cities burned and their children enslaved. This is how Rome keeps peace, by military might and violent force. They make a desolation and call it peace.

"Their favorite symbol for peace is the cross, on which they condemn those who resist their rule to an excruciating death. This is the peace they bring. This is the peace that killed Jesus."

There was a shocked silence. "You don't mean to tell me," said Trolius, "that this Jesus you worship was killed as a political rebel!"

"Yes, I do," I said. "And through that death, by taking the evil of Rome and the evil of the universe upon himself, he exhausted it and brought a peace and a reconciliation deeper than any peace Caesar can even dream of. By emptying himself in love, he reconciled all things, in heaven, on earth, everything in the Roman empire and beyond, between all of creation and all of you and God. That is the kind of peace Jesus brought through the blood of a Roman cross."

"Enough!" It was Lucius again. "I say that not only have we heard enough from this woman's own mouth to condemn her; we have also seen how the actions of her household and community fundamentally challenge the empire and all it stands for. There is now no doubt in my mind that she stands guilty as charged, and all those who confess this Jesus with her.

"Let us now keep her in custody and begin immediately to gather those who meet in her house, before word gets out that we are doing so. These people are a threat to the security of the empire, the security of our society and the security of our wealth. We must not let them continue to meet to spread these seditious teachings."

"Nympha," said Aquila, "you realize that your situation is very grave. Do you wish to change anything you have said?"

"Nothing," I answered, "except to say that Jesus is my Lord, not Caesar, and in my flesh I am happy to complete what is lacking in his afflictions for the sake of his body, the church."

"That's enough!" said Trolius, sharply. "We will send immediately to have her followers rounded up. Who will go to the guards?"

"I will." It was Rufus, who had up until now said nothing. "I will send a slave immediately to notify the guards."

"Good," said Trolius. "Do not delay; they have ears everywhere. The guards will know a few of her followers and by applying torture will discover the rest."

I watched Rufus go with elation in my heart. For a few months now he had been coming secretly to our meetings. I knew that before sending a slave to the guards, Rufus would send another slave, a Christian named Malchus, to go and warn the saints.

Whose Story Is This?

This is, of course, a fictional story. We do not know whether any such trial ever occurred or whether the Nympha we meet in the New Testament ever saw through the implications of her faith in this way. We do know, however, that a poem such as that found in Colossians 1:15-20 would have to be judged as seditious in the context of the Roman empire. And we know that Christians under persecution for their faith were not likely to avail themselves of the defense that faith in Jesus Christ was of no consequence to the empire. No, for both Jews and Christians of the first century, the imperial gospel of Caesar's lordship was in clear conflict with both the Jewish conviction that there is "no Lord but God," and the Christian proclamation that Jesus Christ is Lord.

So whose story is this? It is the story of the church. More precisely, it is the story of the church in conflict with the story of the empire. Two metanarratives, two overarching grand tales of redemption, two gospels, come into conflict precisely in the local story, the little narrative of this community and its sister communities in the Lycus Valley.

Paul makes clear to the Colossian community that they have a place in the metanarrative that he poetically evokes in his letter to them. Indeed he provides transition from the poem's sweeping vision to its localized impact in the life of this community by grammatically echoing the poem's middle strophes. Remember how that middle section is structured (Col 1:17-18):

And he is before all things . . .
And he is the head of the body . . .

Bringing the cosmic claims about Christ to bear on the lives of the Colossian community, in their struggles and their stories, Paul personalizes and localizes the "and he" of the poem by writing, "*And you* who were once estranged and hostile in mind, doing evil deeds, he has now reconciled" (1:21-22). The counterimperial vision of cosmic reconciliation in Christ is the vision that has transformed this community into a subversive body politic, counter to the empire. This metanarrative of creational reconciliation through the blood of a Roman cross—a story that radically contests the imperial metanarrative of violence and oppression—reshapes and reconstitutes this community as citizens of the kingdom rather than subjects of the empire.

But as we have seen, this reconciliation travels the path that leads to a cross. It is therefore not surprising that to be a servant of this gospel, to proclaim this alternative sovereignty in a world of violence, would entail suffering. If the hope of Israel's story is to be found in a suffering servant (Is 53) and Jesus is that suffering servant, it is not surprising that suffering is integral to the life of anyone who embraces this story as their own. So Paul says, "I am now rejoicing in my sufferings for your sake, and in my flesh I am completing what is lacking in Christ's afflictions for the sake of his body, that is, the church" (1:24). This verse has confused and befuddled the church for generations. How can Paul say that he is "completing what is lacking" in Christ's afflictions? How can anything be lacking from what Christ did at the cross? Surely Christians believe that Christ's work on the cross was all-sufficient.

This whole book has been an exercise in hermeneutics. How do we read the ancient text of Colossians in such a way that we maintain its integrity and still hear it speak to us in a very different historical and cultural context? But we have also seen that the question is, how do we read this text in a very different *theological* context? How do we allow this text to challenge the theological presuppositions that we might bring to it? This has especially been the issue in dealing with "absolutes" that may or may not be discerned in the text. Now, coming to the end of our discussion, we meet this passage about filling up what is lacking in Christ's afflictions, and we immediately feel a tension between what Paul is saying and what Christianity, in most of its manifestations, has taught about the sufficiency of Christ's suffering.

This gives rise to a small bit of hermeneutical advice: If in reading Scripture we come up against a text that seems to be in conflict with a received doctrine of our theological tradition, we must hold that doctrine more lightly. Notice what we are saying. We are not saying that we should quickly abandon any doctrine just because we find one text that seems to contradict it. No, we are saying that we should hold the doctrine *more lightly*. We should allow the text to relativize our received traditions. After all, didn't Paul write that "all scripture is inspired by God and is useful for teaching, for reproof, for correction . . ." (2 Tim 3:16)? Well then, that must mean Scripture has authority to correct even our theological traditions.

The Story of Jesus Is a Story of Suffering

What does that mean with regard to this text about "completing what is lacking in Christ's afflictions"? Paul seems to be suggesting that the suffering of Jesus on the cross is not the end of all suffering, especially for the church.

Maybe we need to now go beyond the question *whose story is this?* to *what kind of story is this?* If Paul is preoccupied with the story of Jesus, and if this story shapes the identity and character of the community that receives his gospel as true over against imperial claims, then what kind of a story is this? What kind of a story did Nympha embrace when she threw in her lot with Jesus, and what kind of story is still on offer to us living at the beginning of the twenty-first century?

The answer is that this is a story of suffering. But that suffering neither began nor ended with either Jesus or Paul. We argued earlier in this book that the biblical narrative as a whole is a tale of a suffering God who will stop at nothing to reconcile this broken world. And now we see that if Jesus brings that suffering to a head in the most cosmic conflict between good and evil, then to make his story our story is to embrace a tale of suffering.

That is why in the fiction with which we began this chapter, Nympha was not surprised to find herself called before the authorities on account of her faith. There is a radical identification here between the church and Jesus. Think about it for a moment. Throughout this letter, Paul refers to the church as the "body" of Christ (1:18, 24; 2:19; 3:15). While we have seen that this is a politically loaded term, we also need

to remember that the use of the metaphor of "body" suggests an intimately close identification of the church with Jesus himself. The church is "the body of Christ." God
still takes on flesh in this world, Christ's body is still a life-giving presence—in the
church.

What happened to the body of Christ during his ministry among us? Where did
that ministry, that story of redemption, ultimately lead? To a cross, of course. So is it
any wonder that Paul (or Nympha) would understand such a cross-bearing suffering
to be an integral dimension of what it means to be "the body of Christ" in the world?
Is it any wonder that a community shaped by a narrative of a suffering God would
itself become a cruciform suffering community? The only wonder is that the contemporary church so often is *not* such a community.

Paul seems to think that it his lot to "complete what is lacking in Christ's afflictions"
for the sake of Christ's body, the church. What could this possibly mean? The word *affliction* is never used anywhere else in the New Testament to refer to Christ's suffering
on the cross. So it would seem Paul is not saying that a certain amount of pain or suffering had to be meted out and that that quota wasn't met on Good Friday, so he will
fill it up. This would not be an exegetically supportable interpretation, and it is also
much too mechanistic a view of redemptive suffering to make any biblical sense.

Rather, it would seem Paul is saying that identification with Jesus, and specifically
being his body in a world that is still hostile to his rule, means that *the church will experience affliction.* That's what it means to be the body of Christ. Further, Paul's own
afflictions—remember, he writes this epistle from prison (Col 4:18)!—are for the sake
of the body, for the sake of the church.

On the surface, this is not all that complicated to understand. Paul is in prison because of his ministry on behalf of the body in spreading this empire-threatening story
of Jesus. So in his "flesh," in the suffering he endures as a prisoner of the empire, he
suffers "for the sake of" the church.

We also need to pay attention to the kind of suffering Paul is talking about. As already noted, the word *affliction* that Paul uses here *(thlipseon)* is never actually used
in accounts of Christ's suffering on the cross. But this term is used extensively
throughout the Scriptures to denote various kinds of oppression. Whether we are
talking about the imperial oppression of Egypt and Babylon on Israel, the oppression
of the poor by the rich or the oppression Christians experienced at the hands of the
authorities, all such overtones are carried by this word.[1] Perhaps a better translation
here is "in my flesh I complete what is lacking in the oppression of the Messiah, for
the sake of the body, that is, the church." Insofar as the Messiah, as the representative
of the people, was oppressed, so Paul in his suffering is also oppressed for the sake of

---

[1]Heinrich Shlier, *"thlibo, thlipsis,"* in *Theological Dictionary of the New Testament,* trans. Geoffrey W. Bromiley,
    ed. Gerhard Kittel (Grand Rapids, Mich.: Eerdmans, 1965), 3:130-48.

the Messiah's people, the church, for whom he has become a servant (1:25). This is a recurring theme in Paul's letters. The oppression he experiences is for the sake of the community that also shares in Christ's oppressions (2 Cor 1:3-7). He has suffered the loss of all things in order to share in the Messiah's sufferings, becoming like him in his death, that he may attain the resurrection (Phil 3:8-11). And he calls believers to suffer with the Messiah so that they may be glorified with him (Rom 8:17). Therefore the expectation of those who live this story is that they too will participate in this pattern of dying and new life to which Jesus calls his followers.

Paul's use of *oppression* (*thlipsis*) to describe his own suffering on behalf of the church strikingly underscores again the imperial context of the Colossian Christians. Just as Jesus' death was the result of oppressive political maneuvering on the part of both Jewish leaders and the Romans, who were threatened by the good news of the coming of the kingdom of God, so the continued oppression the Christian community in Colossae faced was the result of their proclaiming an alternative kingdom and living in subjection to a Lord other than Caesar. Paul weaves together the oppression of the Messiah and the oppression he is experiencing in his imprisonment at the hands of the empire, so that his afflictions are identified with the Messiah's and are therefore redemptive for Christ's body, the church.

For Paul the church is one body. It may have various local manifestations—in Colossae, Laodicea, Cape Town, Auckland, Santiago, Belize City, Caledonia—but the church is not plural, it is one. Now this church participates in its Savior's redemption of the world by sharing in his suffering, through radical identification with the "body" of a crucified Lord. As Christ did battle with the "principalities and powers" at the cross, so also the church continues to bear the fury of these powers in anticipation of their final subjugation to Christ at his return.

Paul's claim to joy in the midst of this suffering has the effect of placing the Colossian Christians in a long storyline that stretches from the suffering of God in the Old Testament through the suffering of the Messiah to the suffering of the Christian community in the present. If the grand metanarrative that underlies the Colossian poem in 1:15-20 is to be applied to the local narrative of this community, then it will be a narrative that goes through the sufferings of the cross. So Paul can respond, "Let the empire rage in its fury, let it strike me with all it has, let it throw me into prison, let it mobilize its military and legal structures of oppression! I know that all of this is ultimately disarmed and pacified at the cross."

But for those of us who live at the heart of the empire, this all raises a very uncomfortable question. If, as Paul asserts throughout his letters, we are called to share in the sufferings of Christ, and if such suffering is for the sake of the body of Christ, where does that leave a Christian community that seems to *avoid* any sort of suffering? Where does it leave those of us whose lives seem to be blessed by the empire rather than threatened by it? Where does it leave those of us whose blessings seem to actually be dependent on the oppression of our brothers and sisters elsewhere?

We shall return to these questions at the end of this chapter. But here Paul points toward answers by describing how he himself left a life of inflicting violence for a life of bearing it by becoming the servant of the church. And central to that servanthood was a commission, or a stewardship, from God to make known the "mystery" that had been "hidden throughout the ages" (1:26). Again, this seems to be an imperial reference. The priests of the imperial order used mystery language in reference to sacred rites that usually resulted in a revelation of the image of the emperor.[2] Paul turns this image on its head. Instead of revealing the image of a lord whose rule is demonstrated by violence and oppression over subjugated peoples, Paul's mystery reveals a different Lord—Jesus, the Christ. The Messiah is revealed *among the nations;* it is in their midst that this image of God can be seen.

Paul heightens this point by describing this Messiah as "the hope of glory" (1:27). In Israel's Scriptures, glory language is linked to humanity's bearing the image of God (as in Ps 8). When Israel is unfaithful, it exchanges its glory, its own image-bearing of God, for "graven" images that are futile (Ps 106:20; Jer 2:11; Hos 4:7; Rom 1:23). The hope of glory therefore is a hope in which the Colossian Christians will once again be full image-bearers of God. The mystery the Messiah reveals is that this full image-bearing of God, this glory, will be found among both Gentiles and Jews, breaking down the ethnic divisions that have led to one people's continued oppression of another.

Because "glory" is linked closely to "suffering" in Paul's letters, it is no surprise that they are found in close proximity here. Paul is most explicit on this connection in Romans 8: we will be heirs of Christ "if, in fact, we suffer with him so that we may also be glorified with him" (Rom 8:17). The dynamic of the Colossians passage makes this same movement from sharing in Jesus' suffering to the hope of glory, from sharing in the dehumanizing oppression of the empire to realization of our full humanness in the kingdom of God. Entering the story of the suffering God, following the Messiah who brings peace through the blood of the cross by sharing in his suffering, this community bears the image of that God and that Messiah and thereby becomes mature, complete and whole in Christ (Col 1:28).

Paul's overriding concern in this letter is the community's maturity in Christian faith. They have received a radical hope in the gospel that is counter to the imperial optimism and arrogance all around them. He writes so that they will not shift from that hope (1:23). That is why he writes that God has revealed to them "the riches of the glory of this mystery, which is Christ in you, the hope of glory." The whole story is about Jesus.

---

[2]S. R. F. Price, *Rituals and Power: The Roman Imperial Cult in Asia Minor* (Cambridge: Cambridge University Press, 1984), pp. 190-91.

If William, Elanna and Eric are to find their way in a postmodern world into some kind of Christian commitment, it will have to be because they find Jesus as attractive as Nympha did in our first narrative. The hope that can break through the despair of postmodern anomie and the numbness of oversatiated consumerism is not fundamentally a matter of "adopting" a worldview or even of "accepting" an alternative metanarrative. More foundationally, this hope is realized in a person and in a relationship: "Christ in you."

Our Story

If Colossians 1:21-29 provides a transition from the cosmic vision of the Colossian poem to the local realities of the Colossian community, Paul's concluding comments in chapter 4 of the letter make it even more personal. Not surprisingly, the themes of suffering, service, mystery and maturity in Christ all reappear in the concluding chapter. After offering a provocative countervision to the empire and calling the community to live out a gospel that challenges the imperial imagination and the social and economic structures of imperial society, Paul reminds his listeners of where this gospel, this alternative discipleship, has landed him: in prison (4:3). The implications are clear: if you, as a community that follows the Messiah, really proclaim this mystery, this good news that overturns the boundaries between Greek and Jew, circumcised and uncircumcised, barbarian, Scythian, slave and free, then you should expect to share in the sufferings of Christ.

Paul's greetings and closing instructions draw to conclusion all the dimensions of the gospel we have explored in this book. Onesimus, runaway slave, is commended as a faithful and beloved brother, sent with Tychicus to report about Paul to the community (4:9). Could Paul have more clearly indicated that the distinction between slave and free is erased in Christ than in giving Onesimus this task? Could he have more powerfully undermined the imperial stigma of runaway slave than he did by calling Onesimus "faithful"? Could he have more powerfully undermined the imperial distinction between slave and master than by calling Onesimus a "beloved brother, who is one of you"?

Similarly, Paul's greeting to Nympha and the church in her house (4:15) indicates a level of female leadership that sits uneasily with both empire and synagogue. And in his references to such a diverse group of people as his coworkers we meet in the flesh the kind of cultural and ethnic diversity that he insists is made one in Christ. In this radical band of coworkers there really is neither Greek nor Jew. Paul's closing greetings therefore give us a glimpse into the way the early Christian community confounded the careful social manipulations of the empire with its racial profiling and socioeconomic and gender restrictiveness.

But Paul ends this letter with two statements that are a call. The first is personally directed to someone named Archippus. Paul's word to him is "See that you complete the task that you have received in the Lord" (4:17). We have offered a fictionalized interpretation of what the ministry was to which Archippus was called. But in fact no one knows what the call was—at least no one except Paul and, presumably, Archippus. Perhaps as a member of Philemon's household, Archippus had the ministry of interpreting the radical implications of Paul's gospel to his slave-owning kinsman or friend (see Philem 1-2). We do know that Paul here moves his attention from the community as a whole to the role of one member of it. Archippus has a call, a service to perform, and Paul reminds him of the ministry he has received "in the Lord." In our story of Nympha, she too had to follow through the implications of her discipleship to the end; this was the ministry she was called to fulfill. And it was a ministry that required suffering.

This brings us to the second and concluding call of this letter. Addressing the community as a whole, Paul writes, "Remember my chains" (4:18). Those who are called to service must remember where that service leads: to chains, suffering, oppression.

What does all of this mean for a church that seems not to suffer, but rather to thrive, under empire? What does it mean to remember the apostle's chains for a community that has made its peace with an enslaving empire? Perhaps we need to over-hear Paul's admonition to Archippus and apply it to ourselves as Christians living at home in the imperial realities of the Pax Americana. We are called to proclaim and embody the gospel of a crucified Messiah. This gospel challenges the principalities and powers of our own age. This gospel proclaims that reconciliation and peace come not through the power of unilateral military force but through the blood of the cross. And such a reconciliation is manifest in a community that is renewed in the image of Jesus, a community that shares in the suffering of Jesus in its attempts to bring peace to the social, economic, political, racial and ethnic divisions that sin has caused in the world. In proclaiming and living that gospel, this community will begin to take on the suffering of those who have been oppressed throughout the ages at the hands of the empire. In taking on that suffering, the Christian community will truly enact peace by sharing in Christ's afflictions.[3] This is the call and the challenge with which Paul ends Colossians. And the letter of Colossians does not function as Scripture in the life of the church if this call is not heard and responded to by the church today.

"Say to Archippus . . ." Paul gets quite personal at the end of this letter. And so do we. We need to end the way we began. William is worried that a theism that reads Scripture will be an oppressive religion full of absolutes punching him in the face. Elanna is ethically paralyzed in the postmodern cacophony. And Eric smells fascism under every truth claim. But Nympha meets in Paul's gospel a Jesus who invites her into a covenantal relationship of wholeness, setting her free from the oppressive ab-

---

[3]An example of such a community is Christian Peacemakers Teams, who have gone throughout the world, including Iraq, to enact the peace of Christ in the face of violent imperial forces.

solutes of the empire. She is set free *into* a subversive praxis of secession from the empire and a communal ethic of full-life restoration in Christ. The truth she encounters in the communities that have been spawned by this gospel is no fascist repression but a radical liberation.

So we say to Eric, come into the embrace of the Other who rules, but from a cross, who is sovereign but wears a crown of thorns. To Elanna we say, give Paul a hearing, and more important, give the Jesus whom Paul proclaims a hearing. See if in his voice you might find a way through the cacophony that will set you free for liberating praxis. And we invite our friend William into a living story recorded both in the pages of Paul's letter to the Colossians and, we pray, in the lives of an alternative community that follows Christ, who is all and in all. Yes, William, Paul's vision is total; he is preoccupied with "all." But that is because everything is at stake in this gospel, and the God we meet in Jesus will not rest until all things are reconciled.

What about me?

Yes, of course, how could we forget you, our faithful dialogue partner? We remind you again that in Christ are hidden all the treasures of wisdom and knowledge. Keep digging for those treasures. Never give up your tenacity for truth. Never trade the riches of Christ for any deceitful worldview that would take you captive. This life-giving story is your story. Go out and make it live.

BIBLIOGRAPHY

I. Modernity, Postmodernity and Globalization

Anderson, Walter Truett. *Reality Isn't What It Used to Be*. New York: Harper and Row, 1990.

Anderson, Walter Truett, ed. *The Truth About the Truth: De-confusing and Re-constructing the Postmodern World*. New York: G. P. Putnam's Sons, 1995.

Barber, Benjamin. *Jihad vs. McWorld*. New York: Times Books, 1995; exp. ed.: New York: Ballantine, 2001.

Batstone, David, Eduardo Medienta, Lois Ann Lorentzen and Dwight N. Hopkins, eds. *Liberation Theologies, Postmodernity and the Americas*. New York: Routledge, 1997.

Beaudoin, Tom. *Virtual Faith: The Irreverent Spiritual Quest of Generation X*. San Francisco: Jossey-Bass, 1998.

Berger, Peter. *The Sacred Canopy: Elements of a Sociological Theory of Religion*. New York: Doubleday, 1967; Anchor, 1969.

Berger, Peter, and Thomas Luckman. *The Social Construction of Reality: A Treatise on the Sociology of Knowledge*. Garden City, N.Y.: Doubleday, 1966.

Bernstein, Richard J. *Beyond Objectivism and Relativism: Science, Hermeneutics and Praxis*. Philadelphia: University of Philadelphia Press, 1983.

Berry, Wendell. *Another Turn of the Crank*. Washington, D.C.: Counterpoint, 1995.

———. *Citizenship Papers*. Washington, D.C.: Shoemaker and Hoard, 2003.

———. *Sex, Economy, Freedom, and Community*. New York: Pantheon, 1992.

———. *The Unsettling of America: Culture and Agriculture*. New York: Avon Books, 1997.

Best, Steven, and Douglas Kellner. *Postmodern Theory: Critical Interrogations*. New York: Guilford Press, 1991.

Bloom, Allan. *The Closing of the American Mind*. New York: Simon and Schuster, 1987.

Borgmann, Albert. *Crossing the Postmodern Divide*. Chicago: University of Chicago Press, 1992.

Boyle, Nicholas. *Who Are We Now? Christian Humanism and the Global Market from Hegel to Heaney*. Edinburgh: T & T Clark, 1998.

Caputo, John D. *Against Ethics: Contributions to a Poetics of Obligation with Constant Reference to Deconstruction*. Bloomington: Indiana University Press, 1993.

Cherry, Conrad, ed. *God's New Israel: Religious Interpretation and American Destiny*. Rev. ed. Englewood Cliffs, N.J.: Prentice Hall, 1998.

Chomsky, Noam. *Hegemomy or Survival: America's Quest for Global Dominance*. New York: Metropolitan Books, 2003.

———. *Manufacturing Consent: Noam Chomsky and the Media*. Edited by Mark Achbar. Montreal: Black Rose Press, 1994.

Clapp, Rodney. *Border Crossings: Christian Trespasses on Popular Culture and Public Affairs*. Grand Rapids: Brazos Press, 2000.

Clouser, Roy. *The Myth of Religious Neutrality: An Essay on the Hidden Role of Religious Belief in Theories*. South Bend, Ind.: University of Notre Dame Press, 1992.

Coupland, Douglas. *Life After God*. New York: Pocket Books, 1994.

Cox, Harvey. "The Market as God: Living in the New Dispensation." *Atlantic Monthly* 283, no. 4 (March 1999).

Eagleton, Terry. "Awakening from Modernity." *Times Literary Supplement,* February 20, 1987.

Foucault, Michel. *An Archaeology of Knowledge*. Translated by A.M. Sheridan Smith. New York: Pantheon, 1972.

———. *Discipline and Punish: The Birth of the Prison*. Translated by A.M. Sheridan. New York: Vintage, 1979.

———. *The Order of Things*. New York: Pantheon, 1970.

———. *Power/Knowledge: Selected Interviews and other writings, 1972-1977*. Edited by C. Gordon. New York: Pantheon, 1980.

Gergen, Kenneth. *The Saturated Self: Dilemmas of Identity in Contemporary Life*. New York: Basic Books, 1991.

Gilkey, Langdon B. *Society and the Sacred: Toward a Theology of Culture in Decline*. New York: Seabury, 1981.

Giroux, Henry. *Border Crossings: Cultural Workers and the Politics of Education*. New York: Routledge, 1992.

Goddard, Andrew. "Something Still Stands." *Third Way* 24, no. 8 (November 2001): 13-17.

Goudzwaard, Bob. *Aid for the Overdeveloped West*. Toronto: Wedge Publishing, 1975.

———. *Capitalism and Progress: A Diagnosis of Western Society*. Translated by J. Van Nuis-Zylstra. Grand Rapids: Eerdmans, 1979.

———. *Idols of our Time*. Translated by Mark Vander Vennen. Downers Grove, Ill.: InterVarsity Press, 1984.

Hardt, Michael, and Antonio Negri. *Empire*. Cambridge, Mass.: Harvard University Press, 2000.

Harvey, David. *The Condition of Postmodernity: An Inquiry into the Origins of Cultural Change*. Oxford: Basil Blackwell, 1989.

Hauerwas, Stanley. "The Christian Difference: Or Surviving Postmodernism." In *Anabaptists and Postmodernity,* edited by Susan and Gerald Biesecker-Mast, pp. 41-59. Telford, Penn.: Pandora, 2000.

———. "Nonviolence and the War Without End." *The Other Side* 38, no. 6 (November/December 2002): 30-31.

Hutcheon, Linda. *The Politics of Postmodernism*. New York: Routledge, 1989.

Jameson, Frederick. *Postmodernism, or, The Cultural Logic of Late Capitalism*. Durham, N.C.: Duke University Press, 1991.

Kenneson, Philip. "There's No Such Thing as Objective Truth and It's a Good Thing Too." In *Christian Apologetics in the Postmodern World,* edited by Timothy R. Phillips and Dennis L. Okholm, pp. 155-70. Downers Grove, Ill.: InterVarsity Press, 1995.

Kingsolver, Barbara. *The Poisonwood Bible*. New York: HarperCollins, 1998.

————. *Small Wonder: Essays.* New York: HarperCollins, 2002.

Klein, Naomi. *No Logo: Taking Aim at the Brand Bullies.* Toronto: Vintage, 2000.

Lasch, Christopher. *The Minimal Self: Psychic Survival in Troubled Times.* New York: W. W. Norton, 1984.

Lasn, Kalle. *Culture Jam: the Uncooling of America™.* New York: Eagle Brook, 1999.

Lifton, Robert J. *Boundaries: Psychological Man in Revolution.* New York: Vintage, 1970.

Lyon, David. *Postmodernity.* Minneapolis: University of Minnesota Press, 1994.

Lyotard, Jean François. *The Postmodern Condition: A Report on Knowledge, Theory and History of Literature.* Translated by G. Bennington and B. Massumi. Minneapolis: University of Minnesota Press, 1984.

MacIntyre, Alasdair. *After Virtue: A Study in Moral Theory.* 2nd ed. Notre Dame, Ind.: University of Notre Dame Press, 1984.

————. *Whose Justice? Which Rationality?* Notre Dame, Ind.: University of Notre Dame Press, 1988.

McKibben, Bill. *The Age of Missing Information.* New York: Plume, 1993.

————. *The End of Nature.* New York: Doubleday, 1989.

————. *Enough: Staying Human in an Engineered Age.* New York: Henry Holt/Owl, 2004.

————. *Hope, Human and Wild.* St. Paul, Minn.: Hungry Mind Press, 1995.

McLaren, Peter. *Critical Pedagogy and Predatory Culture: Oppositional Politics in a Postmodern Age.* New York: Routledge, 1995.

Middleton, J. Richard, and Brian J. Walsh. *Truth Is Stranger Than It Used to Be: Biblical Faith in a Postmodern Age.* Downers Grove, Ill.: InterVarsity Press, 1995.

Moore, Stephen D. *Poststructuralism and the New Testament: Derrida and Foucault at the Foot of the Cross.* Minneapolis: Fortress, 1994.

Natoli, Joseph. *A Primer to Postmodernity.* Oxford: Blackwell, 1997.

Nietzsche, Friedrich. *Twilight of the Idols and the Anti-Christ.* Translated by R. J. Hollingdale. London: Penguin, 1990.

Olthuis, James H. "A Cold and Comfortless Hermeneutic or a Warm and Trembling Hermeneutic: A Conversation with John D. Caputo." *Christian Scholars Review* 19, no. 4 (1990): 345-62.

Olthuis, James H. "On Worldviews." *Christian Scholars Review* 14, no. 2 (1985): 153-64.

Pahl, John. *Shopping Malls and Other Sacred Spaces: Putting God in Place.* Grand Rapids: Brazos, 2003.

Postman, Neil. *Amusing Ourselves to Death: Public Discourse in the Age of Show Business.* New York: Penguin, 1985.

Reuther, Rosemary Radford. *To Change the World: Christology and Cultural Criticism.* New York: Crossroads, 1983.

Richard, Pablo, et al. *The Idols of Death and the God of Life.* Translated by Barbara E. Campbell and Bonnie Shepard. Maryknoll, N.Y.: Orbis, 1983.

Ricoeur, Paul. *The Symbolism of Evil.* Translated by E. Buchanan. Boston: Beacon, 1967.

Robertson, Stephen. *The Paradigm of Relationship: Speaking the Scriptural Language of Covenantal Relationship to a Postmodern World.* Unpublished MTS thesis. Toronto: Wycliffe College, 2001.

Rorty, Richard. "Ironists and Metaphysicians." In *The Truth About the Truth: De-confusing and Reconstructing the Postmodern World,* edited by Walter Truett Anderson, pp. 100-106. New York: G. P. Putnam's Sons, 1995.

———. *Philosophy and the Mirror of Nature.* New York: Princeton University Press, 1979.

———. "Pragmatism and Philosophy." In *After Philosophy: End or Transformation?* edited by K. Baynes, J. Bohman and T. McCarthy, pp. 26-66. Cambridge, Mass.: MIT Press, 1987.

Rust, Godfrey. "September 11, 2001." *Third Way* 24, no. 8 (November 2001): 14-15.

Schwartz, P., and P. Leyden, "The Long Boom," *Wired,* July 1997.

Scott, James C. *Domination and the Arts of Resistance.* New Haven, Conn.: Yale University Press, 1990.

Stephenson, Anders. *Manifest Destiny: American Expansion and the Empire of Right.* New York: Hill and Wany, 1995.

Stiglitz, Joseph E. *Globalization and Its Discontents.* New York: W. W. Norton, 2003.

Stout, Jeffrey. *Ethics After Babel: The Languages of Morals and Their Discontents.* Boston: Beacon, 1988.

Taylor, Mark McClain. "Vodou Resistance/Vodou Hope: Forging a Postmodernism That Liberates." In *Liberation Theologies, Postmodernity and the Americas,* edited by David Batstone, Eduardo Medienta, Lois Ann Lorentzen and Dwight N. Hopkins, pp. 169-87. New York: Routledge, 1997.

Usher, Robin, and Richard Edwards. *Postmodernism and Education: Different Voices, Different Worlds.* New York: Routledge, 1994.

Vattimo, G. *The End of Modernity: Nihilism and Hermeneutics in Post-modern Culture.* Cambridge: Polity Press, 1988.

Volf, Miroslav. *Exclusion and Embrace: A Theological Exploration of Identity, Otherness and Reconciliation.* Nashville: Abingdon, 1996.

Walsh, Brian J. "The Church in a Postmodern Age: Ten Things You Need to Know." *Good Idea! A Resource Sheet on Evangelicalism and Church Growth* 3, no. 4 (winter 1996): 1-5.

———. "Derrida and the Messiah: The Spiritual Face of Postmodernity." *Re:Generation Quarterly* 5, no. 1 (spring 1999): 29-33.

———. "Education in Precarious Times: Postmodernity and a Christian World View." In *The Crumbling Walls of Certainty: Towards a Christian Critique of Postmodernity and Education,* edited by Ian Lambert and Suzanne Mitchell, pp. 8-24. Sydney: Centre for the Study of Australian Christianity, 1997.

———. "Lamenting the End of the Empire." *Church Times,* September 21, 2001, p. 9.

———. *Subversive Christianity: Imaging God in a Dangerous Time.* Seattle: Alta Vista College Press, 1994.

———. "Transformation: Dynamic Worldview or Repressive Ideology." *Journal of Education and Christian Belief* 4, no. 2 (autumn 2000): 101-14.

———. "Will You Have Fries with That Faith?" *The Varsity* 120, no. 41 (1997).

———. "Worldviews." In *The Complete Book of Everyday Christianity,* edited by Robert Banks and R. Paul Stevens, pp. 1135-38. Downers Grove, Ill.: InterVarsity Press, 1997.

Walsh, Brian J, and J. Richard Middleton. *The Transforming Vision: Shaping a Christian Worldview.* Downers Grove, Ill.: InterVarsity Press, 1984.

Wolterstorff, Nicholas. *Reason Within the Bounds of Religion*. Grand Rapids: Eerdmans, 1976.

II. Biblical Studies and First-Century Context

Alexander, Philip S. "Targum, Targumim." In *The Anchor Bible Dictionary,* edited by David Noel Freeman, 6:329-30. New York: Doubleday, 1992.

Anderson, Bernhard. *The Unfolding Drama of the Bible*. 3rd edition. Philadelphia: Fortress, 1988.

Ansell, Nik. "Commentary: Col. 3.1." *Third Way* 22, no. 1 (1999): 22.

Arnold, Clinton. *The Colossian Syncretism: The Interface Between Christianity and Folk Belief at Colossae*. Grand Rapids: Baker, 1996.

————. *Powers of Darkness: Principalities and Powers in Paul's Letters*. Downers Grove, Ill.: InterVarsity Press, 1992.

Barclay, John M. G. *Colossians and Philemon*. Sheffield: Sheffield Academic Press, 1997.

Berkhof, Hendrikus. *Christ and the Powers*. Scottdale, Penn.: Herald Press, 1962.

Bible and Culture Collective. *The Postmodern Bible*. New Haven, Conn.: Yale University Press, 1995.

Birch, Bruce C. *Let Justice Roll Down: The Old Testament, Ethics, and Christian Life*. Louisville, Ky.: Westminster John Knox, 1991.

Brueggemann, Walter. "A Shape for Old Testament Theology II: Embrace of Pain." *Catholic Biblical Quarterly* 47, no. 3 (July 1995): 395-415.

————. "Always in the Shadow of Empire." In *Texts That Linger, Words That Explode: Listening to Prophetic Voices,* edited by Patrick Miller, pp. 73-87. Minneapolis: Fortress Press, 2000.

————. *The Creative Word*. Philadelphia: Fortress, 1982.

————. *Hopeful Imagination: Prophetic Voices in Exile*. Philadelphia: Fortress, 1986.

————. *Interpretation and Obedience*. Minneapolis: Fortress, 1991.

————. *Israel's Praise: Doxology Against Idolatry and Ideology*. Philadelphia: Fortress, 1988.

————. *The Land*. 2nd Edition. Overtures to Biblical Theology. Minneapolis: Fortress, 2002.

————. *The Message of the Psalms: A Theological Commentary*. Minneapolis: Augsburg, 1984.

————. *The Prophetic Imagination*. Philadelphia: Fortress, 1978.

————. *The Psalms and the Life of Faith*. Edited by Patrick D. Miller. Minneapolis: Fortress, 1995.

————. "'Vine and Fig Tree': A Case Study in Imagination and Criticism." In *A Social Reading of the Old Testament: Prophetic Approaches to Israel's Communal Life,* edited by Patrick D. Miller, pp. 91-110. Minneapolis: Fortress, 1994.

Caird, George B. *Principalities and Powers*. Oxford: Clarendon, 1956.

Callahan, Dwight. *Embassy of Onesimus: the Letter of Paul to Philemon*. Valley Forge, Penn.: Trinity Press International, 1997.

Cameron, Averil, and Amelia Kuhrt. *Women in Roman Law and Society*. London: Colin Helm, 1986.

Carter, Warren. *Matthew and Empire: Initial Explorations*. Valley Forge, Penn.: Trinity Press International, 2001.

Castelli, Elizabeth. *Imitating Paul: A Discourse of Power*. Louisville, Ky.: Westminster John Knox, 1991.

———. "Interpretations of Power in 1 Corinthians." *Semeia* 54 (1992): 197-222.

Chang, Curtis. "Images of Judaism and Empire in Colossians." Unpublished essay, Harvard Divinity School, December 13, 1999.

Crook, J. A. *Law and Life of Rome, 90 B.C.-A.D. 112.* Ithaca, N.Y.: Cornell University Press, 1967.

D'Angelo, Mary Rose. "Colossians." In *Searching the Scriptures.* Vol. 2. *A Feminist Commentary.* New York: Crossroad, 1994.

Dunn, James D.G. *The Epistles to the Colossians and Philemon.* New International Greek Testament Commentary. Grand Rapids: Eerdmans, 1996.

Elliot, Neil. *Liberating Paul: The Justice of God and the Politics of the Apostle.* Sheffield, U.K.: Sheffield Academic Press, 1995.

———. "Romans 13.1-7 in the Context of Imperial Propaganda." In *Paul and Empire: Religion and Power in Roman Imperial Society,* edited by Richard A. Horsely, pp. 196-203. Harrisburg, Penn.: Trinity Press International, 2001.

Fishbane, Michael. *Biblical Interpretation in Ancient Israel* Oxford: Clarendon, 1985.

———. *The Garments of Torah: Essays in Biblical Hermeneutics.* Bloomington: Indiana University Press, 1989.

Fretheim, Terence E. "Nature's Praise of God in the Psalms." *Ex Auditu* 3 (1987): 16-30.

———. *The Suffering of God.* Philadelphia: Fortress, 1984.

Gorday, Peter, ed. *Colossians, 1-2 Thessalonians, 1-2 Timothy, Titus, Philemon.* Ancient Christian Commentary on Scripture. Downers Grove, Ill.: InterVarsity Press, 2000.

Gordon, Richard. "The Veil of Power." In *Paul and Empire: Religion and Power in Roman Imperial Society,* edited by Richard A. Horsely. Harrisburg, Penn.: Trinity Press International, 1997.

Hanson, Paul. *The People Called: The Growth of Community in the Bible.* San Francisco: Harper & Row, 1986.

Hays, Richard. *Echoes of Scripture in the Letters of Paul.* New Haven, Conn.: Yale University Press, 1989.

Hooker, Morna D. "Interchange and Suffering." In *From Adam to Christ: Essays on Paul,* pp. 42-55. Cambridge: Cambridge University Press, 1990.

———. "Were There False Teachers in Colossae?" In *Christ and Spirit in the New Testament,* edited by B. Linders and S. S. Smalley, pp. 315-31. Cambridge: Cambridge University Press, 1973.

Horsely, Richard A. *1 Corinthians.* Abingdon New Testament Commentaries. Nashville: Abingdon, 1998.

———. *Galilee: History, Politics, People.* Valley Forge, Penn.: Trinity Press International, 2001.

———. "The Gospel of the Savior's Birth." In *Christmas Unwrapped: Consumerism, Christ, and Culture,* edited by Richard A. Horsely and James Tracy. Harrisburg, Penn.: Trinity Press International, 2001.

———, ed. *Paul and Empire: Religion and Power in Roman Imperial Society.* Harrisburg, Penn.: Trinity Press International, 1997.

———, ed. *Paul and Politics: Ekklesia, Israel, Imperium, Interpretation. Essays in Honor of Krister Stendahl.* Harrisburg, Penn.: Trinity Press International, 2000.

———. *Paul and the Roman Imperial Order.* Harrisburg, Penn.: Trinity Press International, 2004.

————. "Paul and Slavery: A Critical Alternative to Recent Readings." In *Slavery in Text and Interpretation. Semeia* 83/84 (1998): 153-200.

————. *The Politics of Plot in Mark's Gospel.* Louisville, Ky.: Westminster John Knox, 2001.

————. "Submerged Biblical Histories and Imperial Biblical Studies." In *The Postcolonial Bible,* edited by R. S. Sugirtharajah. Sheffield, U.K.: Sheffield Academic Press, 1998.

Johnson, Luke Timothy, with Todd C. Penner. *The Writings of the New Testament: An Interpretation.* Rev. ed. Minneapolis: Augsburg, 1999.

Keesmaat, Sylvia C. "In the Face of Empire: Paul's Use of the Scriptures in the Shorter Epistles." In *The Use of the Old Testament in the New Testament,* edited by Stanley Porter. Grand Rapids: Eerdmans, 2004.

————. *Paul and His Story: (Re)Interpreting the Exodus Tradition.* Sheffield, U.K.: Sheffield Academic Press, 1999.

————. "Psalms in Romans and Galatians." In *The Psalms in the New Testament,* edited by Steve Moyise and Maarten Menkes, pp. 139-61. Edinburgh: T & T Clark, 2004.

————. "Scripture, Law and Fruit: Paul and the Biblical Story." *Pro Rege* 27, no. 4 (1999): 10-19.

Lincoln, Andrew T. "Household Code and Wisdom Mode of Colossians." *Journal for the Study of the New Testament* 74 (1999): 93-112.

————. *The Letter to the Colossians. The New Interpreters Bible.* Vol. 11. Nashville: Abingdon, 2000.

————. "Liberation from the Powers: Supernatural Spirits or Societal Structures?" In *The Bible in Human Society,* edited by M. D. Carroll, D. Clines, and P. R. Davies, pp. 335-54. Sheffield, U.K.: Sheffield Academic Press, 1995.

————. *Truth on Trial: The Lawsuit Motif in the Fourth Gospel.* Peabody, Mass.: Hendrickson, 2001.

MacMullen, Ramsey. *Roman Social Relations: 50 B.C. to A.D. 285.* New Haven, Conn.: Yale University Press, 1974.

Melick, Richard R., Jr. *Philippians, Colossians, Philemon.* The New American Bible Commentary. Vol. 32. Nashville: Broadman Press, 1991.

Middleton, J. Richard. "The Liberating Image? Interpreting *Imago Dei* in Context." *Christian Scholar's Review* 24 (1994): 8-25.

————. *The Liberating Image.* Grand Rapids: Brazos, 2005.

Moule, C. F. D. *The Epistles to the Colossians and Philemon.* The Cambridge Greek Testament Commentary. Cambridge: Cambridge University Press, 1957.

Murphy, Roland. "Wisdom and Creation." *Journal of Biblical Literature* 104, no. 1 (1984): 3-11.

Neill, Stephen C., and N. Thomas Wright. *The Interpretation of the New Testament 1861-1986.* 2nd ed. Oxford: Oxford University Press, 1998.

O'Brien, Peter T. *Colossians, Philemon.* Word Bible Commentary. Vol. 44. Waco, Tex.: Word, 1982.

Price, S. R. F. *Rituals and Power: The Roman Imperial Cult in Asia Minor.* Cambridge: Cambridge University Press, 1984.

Riciutti, Anthony J. "An Open Letter to Onesimus of Colossae: An Examination of Colossians 3.18—4.1 in Context." Unpublished paper. Toronto: Institute of Christian Studies, 1999.

Riciutti, Anthony J. *The Economics of the Way: Jubilee Practice Among the Early Christians According to the Acts of the Apostles.* Unpublished M.Phil.F. thesis. Toronto: Institute for Christian Studies, 2001.

Sanders, James. *From Sacred Story to Sacred Text.* Philadelphia: Fortress, 1987.

Schweitzer, Eduard. *The Letter to the Colossians: A Commentary.* Translated by Andrew Chester. Minneapolis: Augsburg, 1976.

Seerveld, Calvin G. "Footprints in the Snow." *Philosophia Reformata* 56 (1991): 1-34.

———. *For God's Sake Run with Joy.* Toronto: Wedge Publishing, 1972.

Segovia, Fernando F., and Mary Ann Tolbert, eds. *Reading from this Place.* Vol. 1: *Social Location and Biblical Interpretation in the United States.* Vol. 2: *Social Location and Biblical Interpretation in Global Perspective.* Minneapolis: Fortress, 1995.

Shlier, Heinrich. *"thlibo, thlipsis."* In *Theological Dictionary of the New Testament,* edited by Gerhard Kittel; translated by Geoffrey W. Bromiley, 3:130-48. Grand Rapids: Eerdmans, 1985.

Stern, Menahem. *Greek and Latin Authors on Jews and Judaism. I. From Herodotus to Plutarch.* Jerusalem: The Israel Academy of Science and Humanities, 1974.

———. *Greek and Latin Authors on Jews and Judaism. II. From Tacitus to Simplicitus.* Jerusalem: The Israel Academy of Science and Humanities, 1980.

———. "The Jews in Greek and Latin Literature." In *The Jewish People in the First Century: Historical Geography, Political History, Social, Cultural and Religious Life and Institutions,* pp. 1101-59. Vol. 2. Compendia rerum Iudaicarum ad Novum Testamentum. Assen: Van Gorcum, 1976.

Stowers, Stanley K. "Greeks Who Sacrifice and Those Who Do Not: Toward an Anthropology of Greek Religion." In *The Social World of the First Christians: Essays in Honor of Wayne A. Meeks,* edited by L. Michael White and O. Larry Yarbrough, pp. 319-29. Minneapolis: Fortress, 1995.

Sugirtharajah, R. S., ed. *The Postcolonial Bible.* Sheffield, U.K.: Sheffield Academic Press, 1998.

Tcherikover, V. *Hellenistic Civilization and the Jews.* New York: Atheneum, 1975.

Thiessen, Gerd. *The Social Setting of Pauline Christianity.* Philadelphia: Fortress, 1982.

Thiselton, Anthony. *New Horizons in Hermeneutics: The Theory and Practice of Transforming Biblical Reading.* Grand Rapids: Zondervan, 1992.

Torrance, Thomas. "One Aspect of the Biblical Conception of Faith." *Expository Times* 68, no. 4 (January 1957): 111-14.

Van Bremen, Riet. "Women and Wealth." In *Images of Women in Antiquity,* edited by Averil Cameron and Amelia Kuhrt, pp. 223-42. New York: Routledge, 1998.

Vermes, Geza, and Martin Goodman. *The Essenes According to the Classical Sources.* Sheffield, U.K.: JSOT Press, 1989.

Wallace-Hadrill, Andrew, ed. *Patronage in Ancient Society.* New York: Routledge, 1989.

Walsh, Brian J. "Commentary: Col. 1.15-20." *Third Way* 24, no. 4 (June 2001): 20.

———. "Late/Post Modernity and Idolatry: A Contextual Reading of Colossians 2.8—3.4." *Ex Auditu* 15 (1999): 1-17.

———. "Regimes of Truth and the Rhetoric of Deceit: Colossians 2 in Postmodern Context." *Pro Rege* 28, no. 3 (March 2000): 1-17. Also in *Interface: A Forum for Theology in the World* 2, no. 1 (May 1999): 23-37.

————. "Reimaging Biblical Authority." *Christian Scholar's Review* 26, no. 2 (winter 1996): 206-20.

————. "Subversive Preaching in a Postmodern World." *The Banner* 136, no. 13 (2001).

Wengst, Klaus. *Pax Romana and the Peace of Jesus Christ,* translated by J. Bowden. London: SCM Press, 1987.

Whittaker, Molly. *Jews and Christians: Graeco-Roman Views.* Cambridge: Cambridge University Press. 1984.

Wiedemann, Thomas. *Greek and Roman Slavery.* London: Billing and Sons, 1981.

Wilson, Walter T. *The Hope of Glory: Education and Exhortation in the Epistle to the Colossians.* Supplements to Novum Testamentum, vol. 88. New York: Brill, 1997.

Wink, Walter. *Naming the Powers: The Language of Power in the New Testament.* Philadelphia: Fortress, 1984.

Wright, N. T. *Climax of the Covenant: Christ and the Law in Pauline Theology.* Edinburgh: T & T Clark, 1991.

————. *Colossians and Philemon.* Tyndale New Testament Commentary. Grand Rapids: Eerdmans, 1986.

————. *Following Jesus: Biblical Reflections on Discipleship.* Grand Rapids: Eerdmans, 1994.

————. "How Can the Bible Be Authoritative?" *Vox Evangelica* 21 (1991): 7-32.

————. *Jesus and the Victory of God.* Minneapolis: Fortress, 1996.

————. *New Tasks for a Renewed Church.* London: Hodder & Stoughton, 1992.

————. *The New Testament and the People of God.* Minneapolis: Fortress, 1992.

————. "Paul's Gospel and Caesar's Empire." *Reflections* 2 (spring 1999):42-65. Reprinted in *Paul and Empire: Religion and Power in Roman Imperial Society,* edited by Richard A. Horsely, pp. 160-83. Harrisburg, Penn.: Trinity Press International, 1997.

Yamauchi, Edward. *The Archaeology of New Testament Cities in Western Asia Minor.* Grand Rapids: Baker, 1980.

Zanker, Paul. *The Power of Images in the Age of Augustus,* translated by Alan Shapiro. Ann Arbor: University of Michigan Press, 1990.

III. Praxis

Austin, R., *Baptized into Wilderness: A Christian Perspective on John Muir.* Atlanta: John Knox Press, 1987.

Banks, Robert, and R. Paul Stevens, eds. *The Complete Book of Everyday Christianity.* Downers Grove, Ill.: InterVarsity Press, 1997.

Berry, Wendell. *Home Economics.* New York: Northpoint, 1987.

————. *The Selected Poems of Wendell Berry.* Washington, D.C.: Counterpoint, 1998.

————. *What Are People For?* New York: North Point, 1990.

Birch, Charles, and John B. Cobb Jr. *The Liberation of Life: From the Cell to the Community.* Cambridge: Cambridge University Press, 1981.

Borgmann, Albert. *Lifeworld and Technology.* Washington, D.C.: University Press of America, 1990.

————. *Power Failure: Christianity in the Culture of Technology.* Grand Rapids: Brazos, 2003.

Bouma-Prediger, Steven. *For the Beauty of the Earth: A Christian Vision for Creation Care.* Grand

Rapids: Baker, 2001.

Bouma-Prediger, Steven, and Brian J. Walsh. "Educating for Homelessness or Homemaking? The Christian College in a Postmodern Culture." *Christian Scholar's Review* 32, no. 3 (spring 2003): 281-96.

Bouma-Prediger, Steven, and Brian J. Walsh. "If It Ain't Broke, Don't Fix It: A Reply to Robin Lunn and John Klay." *Christian Scholar's Review* 33, no. 4 (Summer 2004): 443-50.

Canadian Ecumenical Jubilee Initiative. *Jubilee, Wealth and the Market.* Toronto: CEJI, 1999.

————. *Making a New Beginning: Biblical Reflections on Jubilee.* Toronto: CEJI, 1998.

————. *Sacred Earth, Sacred Community: Jubilee, Ecology and Aboriginal Peoples.* Toronto: CEJI, 2000.

Clapp, Rodney. *The Consuming Passion: Christianity and Consumer Culture.* Downers Grove, Ill.: InterVarsity Press, 1998.

————. *Families at the Crossroads: Beyond Traditional and Modern Options.* Downers Grove, Ill.: InterVarsity Press, 1993.

————. *A Peculiar People: The Church as Culture in a Post-Christian Society.* Downers Grove, Ill.: InterVarsity Press, 1996.

Cochrane, James., John de Gruchy, and Stephen Martin, eds. *Facing the Truth: South African Faith Communities and the Truth and Reconciliation Committee.* Athens: Ohio University Press, 1999.

Crites, Stephen. "The Narrative Quality of Experience." In *Why Narrative? Readings in Narrative Theology,* edited by Stanley Hauerwas and L. Gregory Jones, pp. 65-88. Grand Rapids: Eerdmans, 1989.

Daly, Herman, and John B Cobb Jr. *For the Common Good.* Boston: Beacon, 1990.

Dicum, Gregory, and Nina Luttinger. *The Coffee Book: Anatomy of an Industry from Crop to the Last Drop.* New York: The New Press, 1999.

Dillard, Annie. *Pilgrim at Tinker Creek.* New York: HarperPerennial, 1992.

Freire, Paulo. *Pedagogy of the Oppressed,* translated by M. Bergman Ramos. New York: Continuum Press, 1986.

Fox Keller, Evelyn. *Reflections on Gender and Science.* New Haven, Conn.: Yale University Press, 1985.

Gatto, John T. *Dumbing Us Down: The Hidden Curriculum of Compulsory Schooling.* Gabriola Island, B.C.: New Society Publishers, 1992.

Gatto, John T., ed. *The Exhausted School.* New York: Oxford Village Press, 1993.

Gilligan, Carol. *In a Different Voice: Psychological Theory and Women's Development.* Cambridge, Mass.: Harvard University Press, 1982.

Gornik, Mark R. *To Live in Peace: Biblical Faith and the Changing Inner City.* Grand Rapids: Eerdmans, 2002.

Goudzwaard, Bob, and Harry de Lange. *Beyond Poverty and Affluence: Toward a Canadian Economy of Care,* translated and edited by Mark Vander Vennen. Toronto: University of Toronto Press, 1995.

Hauerwas, Stanley. *A Community of Character: Toward a Constructive Christian Social Ethic.* Notre Dame, Ind.: University of Notre Dame Press, 1981.

————. *Truthfulness and Tragedy: Further Investigations into Christian Ethics.* Notre Dame, Ind.:

University of Notre Dame Press, 1977.

————. *Vision and Virtue: Essays on Christian Ethical Reflection.* Notre Dame, Ind.: Fides Publications, 1974.

Hauerwas, Stanley, and David Burrell. "From System to Story: An Alternative Pattern for Rationality in Ethics." In *Why Narrative? Readings in Narrative Theology,* edited by Stanley Hauerwas and L. Gregory Jones, pp. 158-90. Grand Rapids: Eerdmans, 1989.

Hauerwas, Stanley, and L. Gregory Jones, eds. *Why Narrative? Readings in Narrative Theology.* Grand Rapids: Eerdmans, 1989.

Hoezee, Scott. *Remember Creation: God's World of Wonder and Delight.* Grand Rapids: Eerdmans, 1998.

Holt, John. *How Children Learn.* Rev. ed. Reading, Mass.: Perseus, 1983.

Illich, Ivan. *Deschooling Society.* New York: Harper & Row, 1971.

Jackson, Wes. *Becoming Native to This Place.* Washington, D.C.: Counterpoint, 1994.

Kavanaugh, John Francis. *Following Christ in a Consumer Society: The Spirituality of Cultural Resistance.* Maryknoll, N.Y.: Orbis, 1981.

Keesmaat, Sylvia C. "Gardening in the Empire," *The Banner* 137, no. 3 (2002): 28-30.

————. "In Defense of Hermeneutics and Compassion: A Response to Allen Verhey." In *The Ethos of Compassion and the Integrity of Creation,* edited by Brian J. Walsh, Robert Vandervennen, and Hendrik Hart, pp. 158-65. Lanham, Md.: University Press of America, 1995.

————. "Sabbath and Jubilee: Radical Alternatives for Being Human." In *Making a New Beginning: Biblical Reflections on Jubilee,* pp. 15-23. Toronto: Canadian Ecumenical Jubilee Initiative, 1998.

Keesmaat, Sylvia C., Richard Middleton, Mark Vander Vennen and Brian Walsh. *The Advent of Justice: A Book of Meditations.* Toronto: CJL Foundation, 1993. [Rev. ed. Sioux Centre, Iowa: Dordt College Press, 1994.]

Kneen, Brewster. *Farmaggedon: Food and the Culture of Biotechnology.* Gabriola Island, B.C.: New Society Publishers, 1999.

Kumar, Satish. "Human-Scale Education: Re-inventing Schools to Meet Real Needs." *Green Teacher* 73 (2004): 9-13.

Kuyek, Devlin. "Rice Is Life." *New Internationalist* 349 (September 2002): 15-17.

Kuyper, Abraham. *The Problem of Poverty,* edited by James W. Skillen. Grand Rapids: Baker, 1991.

Leddy, Mary Jo. *Radical Gratitude.* Maryknoll, N.Y.: Orbis, 2002.

————. *Say to the Darkness, "We Beg to Differ."* Toronto: Lester and Orpen Dennys, 1990.

Lewis, C. S. *The Lion, the Witch, and the Wardrobe.* London: Fontana, 1950.

Longacre, Doris. *Living More with Less.* Scottdale, Penn.: Herald Press, 1980.

McDaniel, Jay. *Of God and Pelicans: A Theology for Reverence for Life.* Louisville, Ky.: Westminster John Knox, 1987.

Meeks, Esther. *Longing to Know.* Grand Rapids: Brazos, 2004.

Middleton, J. Richard, and Brian J. Walsh. "Dancing in the Dragon's Jaws: Imaging God at the End of the Twentieth Century." *The Crucible* 2, no. 3 (1992): 11-18.

————. "Theology at the Rim of a Broken Wheel: Bruce Cockburn and Christian Faith in a Postmodern World." *Grail* 9, no. 2 (June 1993): 15-39.

Mouw, Richard. *He Shines in All That's Fair: Culture and Common Grace.* Grand Rapids: Eerdmans, 2001.

Nash, James. *Loving Nature: Ecological Integrity and Christian Responsibility.* Nashville: Abingdon, 1991.

Orr, David. *Earth in Mind: On Education, Environment and the Human Prospect.* Washington, D.C.: Island Press, 1994.

————. *Ecological Literacy.* Albany, N.Y.: SUNY Press, 1992.

Osborn, Bud. *Hundred Block Rock.* Vancouver: Arsenal Pulp Press, 1999.

————. *Keys to Kingdoms.* Vancouver, B.C.: Get to the Point Publishing, 1999.

————. *Lonesome Monsters.* Vancouver, B.C.: Anvil Publishers, 1995.

Pallmeyer, Jack Nelson. "By the Sword." *The Other Side* 38, no. 6 (2002): 24-27.

Palmer, Parker. *To Know as We Are Known.* San Francisco: Harper, 1983.

Polk, Emily. "Children: The Other Side of the Coffee Trade." *Whole Earth* 108 (Summer 2002): 16-17.

Ruskin, Gary. "Why They Whine: How Corporations Prey on Our Children." *Mothering* 97 (November/December 1999): 40-49.

Santmire, Paul. *The Travail of Nature: The Ambiguous Promise of Christian Theology.* Philadelphia: Fortress, 1985.

Schlosser, Eric. *Fast Food Nation: The Dark Side of the All-American Meal.* New York: Harper Collins, 2001.

Schmitt, L. "Crazy for Cloth: The Benefits of Cloth Diapers." *Mothering* 116 (January/February 2003): 36-39.

Schut, M., ed. *Food and Faith.* Denver: Living the Good News, 2001.

————, ed. *Simpler Living; Compassionate Life.* Denver: Living the Good News, 1999.

Seabrook, Jeremy. "Unchaining Captive Hearts." *New Internationalist* 342 (January/February 2002): 15-17.

Seerveld, Calvin G. *Rainbows for the Fallen World.* Toronto: Tuppence Press, 1980.

Sine, Tom. *Mustard Seed Versus McWorld: Reinventing Life and Faith for the Future.* Grand Rapids: Baker, 1999.

————. *Wild Hope.* Dallas: Word, 1991.

Sittler, Joseph. "Call to Unity." In *Evocations of Grace: The Writings of Joseph Sittler on Ecology, Theology and Ethics,* edited by Steven Bouma-Prediger and Peter Bakken, pp. 38-50. Grand Rapids: Eerdmans, 2000.

Sobel, David. *Place-Based Education: Connecting Classrooms and Community.* Nature and Listening 4. Great Barrington, Mass.: Orion Books, 2004.

Stott, John. "The Works of the Lord." In *The Best Preaching on Earth: Sermons for Caring for Creation,* edited by Stan L. LeQuire, pp. 78-83. Valley Forge, Penn.: Judson, 1996, pp. 78-83.

Tutu, Desmond. *No Future Without Forgiveness.* New York: Doubleday, 2000.

Ucko, Hans, ed. *The Jubilee Challenge: Utopia or Possibility? Jewish and Christian Insights.* Geneva: WCC Publications, 1997.

Vorisek White, A. "Breaking Out of the Box: Turn Off TV, Turn On Life." *Mothering* 107 (July/August 2003): 70-75.

Walsh, Brian J. "Education, Tall Tales and the End of an Era." *Christian Teachers Journal* 8, no.

2 (May 2000): 4-9.

————. "One Day I Shall Be Home." *Christianity and the Arts* 7, no. 1 (Winter 2000): 28-32.

Walsh, Brian J. Marianne Karsh, and Nik Ansell. "Trees, Forestry and the Responsiveness of Creation. *Cross Currents* 44, no. 2 (summer 1994): 149-62. Reprinted in *This Sacred Earth: Religion, Nature, Environment,* edited by Roger S. Gottlieb, pp. 423-45. New York: Routledge, 1995.

Webb, Stephen. *Good Eating.* Grand Rapids: Brazos, 2001.

Wilkinson, Loren, et al. *Earthkeeping in the 90's: Stewardship of Creation.* Grand Rapids: Eerdmans, 1991.

Wilkinson, Loren, and Mary Ruth Wilkinson. *Caring for Creation in Your Own Backyard.* Ann Arbor, Mich.: Servant Publications, 1992.

Williams, Deedee. "Living into the Hard Choices." *The Other Side* 38, no. 6 (2002): 10-15.

Wolterstorff, Nicholas. *Until Justice and Peace Embrace.* Grand Rapids: Eerdmans, 1984.

Yoder, John Howard. *The Politics of Jesus.* Grand Rapids: Eerdmans, 1972.

Author Index

Subject Index